# Developing Early Comprehension Skills Through Picture Book Talk

*Developing Early Comprehension Skills Through Picture Book Talk* demonstrates how strategic 'picture reading' and playful sensory learning can develop young children's explicit and implicit comprehension skills, regardless of their decoding ability. Offering an inclusive teaching and assessment approach that aligns with the Early Years Foundation Stage (EYFS) framework and supports the early adopter school initiative, it will help readers to guide children's use of picture-reading-for-meaning strategies in preparation for more complex comprehension instruction in Year 1.

The book also contains useful resources such as colour picture booklets and downloadable family workshop sessions to help guide parents in more effective 'picture book talk' at home. It offers corresponding steps for planning, teaching, and assessing children's 'picture book talk', multisensory learning, self-questioning skills, and early reading for meaning. The methods and activities within this book specifically help to develop:

- vocabulary (setting vocabulary, character vocabulary, general vocabulary)
- communication and language skills
- critical thinking and inference skills
- metacognition (personal learning awareness)
- self-confidence and self-regulation skills

Providing examples of practice, photocopiable resources, and step-by-step guidance for teaching key comprehension strategies and early self-regulation skills, this book is essential reading for all those who work with young children and wish to encourage a love of reading.

**Donna Thomson** is a primary reading skills specialist, researcher, and educational author with a background in SEN, reading recovery, and early literacy skills development. She is also the founder of Think2Read, an e-learning not-for-profit platform which offers primary schools early inference skills teaching and assessment provision for all abilities.

T0383632

'This accessible book, underpinned by theory, offers foundation stage practitioners a practical and engaging approach to developing young children's comprehension skills, using picture fiction and multisensory tools. Reading for meaning, metacognition and booktalk are highlighted throughout and there is rich support for leading parent workshops in a manner which engages and informs. Packed with guidance, activities, book recommendations and evidence of the benefits of the approach, this is a book for all adults who want to develop their instructional skills teaching and support our youngest readers.'

**Teresa Cremin,** Co-Director of Literacy and Social Justice Centre

'To be able to read, to really read, is to explore, to learn, to laugh, to cry, to feel, be and to dream. To learn to really read, we need to ensure that our children love what they are doing and why. It is so much more than decoding the words on a page, it is to comprehend and to be able to immerse themselves in the context, the content and the meaning of the language. This is a special book, written by an EYFS expert for EYFS experts, but its relevance, its wisdom, pragmatism and resources are far more wide reaching. This is an impeccably researched work, filled with practical advice and approaches that will help all of our children, discover the lifelong magic of reading. Thank you Donna.'

**Dr Richard Gerver,** President of The School Library Association

'Donna Thomson offers teachers a wealth of strategies and resources intended to guide young readers on their journey to thinking and learning - and talking - through great picture books. This book is needed by any educator or parent who values children's literature as a vehicle to help students to read, read, read.'

**Larry Swartz,** OISE, University of Toronto, author of *Better Reading Now* and *Teaching Tough Topics*

'One of those rare penny-drop moments that makes you look at the world through a new lens. Donna Thomson explores our history with pictures, dating back to cave drawings, and poses the question, have we missed a link in our early years' learning steps?

A beautifully crafted and comprehensively written guide, questioning what we think we know for sure.

Donna has done an extraordinary job covering the wide scope of early years development of comprehension skills, leaving no stone unturned in her research. A fantastic read and one for every teacher and parent trying to build confidence and foundation skills in young people.'

**Andrew Kay,** CEO of World Literacy Foundation

# Developing Early Comprehension Skills Through Picture Book Talk

## A Step-By-Step Guide for the Early Years Foundation Stage

Donna Thomson

Routledge
Taylor & Francis Group

LONDON AND NEW YORK

Designed cover image: © tiero / Getty Images

First published 2024
by Routledge
4 Park Square, Milton Park, Abingdon, Oxon, OX14 4RN

and by Routledge
605 Third Avenue, New York, NY 10158

Routledge is an imprint of the Taylor & Francis Group, an informa business

British Library Cataloguing-in-Publication Data
A catalogue record for this book is available from the British Library

ISBN: 978-1-032-12803-0 (hbk)
ISBN: 978-1-032-12802-3 (pbk)
ISBN: 978-1-003-22630-7 (ebk)

DOI: 10.4324/9781003226307

Typeset in Helvetica
by Newgen Publishing UK

Access the support material: www.routledge.com/cw/Thomson

This book is dedicated to
my grandson Rio,
to children everywhere
and to all the teachers who inspire them

# Contents

# Acknowledgements

I am grateful to all the people who have inspired me and helped me to complete this book. Warm thanks go firstly to my colleagues Ruth Nixey and Bea Gill, for their invaluable input and support during the development and delivery of the Key Stage 2, then Key Stage 1 comprehension skills programmes.

My gratitude also to Annie Tempest (Dartington Primary School Head), Dr Maureen Lewis (National Primary Strategy Advisor), Judy Clarke (National Literacy Trust Primary Advisor), Rebecca Cosgrave (Devon Education Services Literacy Lead), Beverley Bannon (Blaenau Gwent Local Education Authority Literacy Advisory Teacher) and Ed Whitelaw (Development Officer for Creative Partnerships, British Art Council – funder of the three-year Think2read School project, 2008–2010) for their valued direction and endorsement of the Key Stages 1 and 2 comprehension skills programme.

I am also thankful to Dr Joanna Haynes for leading the philosophical and dialogic elements of the Year 2 project, and to Bea Gill and Elise Sadler for their practical expertise and feedback which greatly informed how we developed the teaching approach for a foundation setting; to EYFS practitioner Georgina Flack for her expert early year's advice, to head teacher Nic Thorpe, class teacher Kathy Smith, EYFS lead Josie Jay and all the teachers and parents who participated in the Think2Read projects. This particularly includes the children at Dartington Primary School, the reception children at Coed-y-lan Primary, Worsborough Bank End Primary, and Exwick Heights Primary whose shared thinking and insightful ideas about how they question, think, and learn, helped me to shape the teaching and assessment methods in this book.

I would especially like to thank Jake Biggin and Chrissy Morgan-Grant for their stunning picture book illustrations; photographers Mike Thomson and Mark Hawkins for capturing some wonderful 'book talk' moments, and the Coed-y-lan school parents and John and Amy Sargent for giving us kind permission to use the photographs of their children.

I would like to extend a special thank you to Chris and Catherine Parkin for meeting in 2006 and granting permission for me to adapt their comprehension assessment and analysis framework to support the development of enquiry and retelling skills using picture narrative (Parkin, C. Parkin, C. and Poole, B. 1999. *PROBE Reading Assessment*. Truine Initiatives).

Finally, I extend my warmest thanks to my husband Andrew, my Mum, my daughters Katie and Jessie, and all my family for their constant love, encouragement, and good advice.

I have learned so much from you all. Without you this book would not have been written.

# Preface

The early learning steps and teaching sequences in this book have grown out of two decades of primary school action-research and development. The aim of this foundation stage comprehension skills approach is to increase young readers' knowledge and conscious use of comprehension strategies to support their understanding in preparation for learning and reading in Key Stages 1 and 2.

Following a review of our pupils' reading skills in 2002, we noticed that the disparity between their reading fluency and reading comprehension skills was widening. It was clear that this was undermining their learning and affecting their depth of understanding and enjoyment of reading. At that time, there was little in the way of explicit inference skills instruction for primary teachers. So, with the support of colleagues and pupils across the school, I designed a self-regulation comprehension skills instruction model based on Palincsar and Brown's (1984) reciprocal reading framework, Parkin, Parkin and Poole's (2002) taxonomy of question types, and elements of Lipman's (1981) Philosophy for Children (P4C) to help solve the problem. The Year 6 programme developed into an effective whole school reading comprehension model. The addition of a metacognitive teaching approach (Clay 2002) also helped to increase our children's inference skills because it provided them with a strategic self-questioning framework for monitoring their understanding as they read (Thomson and Nixey 2005).

The programme was first endorsed by a member of the National Primary Strategy team in 2005 and published as a Year 6 teaching and assessment resource (Thomson and Nixey 2007). Following the improvement in our school and positive reports from our local education authority regarding its impact on other schools, we adapted the model for Year 2 children. These modifications helped to build knowledge and application of reading comprehension strategies over a longer period of instruction to help embed the skills by Year 6. The Year 2 Think2Read programme was evaluated in a small pilot study in 2007/2008 which involved three Devon schools. The encouraging results (borne out by national test results) showed that when teachers followed the programme closely and were committed to it, children across the ability range made better progress in reading than their peers in the parallel class. However, the study revealed limitations regarding the time-period for instruction and aspects of the comprehension assessment that needed further development to include summarising and retelling skills.

Further action-research and development of the programme helped to address these limitations, and the scheme eventually evolved into a funded whole school teaching and assessment project (Creative Partnerships in Association with Think2Read and the Real Ideas Organisation 2008–2010). During this period the programme was also supported by Devon Education Services, Blaenau-Gwent Local Education Authority, and the National Literacy Trust. The teaching and assessment materials were then published as Key Stages 1 and 2 teacher resources following each phase of effective development and delivery in schools (Thomson and Graham 2009–2016, Thomson et al. 2009).

The far-reaching impact of the reading skills intervention encouraged us to explore the possibility of developing comprehension skills at an earlier stage using picture narrative and multisensory tools in the classroom and at home. With the support of Early Years Foundation Stage practitioners, children, and parents from schools in Devon, Wales, and Yorkshire, we created and successfully trialled the Early Years Comprehension Sensory Skills model that is outlined in this book.

My special relationship with picture books began during my time as a reading recovery teacher. A struggling young reader, who we will call Josh, showed me how well-crafted picture books introduce the early reading process in a way I had not considered before.

'I hate books. They are stupid' he blurted out one day. I looked through the book he had chosen. The text and pictures were rather average I thought – but the book was something he would normally have read without too much difficulty. His anger was baffling, until he told me that he had selected the book because 'it was about volcanoes'. He explained that when he tried to read the words, he couldn't find the letter 'v' anywhere.

I glanced at the picture on the cover of the book. The scene depicted a volcano-shape in a barren, grey landscape. The dark sky contained a vague flash of purple and orange. I opened the book again at the image on page one. It was a line drawing rather like the image on the cover. Josh talked about the details in the picture and their meaning. Then we tackled the story in print.

The opening line of text centred on a word beginning with the letter 'c'. The story was set on a planet and the word was 'crater'. However, it seems the illustrator had not seen the text, because nothing in the picture related to the words. No wonder Josh was upset. In the early stages of reading, it is only fair to expect the pictures and text to connect in a meaningful way.

This was the beginning of our picture book journey. We looked for well-crafted stories and talked about how the images and words worked together (Ayra and Feathers 2012). We focused on Josh's favourite topics and how the text left gaps sometimes for pictures to tell the story. Josh's vocabulary grew as our discussions about picture narrative drew him further into word meanings and the author's intention. This developed into a wider investigation. A framework and a web of questions gradually emerged for developing reading comprehension strategies alongside decoding skills, first through picture book talk, then talk about text.

Josh became a confident reader by the end of his primary years. However, he was always proud to acknowledge that his love of reading had initially grown out of his gift for reading images, and his innate understanding of how stories are told (with or without words).

# References

Ayra, P., and Feathers, K. (2012). Reconsidering children's readings: Insights into the reading process. *Reading Psychology*, 33(4), 301–322.

Clay, M.M. (2002). *An observation survey of early literacy achievement*. Heinemann.

Creative Partnerships in Association with Think2Read and the Real Ideas Organisation (2008–2010). *3-year change school project*. British Arts Council.

Lipman, M. (1981). Philosophy for children. In A.L. Costa (Ed.), *Developing minds: Programs for teaching thinking* (2nd edn). Association for Supervisions and Curricular Development.

Palincsar, A.S., and Brown, A. (1984). Reciprocal teaching of comprehension-fostering and comprehension-monitoring activities. *Cognition and Instruction*, 1, 117–175.

Parkin, C., Parkin, C., and Pool, B. (2002). *PROBE – taxonomy of question types, reading assessment New Zealand*. Triune Initiatives.

Thomson, D., and Graham, E. (2009–2016). *Literacy skills – Comprehension series Years 1–6*. Scholastic.

Thomson, D., and Nixey, R. (2005). Thinking to read, reading to think: Bringing meaning, reasoning and enjoyment to reading. *Literacy Today*, 44, 12–13.

Thomson, D., and Nixey, R. (2007). *Quick fix for Year 6 comprehension*. Scholastic.

Thomson, D., Wren, W., Lindsay, S., and Dickinson, D. (2009). *Nelson comprehension series – Primary years* (J. Jackman, Ed.). Nelson Thornes, Oxford University Press.

# PART 1

# Theory: Early reading comprehension and sensory learning instruction

# CHAPTER 1

# Introduction

As all readers know, there is little joy in reading without understanding. Comprehension is the purpose for reading and the cornerstone of learning. It is a complex process which supports understanding and enables us to acquire and apply knowledge, generate new ideas, communicate effectively, relate to others, and successfully participate in the world. It therefore makes sense that we introduce these vital cognitive skills to our children as early as possible.

Arguably, teaching in the Early Years Foundation Stage (EYFS) setting already includes this type of comprehension instruction. Early years educators are experts at bringing stories to life for children and engaging them in daily reading-for-meaning activities – such as role-play, discussion, and lively question-and-answer activities about the story settings, characters, and plots. They understand that involving children from the beginning in meaning-making promotes reading and the enjoyment of books. However, recent evidence shows that although modelling of comprehension skills and talking about stories is essential practice for early literacy development, it is the transference of strategic knowledge to pupils and their *ownership* of the skills which significantly increases their comprehension and motivation to read. In my experience, reading independence only truly begins when young children are shown how to reliably identify and apply specific strategies for themselves to self-monitor their understanding as they learn to read (Block et al. 2008, Lysaker and Hopper 2015).

Of course, this type of skills instruction is complicated for beginner readers and requires small explicit steps, conscious application, and plenty of guided and independent practice for them to grasp the concepts involved. In addition, experience has shown me that early comprehension teaching is more effective when it includes 1) a metacognitive approach, 2) initial focus on visual narrative, 3) in-depth back-and-forth discussion, and 4) playful multisensory activities. The sooner, therefore, that young children are taught how to think and question for themselves and articulate their ideas with confidence, the more empowered, independent, and self-regulatory they will become as readers and learners (Janssen 2002, Chambers 2011, Joseph et al. 2015).

DOI: 10.4324/9781003226307-2

## What does this book offer foundation stage practitioners?

The purpose of this book, therefore, is to build on existing good practice by providing early years practitioners with the strategies, practical guidance, and resources to increase core reading for meaning ability in preparation for Year 1. The 'picture book talk', multisensory learning, and self-questioning techniques that underpin the book's instructional model offer sound and logical steps for achieving this. For example, the model provides a succession of practical easy-to-follow steps for planning, teaching, and assessing children's early reading for meaning, communication, and self-questioning skills. In addition, the book offers a clear meta-cognitive framework for developing oral language ability, critical thinking, visual literacy, and learning self-regulation. The teaching and assessment framework in Part 3, for example (see Chapter 8 p. 87 for overview), demonstrates how this instructional model supports the aims of the EYFS early adopter school initiative (2021) and relates to the characteristics of effective learning and early learning goals.

Furthermore, the unique strength of this instructional approach is that it offers a simple framework for teaching the four key comprehension strategies: Summarising, Predicting, Enquiry, and Clarifying. This inclusive approach ensures that all young readers are equipped with the basic skills to demonstrate their understanding of key comprehension strategies by the end of the reception year – which helps to prepare them for more complex text comprehension instruction later (Lysaker and Hopper 2015).

In addition, foundation stage practitioners are provided with a family reading skills framework and resources to help them guide parents in more strategic 'picture book talk' at home. The family reading-for-meaning activities and Power Point workshop guidance for parents also reinforce classroom instruction and help to narrow the gap between disadvantaged and non-disadvantaged children's reading attainment.

## Early comprehension instruction and the new EYFS framework reforms (2021)

Growing evidence shows that high-quality discussion and explicit teaching of language comprehension skills help young readers to engage in the reading-for-meaning process with much greater ease (Education Endowment Foundation 2021). This type of adult–child interaction is central to the book's teaching and assessment objectives and actively reflects the dialogic aims of the EYFS framework reforms (DfE 2020 cited in DfE 2021: 8). The DfE emphasise for example, that 'children's back and forth interactions from an early age' improve communication, literacy, and the learning progress significantly and help 'to reduce the language gap for those children who do not come from language-rich homes'.

In addition, the recent changes to DfE Language and Communication guidance (2021) which puts 'understanding' alongside the 'listening, attention and speaking' learning goals, emphasises the crucial 'link between language comprehension and later reading'. As our comprehension model demonstrates, the earlier young children are shown how to develop oral skills and cognition by engaging their senses to support their learning (Baines 2008), the sooner they will grasp language, understanding, and communication to strengthen literacy outcomes in readiness for Year 1.

# How this book works

The nine chapters in the book are divided into four main parts. These sections include a review of the theory behind the early comprehension skills model, planning guidance for teaching and assessment and examples of pre-planned teaching sequences and assessments. Parts 1–4 in the book consist of the following chapters.

## Part 1 (Chapters 2–5) – Theory: early reading comprehension and sensory learning instruction

Chapters 2–4 explain 1) the concept of emergent comprehension, 2) the different components and objectives of the multisensory comprehension skills model, and 3) how metacognitive teaching builds language, communication, understanding, and reading self-regulation. In addition, Chapter 5 provides examples of family reading skills workshop activities, and explains how they help parents to engage their children more deeply in the reading-for-meaning process at home to reinforce activities in the classroom.

## Part 2 (Chapters 6–7) – Putting theory into practice: Teaching and reviewing skills

Chapter 6 offers practitioners a step-by-step structure for planning comprehension self-questioning activities using picture books. This includes advice about 1) choosing picture books to support the teaching of specific strategies, and 2) how this instructional approach builds on good EYFS practice and helps to develop:

- vocabulary (setting vocabulary, character vocabulary, general vocabulary),
- communication and language skills,
- critical thinking and self-questioning skills,
- metacognition – personal learning awareness, and
- self-confidence and self-regulation skills.

Chapter 7 provides examples of assessment methods, their purpose and how to plan, deliver and analyse comprehension skills reviews before, during and after instruction.

## Part 3 (Chapters 8–9) – Reception resources: Teaching and assessing comprehension

Chapters 8 and 9 offer an overview of the book's pre-planned lesson resources and learning objectives. This includes a summary of how each teaching sequence and post-unit assessment links to and works towards 1) EYFS early learning goals and 2) Year 1 comprehension objectives.

Sections 1–3 in Chapter 9 provide practitioners with teaching and assessment resources which consist of:

- a systematic series of explicit, pre-planned comprehension teaching units (1–4) and post-unit assessments for daily teaching,
- print-out picture booklets for teaching and assessment,
- comprehension skills assessment resources, with answers to questions,

- guidance on review procedure and how to analyse the children's responses,
- pupil self-assessment sheets (with adult guidance),
- graphic organisers, posters, and
- cut-out templates for the multisensory tools.

### Part 4 – Downloadable resources: Foundation family reading workshop programme

The book's foundation family learning resources, PowerPoint sessions and teacher guidance associated with the family learning studies in Chapter 4 can be found on the Routledge website (www.routledge.com/cw/Thomson). This includes a framework and timetable, plus guidance and resources for setting up a series of family reading skills workshops.

# References

Baines, L. (2008). *A teacher's guide to multisensory learning: Improving literacy by engaging the senses.* Association for Supervision & Curriculum Development.

Block, C., Parris, S., and Whiteley, C. (2008). CPMs: A kinesthetic comprehension strategy. *The Reading Teacher*, 61(6), 460–470.

Chambers, A. (2011). *Tell me: Children, reading and talk with the reading environment.* Thimble Press.

Department for Education. (2021). *The reading framework: Teaching the foundations of literacy, Section 2: Language comprehension.* Department for Education.

Education Endowment Foundation. (2021). *EEF toolkit – reading comprehension strategies.* https://educationendowmentfoundation.org.uk/education-evidence/teaching-learning-toolkit/reading-comprehension-strategies

Janssen, T. (2002). Instruction in self-questioning as a literary reading strategy: An exploration of empirical research. *L1 – Educational Studies in Language and Literature*, 2, 95–120.

Joseph, L.M., Alber-Morgan, S., Cullen, J., and Rouse, C. (2015). The effects of self-questioning on reading comprehension: A literature review. *Reading & Writing Quarterly*, 32(2), 152–173.

Lysaker, J., and Hopper, E. (2015). A kindergartner's emergent strategy use during wordless picture book reading. *Reading Teacher*, 68(8), 649–657.

# CHAPTER 2

# The 'developmental bridge': From reading pictures to understanding text

## Why is early reading comprehension important?

Until recently, the development of phonics and decoding skills has remained central to learning to read in the first years of school. However, growing evidence shows that young children's reading improves significantly when they are also taught how to read for meaning alongside decoding (e.g., Keene and Zimmermann 2013, Education Endowment Foundation 2016, Gov.uk 2017). Understanding what we are reading is, after all, the purpose of reading. It enables us to gather information, communicate better, think about others' perspectives, achieve academic success, and enjoy the reading activity for itself (Snowling et al. 2009).

DOI: 10.4324/9781003226307-3

FIGURE 2.1 'Reading pictures together'. Photograph by Mike Thomson. Reproduced with permission

However, meaningful comprehension involves strategic thinking on a variety of levels to achieve full understanding (e.g., Palincsar and Brown 1984, Duke and Pearson et al. 2011). For example, young readers (see Figure 2.1) must learn how to identify clues and integrate their prior knowledge with key information in the text to gain an overall mental picture of what is happening in the narrative (Kintsch 1998, Helder et al. 2016).

Yet, despite widely held acknowledgement that 'visualising' plays a key role in text comprehension (Frey and Fisher 2008) it is only recently that research has focused on the value of visual literacy in relation to the early development of reading comprehension. For many years, educators have been guided by the logical argument that once decoding and word reading is established, the foundations are laid for building comprehension skills (Perfetti et al. 2005). However, a growing body of wordless picture book research shows that pre-school children demonstrate early comprehending abilities before they decode (Crawford and Hade 2000, Lysaker and Hopper 2015). This capability also includes making inferences in response to reading picture narrative (Paris and Paris 2003). Which raises the question: should reading comprehension be synonymous with decoding words, or might there be an initial developmental stage in early reading comprehension instruction that evolves from visual literacy?

## How does reading for meaning begin? Pictures or text?

Evidence shows that visual literacy plays a pivotal role in the development of language and early reading skills and supports text reading later (e.g., Dooley and Matthews 2009, Lysaker and Miller 2013). Furthermore, recent studies have revealed that beginner readers rely on many of the same strategies for reading wordless picture books, as they do when reading written texts (e.g., Lysaker and Hopper 2015, Crawford and Hade 2000). It is surprising, therefore, that despite frequent use of visual texts for early learning activities, picture narrative is rarely used to develop comprehension strategies and visualising skills (Arizpe 2013, Ploetzner et al. 2013). The misconception that the development of comprehension begins with word reading only, strongly suggests we might be missing a fundamental reading-readiness phase in our young children's early learning and development.

For example, it was notable following our Key Stages 1 and 2 comprehension skills projects (Thomson and Nixey 2005) that, despite differences in decoding ability and initial attitudes to visual literacy, most of the pupils who participated in our picture comprehension research went on to become highly motivated and competent readers. This outcome was largely due to the metacognitive teaching approach and range of visual reading material we introduced them to before written texts. The process of thinking and talking about how we make meaning encouraged the mixed ability groups to observe their own and each other's reading behaviour. This involved noting how they 1) gathered specific information and 2) made deductions about pictures and text to support their understanding. The 10–11-year-olds, for example, noticed that the cognitive processes they used to comprehend complex picture narrative, were comparable to the thinking required to infer from text and make conscious deductions about story outcomes. This revelation encouraged some of the less able decoders to view themselves as 'readers' after all. They realised that although they might struggle with decoding, many of them possessed impressive comprehension strengths. The self-confidence they gained from learning how to understand a variety of visual texts motivated them to tackle written passages and eventually overcome their decoding difficulties.

This should not surprise us. Since the earliest cave drawings man has communicated ideas, told stories, and relayed information through pictures. Nodelman (1988: 5) suggests that we have a long relationship with visual images because 'pictures communicate more universally and more readily than words do'. It seems a reasonable assumption, therefore, that we learn to make meaning of what we see before we can visualise written print. Understanding the immediate world around us is naturally our first preoccupation in life. Researchers and visual literacy practitioners Frey and Fisher (2008:1) remind us of Berger's (2006: 681) observation that 'seeing comes before words. The child looks and recognises before it can speak'. Then they learn the words to label what they see. They *read* the situation and respond. Later this experience of *reading* situations and *reading* people's faces extends to *reading* picture information which they gradually learn to link to words and text. This reference to *reading* as a process of viewing and understanding is fully captured in the expression we use in everyday speech: 'I *see* what you mean', to indicate that we understand someone's meaning. However, although 'visualising' is now considered a reading comprehension strategy (De Koning and Van der Schoot 2013), viewing is rarely mentioned when the collective elements of literacy (reading, writing, speaking, and listening) are described. As Frey and Fisher (2008) note, this is probably because society and schools are predominantly word-centric and tend to 'privilege words over pictures'. Therefore, the potential of the wordless picture book to provide a bridge between image-based comprehension and comprehension of text is too often overlooked (Martínez-Roldán and Newcomer 2011).

## From reading pictures to understanding text – crossing the 'developmental bridge'

I think we can agree that reading is a multicomponent skill which is characterised by two broad categories:

1. **code-related skills**, such as alphabet knowledge and phonological awareness, letter naming, phonological decoding, emergent writing, and print awareness (e.g., Snow et al., 1998), and

2. **oral language skills**, such as comprehension skills which involve knowledge of vocabulary, literal understanding, making inferences, activating prior knowledge, use of world knowledge and story structure, amongst other strategies (Tompkins et al. 2013).

Elements of these decoding and comprehension skills may develop simultaneously in early childhood, sometimes interconnecting, and other times developing independently of each other – depending on the reader's personal experience (e.g., Rapp et al. 2007).

Contrary to the view, therefore, that comprehension occurs once word reading has been mastered, many experts now argue that 'comprehension instruction should begin before children are able to read text' (Hirsch 2003 cited in Tompkins et al. 2013: 404). They explain that early comprehension involves an ongoing process of meaning-making which combines viewing, listening, thinking about, and responding to a variety of visual and written narrative from as early as 12 months (Biemiller 2003). Therefore, it is reasonable to assume that these activities are 'predominant precursors to skilled reading comprehension', as they nurture the language skills and understanding which continue to develop throughout the primary years (Tompkins et al. 2013: 404).

This viewpoint is further explained by Caitlin McMunn Dooley (2011: 169) who provides ample evidence in her review of early literacy skills to show that 'comprehension emerges prior to decoding and continues to develop as a child learns to read'. She emphasises that it is an important part of becoming literate. She refers to this pre-school stage of early meaning-making as *emergent comprehension* and explains that it provides a developmental bridge which 'precedes and extends to later comprehension' (see Figure 2.2). The theoretical connection Dooley (2011) makes between emergent comprehension (reading pictures), and the conventional idea of reading comprehension (reading text), corresponds with our reception and Year 1 action-research findings.

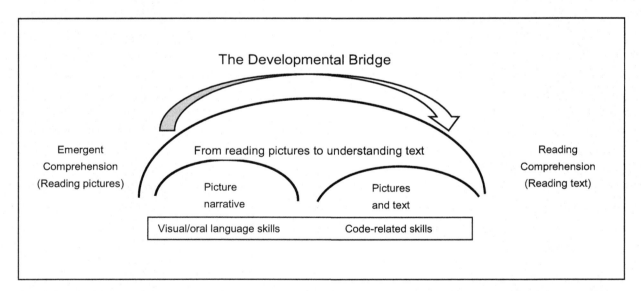

FIGURE 2.2 Example of the 'developmental bridge' (based on theories by Dooley and Matthews 2009 and Tompkins et al. 2013)

She proposes that early interaction with visual texts is important, because, as the teaching sequences in the book indicate, being shown how to link images and word clues to make deductions (see Unit 3, p. 138) encourages the development of strategic reading for meaning which helps to inform early reading instruction (Paris and Paris 2001, 2003, 2007). In addition, she provides examples of how emergent readers begin to comprehend in a variety of ways before conventional reading, by using aural and visual senses to support understanding (e.g., Zimmerman et al. 2009, Riggio and Cassidy 2009, O'Neill and Shultis 2007, Lynch and van den Broek et al. 2008, Flewitt et al. 2009). As Block et al. (2008: 460) demonstrate in their multisensory reading skills research, 'tapping into more than one mode of learning reinforces comprehension for all students'. They conclude that a combination of cognitive and sensory activity helps young readers to 'initiate their own comprehension processes' to support their understanding (see Chapter 3, p. 15). This was also clearly illustrated in our early reading comprehension action-research (see Chapter 5, p. 42). The multisensory learning activities we introduced to help the 5-year-olds and their parents to explore picture narrative in greater depth encouraged them to:

1.  focus more on what they could see on the page,
2.  clarify their ideas, and
3.  ask more questions about the details to make predictions during their picture book enquiry.

These tasks included examining visual texts through a 'Viewer' and learning how to respond to and use specific hand motions to join in 'who, what, where' questioning and discussion about the story (see Chapter 3). By absorbing them in simple visual, physical, and dialogic activities they began to think more deeply about the story and engage in more meaningful 'picture talk' over the six-week study period.

## Creating a picture in your head – who, what, where?

During our family workshops we noticed how the children and their families began to feel more ownership of the comprehension process when they were shown how to identify and apply each comprehension strategy in turn, using an adaptation of Palincsar and Brown's (1984) reciprocal reading framework. This explicit teaching approach is effective because it focuses on specific skills and includes plenty of guided, collaborative, and independent practice – till the reader feels familiar enough with the skills to integrate them automatically.

By introducing the families to pictures first, then a line of text, they realised that 'picture-viewing', like reading written text, requires you to first identify the literal 'who, what, where' information about characters, actions, and places. They found that by following this initial stage, they could then delve more deeply for clues in the narrative. During this process the families also learned that when you use your prior knowledge and wider vocabulary to identify clues, you can make links to explain the 'bigger picture'. This enhances understanding of the narrative and helps young readers to make predictions about what might happen next to the characters, based on their own experience of life and other stories.

The children began to realise that to explain picture narrative, you must turn the images into words to describe what you see, whilst the inverse is true of written text. Comprehending and explaining words involves picturing their meaning before you can discuss the author's ideas (Kintsch 2004). They soon learned that if you do not have a picture in your head when you are reading, listening, or learning, it is likely that you do not understand what you have read, heard, or seen. 'I haven't got a picture in my head' became a useful euphemism for children in my guided reading sessions for 'I don't understand, please explain'.

## Turning pictures into words and words into pictures

The concept of 'turning words into pictures' was made clearer to the children when they were asked to draw the following line of text: 'The boy is playing in the paddling pool'. They were amazed to find that all their drawings matched. Without consciously doing so, they had all identified the key information in the sentence: character (the boy), action (playing), and place (paddling pool). In other words, they had created their own 'situation' model (Kintsch 1998) using the who, what, where information they had heard, to draw their version of 'a boy playing in a paddling pool'. They began to realise that a reader interprets the author's words as they read text in much the same way.

A major report in Ireland, conducted on behalf of the National Council for Curriculum Assessment (2012), supports this view of early literacy. They acknowledge the potential of a pre-school developmental reading and writing stage and refer to Sulzby and Teale's (1991: 729) broader term of 'emergent literacy', which 'ascribes to the child the role of constructor of his or her own literacy'. The report further underlines the significance of emergent literacy, quoting Whitehurst and Lonigan's (1998: 849) definition of the term as:

> the skills, knowledge and attitudes that are presumed to be developmental precursors to conventional forms of reading and writing.

Furthermore, the report demonstrates how oral comprehension, and the thoughtful meaning-making children engage in to interpret picture narrative, may have positive implications for the conventional development of comprehension and inference skills later. Caitlin Dooley (2011) refers to evidence of this in other research where 'oral language has been shown to independently predict (4–5-year-olds) reading comprehension two years later' (Cain and Oakhill 2007 cited in Kendeou et al. 2008, Kendeou et al. 2009). These findings are corroborated by more recent studies. Cohn et al. (2014: 3) suggest, for example, that although wordless books may have little or no text, the separate images come together to 'form complex coherent picture narratives' in much the same way that words combine in language to create text narrative. Both require the active role of the reader in the 'sense-making processes' (Crawford and Hade 2000). Perhaps a reasonable argument can be put forward, therefore, that since '...pictures in picture books provide equality of access to narrative' (Arizpe 2013), many children begin the process of comprehension through picture narrative, before they attempt to interrogate written narrative for meaning.

## References

Arizpe, E. (2013). Meaning-making from wordless (or nearly wordless) picturebooks: What educational research expects and what readers have to say. *Cambridge Journal of Education*, 43(2), 163–176.

Berger, J. (2006). Ways of seeing. In D. McQuade and C. McQuade (Eds), *Seeing and Writing* (4th edn). Bedford/St. Martin's.

Biemiller, A. (2003). Vocabulary: Needed if more children are to read well. *Reading Psychology*, 24(3–4), 323–335.

Block, C., Parris, S., and Whitely, C. (2008). CPMs: A kinesthetic comprehension strategy. *The Reading Teacher*, 61(6), 460–470.

Cohn, N. Jackendoff, R., Holcomb, P.J., and Kuperberg, G.R. (2014). The grammar of visual narrative: Neural evidence for constituent structure in sequential image comprehension. *Neuropsychologia*, 64, 63–70.

Crawford, P.A., and Hade, D.D. (2000). Inside the picture, outside the frame: Semiotics and the reading of wordless picture books. *Journal of Research in Childhood Education*, 15(1), 66–80.

De Koning, B.B., and Van der Schoot, M. (2013). Becoming part of the story! Refueling the interest in visualization strategies for reading comprehension. *Educational Psychology Review*, 25, 261–287.

Dooley, C.M. (2011). The emergence of comprehension: A decade of research 2000–2010. *International Electronic Journal of Elementary Education*, 4(1), 169–184.

Dooley, C.M., and Matthews, M.W. (2009). Emergent comprehension: Understanding comprehension development among young literacy learners. *Journal of Early Childhood Literacy*, 9(3), 269–294.

Duke, N.K., Pearson, P.D., Strachan, S.L., and Biullman, A.K. (2011). *What research has to say about reading instruction* (4th edn) (S.J. Samuels and A.E. Farstrup, Eds). International Reading Association.

Education Endowment Foundation. (2016). *Teaching & learning toolkit reading comprehension strategies*. https://educationendowmentfoundation.org.uk/education-evidence/teaching-learning-toolkit/reading-comprehension-strategies

ernsbacher, M.A. (1985). Surface information loss in comprehension. Cognitive Psychology, 17, 324–363.

Flewitt, R., Nind, M., and Payler, J. (2009). If she's left with books she'll just eat them: Considering inclusive practices. *Journal of Early Childhood Literacy*, 9, 211–233.

Frey, N., and Fisher, D. (2008). *Teaching visual literacy: Using comic books, graphic novels, anime, cartoons, and more to develop comprehension and thinking skills*. Corwin Press.

Gernsbacher, M. A. (1985). Surface information loss in comprehension. Cognitive Psychology, 17, 324–363.

Gov.uk (2017). *Progress in international reading literacy study (PIRLS): National report for England*. www.gov.uk/government/publications/pirls-2016-reading-literacy-performance-in-england

Helder, A., van Leijenhorst, L., and van den Broek, P. (2016). Coherence monitoring by good and poor comprehenders in elementary school: Comparing offline and online measures. *Learning and Individual Differences*, 48, 17–23.

Hirsch, E.D. (2003). Reading comprehension requires the knowledge – of words and the world. *American Educator*, 27(1), 10–13, 16–22, 28–29, 48.

Keene, D.E., and Zimmermann, S. (2013). Years later, comprehension strategies still at work. *The Reading Teacher*, 66(8), 601–606.

Kendeou, P., Bohn-Getter, C., White, M.J., and van den Broek, P. (2008). Children's inference generation across media. *Journal of Research in Reading*, 31, 259–272.

Kendeou, P., Savage, R., and van den Broek, P. (2009). Revisiting the simple view of reading. *British Journal of Educational Psychology*, 79, 353–370.

Kintsch, W. (1998). *Comprehension: A paradigm for cognition*. Cambridge University Press.

Kintsch, W. (2004). The construction-integration model of text comprehension and its implications for instruction. In R.B. Rudell and N.J. Unrau (Eds), *Theoretical models and processes of reading* (5th edn) Unrau, 2004, Newark, DE: International Reading Association.

Lynch, J.S., Van Den Broek, P., Kremer, K.E., Kendeou, P., White, M.J., and Lorch, E.P. (2008). The development of narrative comprehension and its relation to other early reading skills. *Reading Psychology*, 29(4), 327–365.

Lysaker, J., and Hopper, E. (2015). A kindergartner's emergent strategy use during wordless picture book reading. *Reading Teacher*, 68(8), 649–657.

Lysaker, J., and Miller, A. (2013). Engaging social imagination: The developmental work of wordless book reading. *Journal of Early Childhood Literacy*, 13(2), 147–174.

Martínez-Roldán, C., and Newcomer, S. (2011). Reading between the pictures: Immigrant students' interpretations of The Arrival. *Language Arts*, 88(3), 188–197.

National Council for Curriculum Assessment. (2012). *Literacy in early childhood and primary education (3–8 years)*. Report No. 15. Research conducted on behalf of the National Council for Curriculum and Assessment.

Nodelman, P. (1988). *Words about pictures*. University of Georgia Press.

O'Neill, D.K., and Shultis, R.M. (2007). The emergence of the ability to track a character's mental perspective in narrative. *Developmental Psychology*, 43(4), 1032–1037.

Palincsar, A., and Brown, A. (1984). Reciprocal teaching of comprehension-fostering and comprehension-monitoring activities. *Cognition and Instruction*, 1, 117–175.

Paris, A., and Paris, S.G. (2001). *Children's comprehension of narrative picture books* (Technical Report No 3 – 012). Centre for the Improvement of Early Reading Achievement.

Paris, A., and Paris, S.G. (2007). Teaching narrative comprehension strategies to first graders. *Cognition and Instruction*, 25(1), 1–44.

Paris, S., and Paris, S.G. (2003). Assessing narrative comprehension in young children. *Reading Research Quarterly*, 38, 36–76.

Perfetti, C., Landi, N., and Oakhill, J. (2005). The acquisition of reading comprehension skill. In M. J. Snowling & C. Hulme (Eds.) *The science of reading: A handbook*. Blackwell

Ploetzner, R., Lowe, R., and Schlag, S. (2013). A systematic characterization of cognitive techniques for learning from textual and pictorial representations. *Journal of Education and Learning*, 2(2), 78–95.

Rapp, D.N., van den Broek, P., McMaster, K.L., Kendeou, P., and Espin, C.A. (2007). Higher-order comprehension processes in struggling readers: A perspective for research and intervention. *Scientific Studies of Reading*, 11, 289–312.

Riggio, M.M., and Cassidy, K.W. (2009). Pre-schoolers' processing of false beliefs within the context of picture book reading. *Early Education and Development*, 20(6), 992–1015.

Snow, C.E., Burns, M.S., and Griffin, P. (1998). *Preventing reading difficulties in young children*. National Academy Press.

Snowling, M., Cain, K., Nation, K., and Oakhill, J. (2009). *Reading comprehension: Nature assessment and teaching*. Centre for Reading and Language.

Sulzby, E., and Teale, W. (1991). Emergent literacy. In R. Barr, M.L. Kamil, P.B. Mosenthal, and P.D. Pearson (Eds), *Handbook of Reading Research* (2nd edn). Longman.

Thomson, D., and Nixey, R. (2005). Thinking to read, reading to think: Bringing meaning, reasoning, and enjoyment to reading. *Literacy Today*, 44, 12–13.

Tompkins, V., Guo, Y., and Justice, L.M. (2013). Inference generation, story comprehension, and language skills in the preschool years. *Reading and Writing: An Interdisciplinary Journal*, 26(3), 403–429.

Whitehurst, G.J., and Lonigan, C.J. (1998). Child development and emergent literacy. *Child Development*, 69, 848–872.

Zimmerman, F.J., Gilkerson, J., Richards, J.A., Christakis, D.A., Xu, D., Gray, S., and Yapanel, U. (2009). Teaching by listening: The importance of adult–child conversations to language development. *Paediatrics*, 124, 342–349.

# CHAPTER 3

# Engaging the senses to make meaning

## What is multisensory learning?

As we know, children learn through play and use their senses to explore and understand the world around them. They are also diverse learners who make sense of information in distinctly different ways (Gardner 1999). Some learn more easily through seeing, hearing, and speaking – others through touch and movement. These different modes of learning are known as visual, auditory, tactile, and kinaesthetic learning styles (Fleming and Mills 1992, Dunn and Dunn 1993). Figure 3.1 shows how they fall into two fundamental areas of thinking and learning in the classroom:

1. Kinaesthetic and tactile: physical activities that focus on 'doing', and
2. Visual and auditory: observing, listening, and speaking.

These senses support active learning through:

- **seeing** (visual learning) – using the sense of sight to understand information and concepts when they are presented in visual form, e.g., diagrams, concept maps, illustrations, symbols,
- **hearing and speaking** (auditory learning) – using the sense of hearing to understand new ideas. This happens when the information is explained out loud, either by the child doing the speaking, or by others doing the talking,
- **touch** (tactile learning) – using the sense of touch to make meaning of ideas by moving things around and by manipulating objects that represent the concepts they are learning, and
- **body movement** (kinaesthetic learning) – using body movement to keep focused. Movement is also used to support understanding and interpretation of ideas in a variety of ways (e.g., role-play, dance) or to mimic a concept they are learning (e.g., hand and body gestures).

## Active learning – engaging all the senses

Some sensory learning theorists believe that instruction is more effective when it engages children in their preferred learning style (Fleming and Mills 1992, Dunn and Dunn 1993, Dunn and

DOI: 10.4324/9781003226307-4

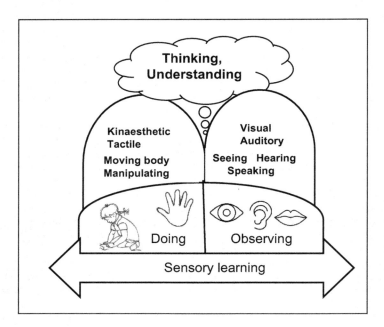

FIGURE 3.1  Example of multisensory learning activities

Griggs 2003). However, it is now more widely accepted that teaching has a greater impact on learning enjoyment and attainment when it involves a combination of senses and learning styles (Gardner 2004, Denig 2004, Shams and Seitz 2008). This is because we absorb and retain multiple sources of information with greater ease and become more actively involved in learning when all four sensory pathways to the brain are engaged at one time (Paivo 1991, Farkas, 2003). The Chinese proverb 'Tell me and I'll forget; show me and I may remember; *involve me and I'll understand*' makes this point well. As Baines (2008) argues, when all the senses work actively together to support thinking, they are as impactful in the classroom as they are in our daily lives. Our senses help us to achieve our objectives and to explore new challenges.

The appeal of multisensory learning, therefore, is clear. With the addition of playful sensory tools, easy-to-use techniques, and intriguing resources, young children are encouraged to actively engage in their own thinking, doing, and learning (Baines 2008, Block et al. 2008: 460–470). Furthermore, research shows that these child-centred activities help early learners to concentrate over longer periods of time and to think more deeply about the task in hand (Aja et al. 2017). This in turn boosts their motivation to learn and helps them to achieve the goals they set themselves (Block et al. 2008). An example of how multimodal teaching can maximise children's enthusiasm for learning is evident in the Rose Review of Early Reading (2006: 16). The report describes how 'the best teaching seen at the review' had 'fired children's interest often by engaging them in multisensory activities' which 'drew upon a mix of stimulating resources'.

## Multisensory reading for meaning

Although multisensory teaching provides significant learning support for children with special educational needs (Kelly and Phillips 2011, Jasmine and Connolly 2015), research shows that a mix of sensory activities helps all learners to process information and self-regulate their understanding (Block et al. 2008). This is particularly the case in the development of early reading skills, which traditionally begins with phonics instruction. As the Rose Review (2006: 16) observes, combining sensory activities such as seeing, speaking, and hearing with a range of physical actions is highly effective for helping young children to recognise and repeat the sound of individual letters in words (Blevins 1997) and sound out words to help them read print. These kinaesthetic and tactile activities, such as bouncing or throwing a ball to letter sounds or clapping to blended sounds in words, are particularly successful.

The Rose Review (2006: 16) also suggests that multisensory activities help to nurture children's 'understanding', although the report provides no further information about this. As Dooley (2011) remarks, developing early comprehension skills through engaging the senses is a relatively new concept. However, an example of successful kinaesthetic teaching is presented in Block et al.'s (2008) pioneering early reading study, which explores whether 5–6-year-olds are capable of learning and portraying comprehension mental processes through the use of specific hand motions. They explain that the purpose of their Comprehension Process Motions design is to make abstract comprehension processes more consciously accessible and to give teachers a way to observe what students have (or have not) comprehended. Their conclusion that even the youngest readers can internalise comprehension processes and know how to elicit them at specific points in a text when they are needed, resonates with our multisensory comprehension projects with reception-aged children (see Chapter 5 pages 46–48).

## SPECtacular reading-for-meaning strategies and multisensory teaching

The acronym 'SPEC' offers teachers, parents, and children a simple way to remember the four key comprehension strategies (Summarising, Predicting, Enquiry, Clarifying) which support the reading-for-meaning process (Palincsar and Brown 1984, Pressley and Wharton-McDonald 2006, Duke and Pearson 2002). By teaching the children how to identify, talk about, and apply each SPEC comprehension strategy themselves to make meaning, they learn how to 1) self-monitor their understanding as they read and 2) how to clarify meanings to make greater sense of texts.

The brief description in Figure 3.2 highlights some of the key features of the four strategies.

---

**Summarise** - *What have I just read?* Summing up and retelling the main points. Ordering events and reorganising information (beginning, middle, end), e.g., Who is involved? What are they doing? Where are they? What is the problem? Why? What is happening? Is the problem solved? How?

**Predict** - *What might happen next?* Using explicit information, clues in the title, pictures, and text with what they already know, to anticipate what might happen next.

**Enquiry/self-questioning** - *What is happening?* Asking and answering their own who, what, where, and why literal and inference questions about the characters, their actions, and events to check their understanding and make predictions about the story.

**Clarify** - *What does this mean?* Making sense of images, words, and concepts by making links with the context and what they already know.

---

FIGURE 3.2 Description of each SPEC comprehension strategy

## The SPEC reading-for-meaning process

The explicit and dialogic instructional process featured in the book's SPEC approach resonates with Kintsch's (1998) construction-integration comprehension model and Alexander's reciprocal approach to 'classroom talk' (2013: 22–29). This type of teaching involves 'building mental representations of what the text means' (Duke et al. 2011: 53) and drawing on one's understanding of the world and knowledge of vocabulary to discuss what you see or infer is happening in picture narrative and text with others (Lysaker and Hopper 2015, Crawford and Hade 2000).

The four strategies are initially taught separately and begin with 'enquiry' (self-questioning skills). Careful teacher modelling shows young readers how to consciously generate and answer simple 'who, what, where' literal questions about the characters, their actions, and the setting. The aim is to encourage them to ask their own questions about texts right from the beginning (Basaraba et al. 2012) to help them establish the key information in a story. Following this, they learn how to search for clues and make connections with their prior knowledge, to predict what might happen next. The process of making predictions introduces the children to causal inference (cause and effect conflicts) in stories. This helps them to understand the steps involved in asking and answering their own inference questions about the narrative, and to think more deeply about the author's meaning and intention. Throughout this procedure they are encouraged to revisit information to clarify for sense and meaning, and to summarise and retell the main points. Once the SPEC strategies are familiar to them, they are shown how to combine the skills to solve comprehension problems as they read.

## Comprehension strategies and multisensory activities

Since the purpose of SPEC comprehension instruction is to show young children how to consciously process their thinking to make meaning of images and text, it is essential that they learn how to 'think aloud about their thinking'. This verbalising of thought processes, listening to, and building on each other's ideas in teacher–pupil discussion about meaning-making involves a metacognitive process which is supported by a variety of sensory activities. All the multisensory activities included in this book (see Figure 3.3) support the process of reasoning, questioning, and making connections with the author to understand narrative. This multisensory comprehension enquiry shows young readers how to:

1.  think and look more closely (visual – viewing),
2.  listen more carefully and articulate ideas with clarity and confidence (auditory – listening and speaking), and
3.  use motor skills more effectively to support learning (tactile/kinesthetic – handling and moving).

For example, see Figure 3.3.

| Multisensory Learning aids | | | | |
|---|---|---|---|---|
| Visual | Audio | | Tactile | Kinaesthetic |
| Looking seeing | Listening hearing | Speaking talking | Touching handling | Moving doing |

| Picture viewer - Visual/tactile tool | Predicting and Clarifying |
|---|---|
| Used to frame details on the page like a magnifying glass or camera. | *Using the 'viewer' like a detective to skim and scan for clues.<br>* Using the viewer's large and small hole like camera lens to:<br>*Zoom in to look closer at details.<br>*Zoom out to see wider context and 'bigger picture'. |
| Hand and body gestures – Kinaesthetic/ aural tool<br>Who is in the story?<br>What are they doing?<br>Where are they?<br>Used to indicate type of literal question and information required to answer. | Enquiry – question and answer prompts<br>*Circling your face to indicate a 'who' question about a character.<br>* Jogging on the spot or your moving arms back and forth to indicate a 'what' question about a character's actions.<br>* Placing your hand above your brow in a searching gesture to indicate a 'where' question about<br>a) the place or<br>b) character's position in relation to characters and objects in a scene. |
| Question cards – Tactile, kinaesthetic, aural<br>Who....? Why....?<br>What...? How do you know?<br>Where?<br>Used to prompt a range of questioning. | Enquiry – question and answer prompts<br>Used to:<br>*Take it in turns to generate and answer your own literal and inference questions about a narrative.<br>*Prompt the use of hand and body gestures to support questioning. |
| Five-finger Retelling – Kinaesthetic, aural<br>Using each finger in succession to retell the main points in the beginning, middle, end of a story. | Summarising<br>* Summarising a story in the correct order as follows:<br>1. In the beginning..... (who, what, where)<br>2. Then .....(problem)<br>3. Next.... (attempts to solve problem)<br>4. After that...(solution)<br>5. In the end.... (outcome) |
| Role-play - Visual, audio, kinaesthetic tool<br>Acting out parts of a story to increase knowledge of story structure and understanding of character's motives | Retelling<br>* Performing or narrating your own version of a narrative to increase your understanding of story themes and plots.<br>* Re-enacting stories to practice summarising events in the correct order. |

FIGURE 3.3 How multisensory learning supports SPEC comprehension

# Multisensory learning aids and activities

FIGURE 3.4 'Modelling how to use the Picture Viewer'. Photograph by Mike Thomson. Reproduced with permission

FIGURE 3.5 'Reception children skimming and scanning pictures for information'. Photograph by Mark Hawkins. Reproduced with permission

**The Picture Viewer** (visual, tactile, and kinaesthetic — using looking, fine motor co-ordination, and body movement). The reader moves this sensory tool around the page to skim and scan for information and frame details for closer examination (see Figures 3.4 and 3.5).

**Hand and body gestures** (visual, kinaesthetic – using looking, fine motor co-ordination and body movement) provide cues for recognising different types of question which supports enquiry and helps readers to retell stories.

Who – circling face (identifying and asking about characters),
What – jogging action (identifying and asking what characters are doing),
Where – searching action – hand over brow (identifying places and characters' positions in a scene)

**Question cards** (visual, tactile, audio – using looking, fine motor co-ordination, listening, speaking) remind the reader of the type of 'Who, What, Where' literal questions and 'Why? How do you know that' detective questions they can ask to support 'book talk' about visual and written texts.

**Five-Finger Retelling** (visual, kinaesthetic, audio – using looking, fine motor co-ordination, speaking). Readers use individual finger movements in sequence to help them summarise and retell the main points of a story in the correct order.

**Role-play** (visual, audio, kinaesthetic – using looking, listening, speaking, fine motor co-ordination and body movements) helps readers to build understanding of story structure through re-enactment of scenes in stories.

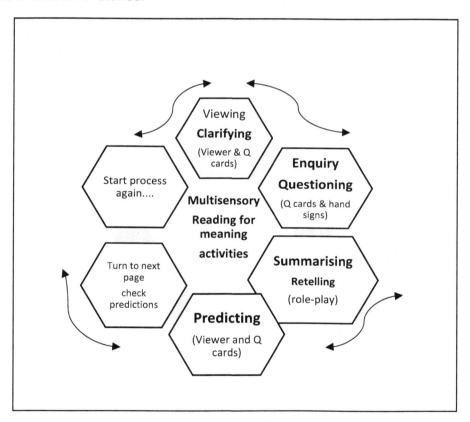

FIGURE 3.6 Example of the SPEC multisensory reading for meaning process in action

Figure 3.6 shows how the SPEC comprehension strategies and multisensory activities help emergent readers to actively take part in the meaning-making process. The reading-for-meaning structure is both versatile and interactive as the table demonstrates. For example, the process might begin with viewing and clarifying and continue through to predicting in a cyclic direction, before the reader begins the process again with the next page. However, more competent readers will learn to move backwards and forwards to different strategies or combine them as they need them.

# How the multisensory comprehension model links to elements of the EYFS framework (2021)

**SPEC** (Summarising/retelling, Predicting, Enquiry/questioning, Clarifying strategies)
**Multisensory learning** (visual, audio, tactile/kinaesthetic techniques, and learning aids)

FIGURE 3.7 'Picture book talk'. Photograph by Mark Hawkins. Reproduced with permission

FIGURE 3.8 'Searching for picture clues using the Viewer'. Photograph by Mark Hawkins. Reproduced with permission

As Figure 3.9 demonstrates, the multisensory activities involved in the SPEC reading-for-meaning process directly relate to the characteristics of effective learning and early learning goals in the EYFS framework (2021). For example, the model's emphasis on playful and explorative active learning using role-play, hand motions, moving and handling objects (e.g., the Viewer, question card prompts) also involves viewing, listening, understanding, and speaking. These are all key elements of the prime areas of learning. In addition, the creative and critical thinking and discussion which is central to this teaching approach helps young readers to build learning self-awareness, reasoning, communication, and language skills which are fundamental aims of the EYFS framework (see Figures 3.7 and 3.8).

Furthermore, this collaborative process fosters self-confidence and a love of reading and helps to build the personal, social, and emotional skills which prepare young readers for learning across the curriculum, and for a more confident transition from Reception to Key Stage 1. Figure 3.9 further outlines how this multisensory comprehension approach includes a structure for developing reading self-regulation, relationship building, and emotional intelligence.

---

How SPEC Multisensory Comprehension Model links to Prime areas of learning and ELGs
Department for Education (2021) Statutory framework for the early years foundation stage

---

Characteristics of effective learning (CEF)

- Playing and exploring – 'engagement'
- Active learning – 'motivation' and empowerment
- Creating and thinking critically – 'Choosing ways to do things and finding new ways' and developing and linking concepts.

Links to Characteristics of effective learning criteria

- Combination of visual, audio, tactile and kinaesthetic activities and strategies support child-centred reading and questioning.
- Class learns how to self-monitor and demonstrate understanding of picture narrative and text using SPEC comprehension strategies and questioning techniques.
- Children learn how to search for clues, identify and apply appropriate strategies to generate and answer their own and respond to other's questions about picture narrative and text.

**Prime areas of learning and Early Learning Goals (ELGs)**

Links to Communication and Language criteria: 'This involves giving children opportunities to speak and listen in a range of situations and to develop their confidence and skills in expressing themselves.'

---

FIGURE 3.9 How SPEC comprehension strategies and sensory learning link to key areas of EYFS framework (2021).

Creating and thinking critically

SPEC comprehension activities include careful looking, listening, and speaking to help them gather information to *ask questions*.

Listening and attention ELG – To be able to '...listen to stories... accurately anticipating key events and respond to what they (see) and hear with relevant comments, questions, or actions.'

- Children are shown how to listen for information and scrutinise pictures and text for clues to respond accurately and relevantly to questions about what they hear and see.

Understanding ELG - 'Children follow instructions involving several ideas or actions. They answer 'how' and 'why' questions about their experiences and in response to stories or events'.

- SPEC comprehension activities include following instructions and constructing meaning from information to ask and answer questions.
- Class is shown how to find meaning as they read and self-monitor their understanding.
- They learn how to *ask and answer* their own literal and inference questions to demonstrate their understanding of what they have read.

Speaking ELG – To be able to: '... express themselves effectively, showing awareness of listeners' needs'.

'They use past, present, and future forms accurately when talking about events that have happened or are to happen in the future. They develop their own narratives and explanations by connecting ideas or events'.

- Children use past, present, and future forms accurately when talking about events in class discussion, retelling stories and making predictions about what might happen next to characters in stories they have read.
- They demonstrate understanding of narrative by explaining connections made between ideas or events in the text.

Links to Physical Development criteria: 'This involves providing opportunities for children to be active and interactive, and to develop their co-ordination, control, and movement.'

Playing and exploring

The SPEC Multisensory approach combines visual, auditory, and physical sensory learning to encourage interactive reading for meaning and pleasure.

Moving and handling ELG – (Using body movements and manipulating objects) To be able to: '.... show good control and co-ordination in large and small movements. They move confidently in a range of ways, safely negotiating space. They handle equipment and tools effectively.'

FIGURE 3.9 (Continued)

- Children are shown how to move and operate SPEC sensory learning tools. For example, how to use:
- Small movements to operate the 'Viewer'- a sensory aid for framing and examining picture details to find and link clues,
- The 'Q cards' sensory aid helps to prompt 'who, what, where, why, how do you know?' questioning about a story. Large movements - drawing 'who, what, where symbols in the air to demonstrate identification of question types and role-play.

Links to Personal, Social and Emotional criteria

This involves 'helping children to:

- develop a positive sense of themselves and others,
- form positive relationships and develop respect for others,
- develop social skills and learn how to manage their feelings,
- understand appropriate behaviour in groups.
- have confidence in their own abilities.'

Active learning

The SPEC model promotes the ethos of co-operation, working together and self-regulated learning to foster self-confidence and empowered learning.

Self-confidence and self-regulation ELG – To '…..feel confident about trying new activities and say why they like some activities more than others. They are confident speaking in a familiar group, will talk about their ideas, and will choose the resources they need for their chosen activities. They say when they do or do not need help.'

- The SPEC model engages children in thinking and talking about learning processes to encourage learning awareness. This helps individuals to recognise and celebrate their strengths and resolve weaknesses through:
- use of 'riskometer' to boost confidence in class discussion,
- use of metacognition - thinking about learning processes and activities,
- learning how to use comprehension skills self-assessment to self-monitor their learning,
- one-to-one SPEC reading skills assessment with their teacher - encouraging children to talk about their learning strengths and weaknesses and how to resolve specific issues.
- Team points chart is used to motivate learning and reward individual and group effort.

Managing feelings and behaviour ELG - To be able to: '….. talk about how they and others show feelings, talk about their own and others' behaviour and its consequences, and know that some behaviour is unacceptable. They work as part of a group or class and understand and follow the rules. They adjust their behaviour to different situations and take changes of routine in their stride.'

FIGURE 3.9 (Continued)

- Children are encouraged to work collaboratively in pairs and in groups - thinking and talking with others about their personal experiences, feelings, reactions to cause and effect conflicts.
- This helps them to empathise and support each other and to better understand character's motives and behaviour in stories.

Making relationships ELG – To be able to: '….. play co-operatively, taking turns with others. They take account of one another's ideas about how to organise their activity. They show sensitivity to others' needs and feelings and form positive relationships with adults and other children.'

- The SPEC teaching activities show pairs and groups of children the rules of interaction and how to work together effectively and co-operatively.
- They are also encouraged to acknowledge their own and each other's skills and talents which teaches them empathy and respect.

FIGURE 3.9 (Continued)

# References

Aja, N., Eze, S., Igba, P., Igba, D., Nwafor, E.C., and Nnamani, S. (2017). Using multi-sensory instruction in managing classroom for effective teaching and learning. *International Journal of Applied Engineering Research*, 12(24), 15112–15118.

Alexander, R.J. (2013). *Improving oracy and classroom talk: Achievements and challenges*. Primary First.

Baines, L. (2008). *A teacher's guide to multisensory learning: Improving literacy by engaging the senses...* Association for Supervision & Curriculum Development.

Basaraba, D., Yovanoff, P., Alonzo, J., and Tindal, G. (2012). Examining the structure of reading comprehension: Do literal, inferential, and evaluative comprehension truly exist? *Reading and Writing*, 26, 349–379.

Blevins, W. (1997). *Phonemic awareness activities for early reading success: Easy, playful activities that help prepare children for phonics instruction*. Scholastic.

Block, C., Parris, S., and Whiteley, C. (2008). CPMs: A kinesthetic comprehension strategy. *The Reading Teacher*, 61(6), 460–470.

Crawford, P.A., and Hade, D.D. (2000). Inside the picture, outside the frame: Semiotics and the reading of wordless picture books. *Journal of Research in Childhood Education*, 15(1), 66–80.

Denig, S.J. (2004). Multiple intelligences and learning styles: Two complementary dimensions. *Teachers College Record*, 106(1), 96–111.

Department for Education. (2021). *Statutory framework for the Early Years Foundation Stage*. www.gov.uk/government/publications/early-years-foundation-stage-framework--2

Dooley, C.M. (2011). The emergence of comprehension: A decade of research 2000–2010. *International Electronic Journal of Elementary Education*, 4(1), 169–184.

Duke, N.K., and Pearson, D. (2002). Effective practices for developing reading comprehension. In A.E. Farstrup and S.J. Samuels (Eds), *What research has to say about reading instruction* (3rd edn). International Reading Association.

Duke, N.K., Pearson, P.D., Strachan, S.L., and Biullman, A.K. (2011). *What research has to say about reading instruction* (4th edn) (S.J. Samuels and A.E. Farstrup, Eds). International Reading Association.

Dunn, R., and Dunn, K. (1993). *Teaching elementary students through their individual learning styles: Practical approaches for Grades 3–6*. Allyn and Bacon.

Dunn, R., and Griggs, S.A. (2003). *Synthesis of the Dunn and Dunn learning-style model research: Who, what, when, where, and so what?* St. John's University's Center for the Study of Learning and Teaching Styles.

Farkas, R.D. (2003). Effects of traditional versus learning-styles instructional methods on middle school students. *The Journal of Educational Research*, 97(1), 42–51. https://doi.org/10.1080/0022067030 9596627

Gardner, H. (1999). *Intelligence reframed: Multiple intelligences for the 21st century*. Basic Books.

Gardner, H. (2004). Audiences for the theory of multiple intelligences*. *Teachers College Record*, 106(1), 212–220. https://doi.org/10.1111/j.1467-9620.2004.00329.x

Jasmine, J., and Connolly, M. (2015). The use of multisensory approaches during center time, through visual, auditory, and kinesthetic-tactile activities, to enhance spelling accuracy of second grade students. *Journal of Education and Social Policy*, 2(1), 12–19.

Kelly, K., and Phillips, S. (2011). *Teaching literacy to learners with dyslexia: A multisensory approach*. Sage Publications.

Kintsch, W. (1998). *Comprehension: A paradigm for cognition*. Cambridge University Press.

Lysaker, J., and Hopper, E. (2015). A kindergardner's emergent strategy use during wordless picture book reading. *Reading Teacher*, 68(8), 649–657.

Paivo, A. (1991). Dual coding theory: Retrospective and current status. *Canadian Journal of Psychology*, 45, 255–287

Palincsar, A., and Brown, A. (1984). Reciprocal teaching of comprehension-fostering and comprehension-monitoring activities. *Cognition and Instruction*, 1, 117–175.

Pressley, M., and Wharton-McDonald, R. (2006). The need for increased comprehension instruction. In M. Pressley (Ed.), *Reading instruction that works: The case for balancing teaching* (3rd edn). The Guilford Press.

Rose, J. (2006). *Independent review of the teaching of early reading: Final report*. Department of Education & Skills. https://dera.ioe.ac.uk/5551/2/report.pdf

Shams, L., and Seitz, A.R. (2008). Benefits of multisensory learning. *Trends in Cognitive Sciences*, 12(11), 411–417.

# CHAPTER 4

# Teaching children *how* to think, speak, and question (for themselves)

## What is active thinking?

Thinking is a difficult concept to define. It is commonly perceived as a continual process of organising information, solving problems, making decisions, and generating ideas. Thinking skills expert Robert Fisher (1990) describes it more succinctly as a creative and critical mental activity through which we make meaning out of life. He also points out that although it is generally a personal and individual action, it is 'not done in isolation'. Thinking is a collaborative, social activity. It is influenced by others, by our culture, experiences, and environment. It is also central to how information in the brain is stored and used as a tool for learning to develop different aspects of our intelligence (Gardner 1993). Active thinking, therefore, involves teaching children how to consciously think for themselves, which as we all know, is an essential activity for personal development, and for life-long reading and learning.

According to Sternberg (1984/1990), success in thinking involves three components to process information which Fisher (1990) agrees is determined by efficiency in these operations which can be developed through instruction (see Chapter 6). For example see Figure 4.1.

DOI: 10.4324/9781003226307-5

| Processing elements for successful thinking – Sternberg (1984: 11) | Developing thinking skills through instruction – Fisher (1990: 12) |
| --- | --- |
| Knowledge acquisition<br>*Learning new material (input)*<br>*e.g., seeing, hearing, physical/sensory experience* | Acquiring knowledge (input)<br>*Learner is taught how to acquire knowledge and skills* |
| Performance<br>*What we do (output)*<br>*e.g., remembering, reflecting, generating ideas, problem solving* | Strategies for using knowledge and solving problems (output)<br>*Learner is taught how to apply skills effectively to solve problems* |
| Strategic thinking<br>*Organising what has been learned (control)*<br>*e.g., control of memory, planning, decision-making, evaluating* | Metacognition and decision-making (executive control)<br>*Learner is taught how to reflect on and make changes to improve own thinking to make effective decisions* |

FIGURE 4.1 Processing information (adapted from Fisher 1990: 11–12, and Sternberg 1984/1990: 11)

The first column in Figure 4.1 suggests the process of acquiring knowledge involves understanding, absorbing, storing, and retaining information in memory. This input may include a physical or sensory experience or information we have seen, heard, or read, which we can recall and apply at a later stage. However, successful retrieval of information relies on how we have encoded it in our memory. The second column in Figure 4.1 suggests it is essential, therefore, for young learners to be shown how to consciously use cognitive strategies and higher order thinking, such as metacognition and multisensory learning, to help them control their use of memory. They are then more able to plan, monitor, and evaluate their learning effectively to gain the most from what they have been taught (Whitebread and Basilio 2012).

## Teaching 'thinking about thinking' - cognition and metacognition

Cognition is essentially the mental process of knowing, understanding, and learning. It relies on strategies or memorisation techniques for learners to successfully develop complex skills, such as reading comprehension and self-questioning (Education Endowment Foundation, 2018). Although cognitive strategies are central to good teaching and learning, problem solving is shown to be more effective when children feel motivated to learn and know how to evaluate and self-regulate their learning (Pascal et al. 2018). Metacognition is a process that supports this conscious thinking, engagement, and monitoring of understanding. The learner is shown 1) how to become aware of what they already know, and 2) how to select and apply appropriate strategies to complete a task successfully (Taylor 2014). Furthermore, years of personal study and practice has shown me that the earlier children are taught *how* to consciously apply metacognitive strategies to support reading for meaning and self-questioning, the more their reading attainment and enjoyment of learning in general improves. Although we usually associate this level of text interrogation with fluent readers, evidence shows that it is within reach of all children. Even very young children have prior knowledge and experience that prompts them to make inferences from stories (Hudson and Slackman 1990), and 'children as young as four years old can generate certain types of inferences during reading' (YARC, Snowling et al. 2009).

Additionally, our action-research and other studies (Whitebread and Basilio 2012, Blair and Razza 2007) indicate that children as young as 3 years old can engage in a wide range of self-regulatory reading-for-meaning tasks, once they have been explicitly shown how to check their understanding. Indeed, a wealth of evidence shows that when teachers model skills using a step-by-step framework, such as Reciprocal Reading (Palincsar and Brown 1984; Chapter 6, pages 55 and 57), children can develop metacognitive knowledge, even at a very young age.

However, this trust in early metacognitive instruction is not shared by all. There is a common mis-conception that young children do not possess the concentration, motivation, and self-knowledge to be able to plan, monitor, and evaluate their own reading for meaning. This probably stems from the long-held view that in the first years of education children do not have the capacity to con-sciously identify and apply cognitive comprehension skills – until they are 8–10 years old (e.g., Flavell 1987, Veneman and Spaans 2005, Gutiérrez-Braojos et al. 2014).

Yet empirical data indicates that delay in teaching comprehension strategies (PIRLS 2006, 2011, 2016) may have contributed to the decline in students' reading performance and infer-ence skills in the period between 2006 and 2011. This has prompted recent research to inves-tigate the potential for earlier strategic comprehension instruction in the primary curriculum. For example, Molly Ness's (2011: 99) paper which examines the impact of teaching early reading comprehension skills reports that 'students who received the direct explanations of reading comprehension strategy instruction outperformed their peers who received no such instruction'. She points specifically to strategies that elicit readers' cognitive, metacognitive, and behavioural knowledge because they have 'consistently high levels of impact' on pupils' learning, reading performance, and self-confidence. She also highlights the importance of teacher facilitation of 'modelling, think-alouds, scaffolding, guided practice and independent practice', which supports this.

## The teacher's role as facilitator

As Ness (2011) emphasises, teacher facilitation of metacognition and self-questioning is key when encouraging young children to consciously think about how they make meaning. It requires practitioners to first be explicit about *how* to apply the core SPEC strategies – then allow plenty of time for 'thinking', interactive discussion, modelling of the skills and practice using them. Reciprocal teachers also need to guide and model the 'language of debate' during discussion to provide a scaffold for purposeful 'talk' and respectful listening when children are working together in groups (see examples in Part 3, Unit 1, pages 112 and 113).

By modelling discussion and enquiry skills – then 'stepping back' to actively listen, the recip-rocal teacher is showing the class that what they have to say is of real importance and interest to them. They are giving them permission to express themselves; to listen and discuss other's perspectives; to think, question, and reason for themselves.

This approach ensures that these sessions are child-led rather than teacher-led – and prepares the children for the responsibility and challenges later in reciprocal reading when they will be man-aging their own group discussions and decision-making to complete group tasks.

# Building skills and 'letting go': Scaffolding and gradual release of responsibility

When teaching and learning involves a metacognitive framework, this usually includes teacher–pupil co-construction of meaning, alongside frequent modelling and scaffolding of how to consciously apply strategies. By gradually facilitating learning independence in this way, teachers can move from assuming 'all the responsibility for performing a task… to a situation in which the students assume all the responsibility' (Duke and Pearson 2002: 211). This instructional approach is described by Askew (2007: 91) as the 'ultimate goal' of teaching because it helps passive learners to become 'independent learners' who know how to select and apply strategies appropriately to support their understanding as they read.

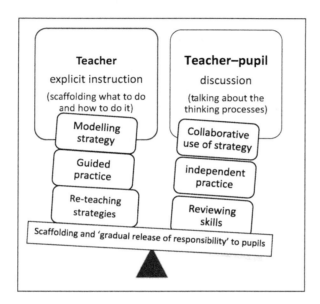

FIGURE 4.2  Example of scaffolding and gradual release of responsibility

As Figure 4.2 indicates, teacher scaffolding is a balance of explicit instruction, modelling of strategies, back-and-forth dialogue between pupils and teacher, and guided practice to support the children's thinking and learning. This 'collaborative use of the strategy in action' (Duke et al. 2011: 65–66) fosters personal responsibility for the tasks and helps young readers to gradually master the skills on their own. This series of progressive steps is effective when they are delivered as follows.

## Explicit strategy instruction (one strategy at a time)

The content is broken down into manageable teaching units based on children's cognitive capabilities (showing them what to do and how to do it). The teacher introduces the children to each set of skills separately. This involves describing the skills explicitly and discussing:

- the reader's previous knowledge of the strategy, and
- the purpose of the strategy and how and when to use it.

## Modelling the strategy

The teacher uses 'think-alouds' to demonstrate how to use a specific strategy (e.g., predicting). They talk through each small step to ensure the children understand what to do and why they are doing it. For instance, after they have introduced the topic of the story (e.g., dressing up for 'Book Day') and asked the children to discuss what they know about the subject, the practitioner might model how the predicting process works as follows:

- 'We make predictions by first asking ourselves simple questions about the characters' actions and whereabouts. We look at the details we can see right there on the page e.g., 'Who are they? What are they doing? Where are they?'
- 'We use this information to ask questions about less obvious details in the scene (the clues). eg '…I can see six characters in this scene… Mmmmh… I wonder why they are all standing together in a huddle?'
- 'When we link this information to our own experiences and what we know about the world, it helps us to make predictions about what might happen next in the story… eg., 'I think the friends are waiting to have a photo taken of them in their Book Day costumes…'
- 'Good Detectives also give reasons for their predictions, using the clues they have found on the page to explain… 'I say that because'… e.g., 'they are all facing one way and smiling or making faces. Also, I can see a hand is holding up a mobile phone like a camera and pointing it in the direction of the group…'

## Collaborative use of strategy and reflection

Directly after the teacher modelling, it is important that the class or groups/pairs are given the opportunity to apply the strategy for themselves, then share their collaborative ideas with the teacher and other children. They might also talk about any successes or difficulties they may have experienced during the task.

## Guided practice supported by teacher scaffolding

Teacher scaffolding involves regular modelling of skills and guided practice. This can be supported effectively using graphic organisers to help the children plan, draw, or write down their ideas. For example, Figure 4.3 shows how the Retelling Map in the book (see graphic organiser p. 239 and Unit 4 p. 164) provides visual cues that indicate how to gather, organise, and retell the main 'who, what, where, why' information about a story in the correct order. This type of guided practice, supported by teacher scaffolding and discussion, helps children to 'think about their thinking', and organise their ideas in a way that is easy for them to comprehend, internalise, and share. The reflective discussion generated by these activities encourages young children to talk about their learning. The shared knowledge and support this generates gradually builds their confidence in initiating the comprehension processes without teacher prompting.

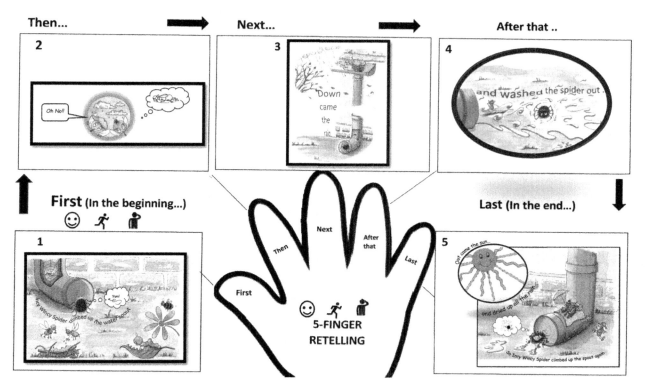

FIGURE 4.3 Example of Five-Finger Retelling Map (images from *Little Fly and the Spider Trap* by Donna Thomson and Chrissy Morgan-Grant)

## Independent practice

Pupils complete their own investigation after they have been shown how to select and combine strategies appropriately to help them self-monitor their understanding as they read (see examples in Teaching Units 3 and 4 pages 139–175). This is followed again by reflective teacher–pupil discussion or sharing of ideas as a class about what they have just read.

The following example of a discussion with a group of 5-year-olds after a paired picture reading activity demonstrates how their knowledge of prediction and clarifying strategies helps them to 1) work out what is happening and may happen in the story, and 2) justify their thinking.

*Teacher:* Who is in the story?
*Will:* Annie
*Teacher:* What is she doing?
*Amy:* Looking out of the window at the lightning.
*Teacher:* Where do you think Annie is?
*Amy:* At home… in her bedroom.
*Teacher:* Why do you think it's her bedroom?
*Amy:* Because it is dark… so, it is bedtime.
*Will:* You might see more of a storm up in your bedroom.
*Teacher:* Interesting Will – why do you say that?
*Will:* Because it's more stormy at night time.

*Jade:* There is the top of a tree outside the window… so she is upstairs. Probably in her bedroom.
*Will:* I think she is scared, and she wants her Mum to come.
*Teacher:* Why do you think she's scared?
*Will:* (Long pause) Because she looks… because she looks unhappy…
*Ruby:* I think Annie's scared because of the storm.
*Jacob:* I think Annie's scared because it is dark.
*Will:* I think Annie's scared because she hasn't heard thunder before.
*Emma:* I think Annie's scared because the thunder was loud.
*Teacher:* What do you think Annie might be thinking?
*Ruby:* (Long pause) She is scared the tree might fall down in the garden… because…

## Reviewing skills

This review stage provides teachers and readers with an opportunity to talk about the pupil's comprehension strengths and weaknesses (see Chapter 7 p. 66). The purpose of this discussion is to assess whether the reader has sufficiently mastered the new skills to be able to move on to the next stage of instruction. For example, the teacher may consider whether:

- their answers relate to the explicit information in the picture narrative,
- they have problems identifying literal information,
- they are engaged in the picture content, e.g., have they looked closely enough at the picture detail?
- Is the pupil's prior knowledge being used in addition to the direct information in the picture narrative?
- Do they understand the phrasing of the question/meaning of the vocabulary used in the story title, text and in the questions?
- Do they have problems with answering or asking literal questions?
- Do they have problems expressing themselves?
- Does the pupil have problems writing down answers to explicit questions or writing their own literal questions?

## Re-teaching strategies or skills where necessary

A review of comprehension skills at the end of each teaching unit provides a useful overview of progress and informs teachers whether to revisit specific elements of instruction to ensure these skills are embedded before progressing to the next strategy.

With consistent teacher modelling of specific strategies and gradual release of responsibility from teacher to pupil, even young children can eventually identify and apply the skills they need to complete a particular comprehension task and monitor whether it has been successful. Teacher scaffolding of skills also provides emergent readers with a structure for learning how to generate and answer their own questions about picture narrative to help them to think more deeply about the author's meaning. For example, the steps involved in this book (see Teaching Units 1–4 pages 108–174) show reception children how to:

- gather data and clues from pictures, text, graphs, diagrams,
- apply this information to help them question and understand direct and inferred meaning on the page,

- retell, summarise, make predictions, and make sense of unknown words from context,
- form simple and complex sentences from their growing knowledge of how language is structured,
- generate a range of their own questions and answers from their knowledge of sentence structure,
- make links between clues in text and their own prior experience to ask inference questions and justify their answers fully,
- use synonyms and antonyms to help them to identify, generate, and answer inference questions from pictures and text, and
- identify and make sense of language to support deeper understanding of unknown words and concepts in text.

## The importance of 'talk' – the 'Language of Discussion'

It is crucial that children understand the role that discussion plays in developing thinking and reading for meaning skills. When they learn how to listen respectfully to others, using a framework for discussion that encourages active 'talk' about how their ideas and experiences link to texts, they enjoy a deeper understanding of each other and the meaning in stories (Chambers 2011, Mercer 2000).

They soon learn that the flow of group discussion is greatly influenced by the way a thought is expressed or received. They understand that it is important that ideas, reasons, and points of view are acknowledged by the next speaker, whether they agree or disagree with what has been said. They begin to realise that when they use 'the Language of Discussion' (see Teaching Unit 1 p. 113), it helps them to slow down their reactions, bring clarity to their thoughts and articulate their ideas more confidently. This in turn fosters respect and consideration for each other and demonstrates that everyone has something of value to contribute.

A step-by-step approach and back-and-forth dialogue between teachers and pupils are also fundamental to successful skills-based instruction. Pupil discussion about their thinking and learning encourages them to reflect on their decision-making, learn from others, extend their thinking further, and become more aware of how they learn (Alexander 2013: 22–29, Mercer 2000). Also, when children possess the metacognitive steps and comprehension strategies to reason, question, plan, evaluate, and monitor their understanding as they read, they learn how to talk about and eventually manage their own thinking to respond independently to a problem (Palincsar 1986, Whitebread et al. 2007).

## Self-belief and self-regulation – engagement and motivation

The impact of self-belief on 'effective intellectual functioning' (Bandura 1993: 117) and emotional well-being was one of the most compelling aspects of our early comprehension case studies. Although there has been a resurgence of interest in how students' self-perception of their ability influences their learning and academic achievement (Pascal et al. 2018), Bandura suggests that a good deal of cognitive research has neglected the 'self-regulatory processes that govern' an individual's 'development and adaption'. He emphasises that these beliefs in one's own capability are central to the way 'people feel, think, motivate themselves, and behave'. He concludes, therefore, that the more a child believes in their ability to achieve a task and the higher they set the goals for themselves, the more likely they are to remain engaged and committed to the task (Whitebread and Basilio 2012). A recent review of effective pedagogical practice in Reception Year (Pascal et al. 2018: 29) also provides conclusive evidence that self-regulation skills and development of self-executive functioning abilities encourages 'greater autonomy in learning', 'long-term well-being', and 'academic attainment'.

## Comprehension strategies and skills – what is the difference?

Explicit reading for meaning instruction is particularly helpful in nurturing cognitive self-regulation because young readers are shown how to consciously choose the most effective tactics to help them understand the text they read. These tactics are known as reading comprehension strategies. Comprehension skills, on the other hand, are the product of this goal-directed practice. These skills become established once readers know how to automatically and flexibly apply strategies to support reading for meaning. For example, Afflerbach et al. (2008: 371) observe that '... while automatic use of reading skills is a goal of reading instruction', readers will only develop effortless use of skills following 'a period of deliberate and conscious application'. Paris and Paris (2003) further explain that readers need to be aware of their comprehension strengths and weaknesses and develop the appropriate knowledge to help them tackle problems as they occur. Their ability to find ways to make sense of the text are the skills they have learned through practising the use of specific strategies. Afflerbach et al. (2008: 370) also emphasise that 'teaching these kinds of reading strategies explicitly helps children to understand what they are doing and why it is important'.

This understanding about the difference between strategies and skills has arisen from observations of proficient readers and how they use effective thinking and problem solving to understand visual and written text. For example, good readers rely on some of the comprehension strategies and skills outlined in Figure 4.4 to clarify meanings as they read.

All these skills (Figure 4.4) are linked to the four SPEC strategies that feature in this book's metacognitive teaching approach (Summarising/retelling, Predicting, Enquiry/questioning and Clarifying; see Chapter 6 and Part 3 Teaching Units 1–4). These strategies are based on the reciprocal reading model, devised by Palincsar and Brown (1984) to support the collaborative development of reading comprehension skills. This interactive approach is widely used in the USA, Australia, New Zealand, and more recently in UK schools.

## SPEC reciprocal teaching method

The reciprocal framework offers young readers a systematic and logical method for making meaning together which is easy to apply after explicit instruction and sustained practice. Emergent readers learn how to identify and re-organise information to support and solve comprehension problems as they explore picture books together. The metacognitive teaching sequences involve a step-by-step process which helps them to build higher order thinking skills to assist their understanding of texts. This begins with exploring visual material, then written texts using co-construction and teacher modelling. This careful scaffolding of strategies eventually leads to release of the teacher's

| Strategies | Skills |
|---|---|
| Activating prior knowledge | Organising and combining general knowledge, past reactions or experiences which are stored in memory with incoming information to help construct meaning (e.g. Carr and Thompson 1996, Kintsch and van Dijk 1978) |
| Visualising | Creating mental images of characters, objects, actions, and places to clarify spoken and written meanings (e.g., Kintsch and Rawson 2005) |
| Using graphic and semantic organisers | Using a visual tool for showing relationship between concepts (Trehearne 2006: 159) e.g., organising, and synthesising information in a concise, logical way to support recall. Drawing or writing down ideas to deepen thinking and understanding |
| Synthesising and integrating | Tracking thinking and new ideas about text - being aware of how thinking changes and evolves during reading to achieve an overall understanding (e.g., Mills 2008) |
| Making connections | Drawing on prior knowledge to make sense of information in text, linking what the reader knows with inferences in text to make deductions about characters, events, and places (Harvey and Goudvis 2007, Hall 2015) |
| Generating and answering questions | Readers ask themselves a range of questions to check their understanding as they read (Bloom 1956, Parkin et al. 2002) |

FIGURE 4.4  Example of some reading comprehension strategies and skills

responsibility for managing the skills to the pupils' conscious use of them to self-monitor their understanding (see Chapter 4, p. 31).

The purpose of this reciprocal approach is to:

- help children across the ability range to grasp the thinking processes involved in interpreting author's meaning,
- teach them the comprehension strategies, inference skills and questioning techniques that encourage 'understanding' of text to grow out of their own enquiry,
- show them how to apply key comprehension strategies to monitor their understanding of the author's meaning before, during, and after reading, and
- bring a sustainable level of meaning, reasoning, and enjoyment of reading to them that is essential to life-long learning.

See the framework in Chapter 6 (p. 57) which provides an overview of the comprehension strategies and the order the learner might initially be shown how to use these skills to explore a page in a picture book.

## Self-questioning instruction – self-monitoring understanding

In her research review on the use of self-questioning instruction as a reading strategy, Janssen (2002: 96) demonstrates how self-questioning plays 'an important role in self-regulative, independent learning'. She explains that when readers attempt to make sense of text, their 'natural response to literature' is to ask questions about it as they read. This is supported by other studies (Hervey 2006, Basaraba et al. 2012, Joseph et al. 2015) which suggest that self-questioning during reading increases reader engagement in the text and improves the reader's understanding of the author's meaning and intention (see Teaching Units 2–4). In addition, evidence from our action-research and other sources (Gavins 2016, PIRLS Report 2011) demonstrates that when literal and inferential reading is mastered, most children, regardless of initial reading ability, can read for meaning with greater ease and monitor their understanding before, during, and after reading. They realise that generating their own questions helps them to understand information on the page, and enables them to discuss the author's purpose, which fully engages them in the story and gives them a personal connection with the author. I have learned that we simply need to start early and be explicit when teaching young children how to identify and apply self-questioning skills to help them think more for themselves (Thomson and Nixey 2005). This early instruction not only boosts literacy skills and encourages reading for pleasure, but also empowers their learning across the curriculum.

## References

Afflerbach, P., Pearson, P., and Paris, S.G. (2008). Clarifying differences between reading skills and reading strategies. *The Reading Teacher*, 61(5), 364–373.

Alexander, R.J. (2013). *Improving oracy and classroom talk: Achievements and challenges.* Primary First.

Askew, B. (2007). A tribute to Marie M. Clay: She searched for questions that needed answers. *Journal of Reading Recovery*, 91. https://readingrecovery.org/wp-content/uploads/2016/12/JRR_7.1Askew.2.pdf

Bandura, A. (1993). *Perceived self-efficiency in cognitive development and functioning.* www.uky.edu/~eushe2/Bandura/Bandura1993EP.pdf

Basaraba, D., Yovanoff, P., Alonzo, J., and Tindal, G. (2012). Examining the structure of reading comprehension: Do literal, inferential, and evaluative comprehension truly exist? *Reading and Writing*, 26, 349–379.

Blair, C.Y., and Razza, R.P. (2007). Relating effortful control, executive function, and false belief understanding to emerging math and literacy abilities in kindergarten. *Child Development*, 78, 647–663.

Bloom, B.S. (1956). *Taxonomy of educational objectives, Handbook I: The cognitive domain.* David McKay Co.

Carr, S., and Thompson, B. (1996). The effects of prior knowledge and schema activation strategies on the inferential reading comprehension of children with and without learning disabilities. *Learning Disability Quarterly*, 19(1), 48–61.

Chambers, A. (2011). *Tell me: Children, reading and talk: With the reading environment.* Thimble Press.

Duke, N., and Pearson, D. (2002). Effective practices for developing reading comprehension. In A. Farstrup and J. Samuels (Eds), *What research has to say about reading instruction* (3rd edn). International Reading Association.

Duke, N.K., Pearson, P.D., Strachan, S.L., and Biullman, A.K. (2011). *What research has to say about reading instruction* (4th edn) (S.J. Samuels and A.E. Farstrup, Eds). International Reading Association.

Education Endowment Foundation. (2018). *Metacognition and self-regulated learning guidance report.* https://educationendowmentfoundation.org.uk/public/files/Publications/Metacognition/EEF_Metacognition_and_self-regulated_learning.pdf

Fisher, R. (1990). *Teaching children to think*. Stanley Thornes.

Flavell, J.H. (1987). Speculations about the nature and development of metacognition. In F.E. Weinert and R.H. Kluwe (Eds), *Metacognition, Motivation and Understanding*. Erlbaum.

Gardner, H. (1993). *Frames of mind: The theory of multiple intelligences* (10th anniversary edn). Basic Books.

Gavins, P. (2016). Tipping the scales of justice in your favour. *Times Educational Supplement*, 6 February.

Gutiérrez-Braojos, C., Fernández, S.R., and Vílchez, P.S. (2014). How can reading comprehension strategies and recall be improved in elementary school students? *Estudios Sobre Educacion*, 26, 9–31.

Hall, C.S. (2015). Inference instruction for struggling readers: A synthesis of intervention research. *Educational Psychology Review*, 28, 1–22.

Harvey, S., and Goudvis, A. (2007). *Strategies that work: Teaching comprehension for understanding and engagement* (2nd edn). Stenhouse House Publishers.

Hervey, S. (2006). Who asks the questions? *Teaching Pre K-8*, 37(1), 68–69. eric.ed.gov/?id=EJ746030

Hudson, J.A., and Slackman, E.A. (1990). Children's use of scripts in inferential text processing. *Discourse Processes*, 13(4), 375–385.

Janssen, T. (2002). Instruction in self-questioning as a literary reading strategy: An exploration of empirical research. *L1 – Educational Studies in Language and Literature*, 2, 95–120.

Joseph, L.M., Alber-Morgan, S., Cullen, J., and Rouse, C. (2015). The effects of self-questioning on reading comprehension: A literature review. *Reading & Writing Quarterly*, 32(2), 152–173.

Kintsch, W., and Rawson, K.A. (2005). Comprehension. In M.J. Snowling and C. Hulme (Eds), *The science of reading: A handbook*. Blackwell.

Kintsch, W., and van Dijk, T.A. (1978). Towards a model of text comprehension and production. *Psychological Review*, 85, 363–394.

Mercer, N. (2000). *Words and minds: How we use language to think together*. Routledge.

Mills, K.A. (2008). The seven habits of highly effective readers. Conference: Stories, Places, Spaces: Literacy and Identity, National conference by the Australian Literacy Educators' Association (ALEA) and Australian Association for the Teaching of English, Adelaide, SA, 6–9 July 2008.

Ness, M. (2011). Explicit reading comprehension instruction in elementary classrooms: Teacher use of reading comprehension strategies. *Journal of Research in Childhood Education*, 25(1), 98–117.

Palincsar, A.S. (1986). The role of dialogue in providing scaffolded instruction. *Educational Psychologist*, 21(1–2), 73–98.

Palincsar, A.S., and Brown, A. (1984). Reciprocal teaching of comprehension-fostering and comprehension-monitoring activities. *Cognition and Instruction*, 1, 117–175.

Paris, S., and Paris, S.G. (2003). Assessing narrative comprehension in young children. *Reading Research Quarterly*, 38, 36–76.

Parkin, C., Parkin, C., and Pool, B. (2002). *PROBE – taxonomy of question types, reading assessment New Zealand*. Triune Initiatives.

Pascal, C., Bertram, T., and Rouse, L. (2018). *Getting it right in the Early Years Foundation Stage*. The British Association for Early Childhood Education.

Progress in International Reading Literacy Study (PIRLS). (2006). *Reading achievement in England*. https://nces.ed.gov/surveys/pirls/

Progress in International Reading Literacy Study (PIRLS). (2011). *Reading achievement in England*. https://nces.ed.gov/surveys/pirls/

Progress in International Reading Literacy Study (PIRLS). (2016). *Reading achievement in England*. https://nces.ed.gov/surveys/pirls/

Sternberg, R.J. (1984/1990). Advances in the psychology of human intelligence. In R. Fisher (Ed.), *Teaching Children to Think*. Stanley Thornes.

Taylor, R. (2014). Meaning between, in, and around words, gestures and postures: Multimodal meaning making in children's classroom communication. *Language and Education*, 28(5), 401–420.

Thomson, D., and Nixey, R. (2005). Thinking to read, reading to think: Bringing meaning, reasoning and enjoyment to reading. *Literacy Today*, 44, 12–13.

Trehearne, M. P. (Ed.). (2006). *Comprehensive literacy research for grades 3–6 teachers*. ETA/Cuisenaire.

Veneman, M.V.J., and Spaans, M.A. (2005). Relation between intellectual and metacognitive skills: Age and task differences. *Learning and Individual Differences*, 15, 159–176.

Whitebread, D., Bingham S., Grau, V. and Pino-Pasternak D. (2007) Development of metacognition and self-regulated learning in young children: Role of collaborative and peer-assisted learning, *Journal of Cognitive Education and Psychology*, 6(3), 433–455.

Whitebread, D., and Basilio, M. (2012). The emergence and early development of self-regulation in young children. *Profesorado: Journal of Curriculum and Teacher Education*, Monograph issue: Learn to learn: Teaching and evaluation of self-regulated learning, 16(1), 15–34.

YARC, Snowling et al. (2009). *Developing reading comprehension: The important role of inferences*. www.yarcsupport.co.uk/documents/devreadcomp.pdf

# CHAPTER 5

# Nurturing family reading and learning: Case studies

It has often been said that 'children are made readers on the laps of their parents'. I think most teachers would agree with this. However, throughout our workshop trials, practitioners have been aware that disadvantaged families, and parents in general, tend to receive little specific guidance about how to support their children's reading-for-meaning skills at home.

Furthermore, concern about young children's reading and learning has escalated since the partial school closures associated with the Covid-19 pandemic. Key findings in the National Foundation for Educational Research (NFER, Twist et al. 2022), for example, report that 'the negative impacts of the pandemic were greatest on reading in Key Stage 1 (and in Year 1 in particular)'. In addition, the report suggests that large attainment gaps have appeared between disadvantaged and non-disadvantaged pupils during this period. The need therefore for more explicit family learning provision to close the gulf between disadvantaged children and pupils from 'more language-rich homes' has become even more urgent (DfE 2020 cited in DfE 2021: 8).

This chapter outlines the long-term benefits of encouraging parental involvement in early reading-for-meaning skills instruction and describes the structure and progression of the family reading and learning activities used in the workshops. In addition, it provides examples of how a multisensory approach can help families to engage more effectively in picture book talk together.

Following the development of our Think2Read Key Stage 1 comprehension skills programme, we embarked on a foundation stage family reading skills project in 2013–2014. It seemed logical that since collaboration between teacher, pupils and parents is central to 'effective teaching and learning' in the primary years (Goodall and Vorhaus 2011), teacher-led workshops in school could help to increase family literacy and encourage more reading for meaning and enjoyment at home.

However, it was clear from our research that disadvantaged children and those who struggled with reading were often from homes where parents felt they lacked the skills to support their child's learning. Many of them revealed they had anxiety about approaching their child's school to ask for help because of their own experiences as young learners. The DfE 'Review of best

DOI: 10.4324/9781003226307-6

practice in parental engagement' (Goodall and Vorhaus 2011: 4–65) underlines how important it is that schools engage with parents and support them with home learning. The report goes on to say how 'family literacy programmes' and home-assisted learning can indeed 'have a positive impact on the most disadvantaged families, including the academic outcomes of the children'. Furthermore, the authors emphasise that this is especially the case when:

1. families have 'a clear and consistent goal' for improving their child's learning,
2. they are shown how to apply specific strategies to support this at home using 'an evidence-based model', and
3. the intervention builds 'relationships across the family, the school and the community'.

The aim of our family 'Story Talk' reading project, therefore, was to consolidate comprehension skills taught in the classroom by showing parents and children how to self-monitor and regulate their understanding using the same reading strategies at home. This was achieved, first, by showing them:

1. how to interrogate pictures for meaning together using multisensory tools to support this, then
2. how to infer from text using similar methods for making meaning.

This focus on the development of strategic speaking, listening, and thinking to support language comprehension, encouraged their children to:

- speak more clearly,
- begin to convey ideas more confidently,
- develop a deeper understanding of pictures and text through knowledge of predicting, clarifying, and summarising skills,
- use these literacy skills to speculate, use their imagination more effectively and explore ideas across the curriculum,
- justify ideas about text using evidence and logical reasoning,
- begin to ask in-depth questions to check understanding,
- develop their knowledge of story structure and extend their vocabulary,
- clarify their thinking and use these skills to organise their ideas for writing,
- negotiate, evaluate, and build on the ideas of others, and
- become more aware of their learning and how to self-correct to make sense as they read.

In 2013 we invited a primary school in Pontypridd, South Wales and a school in Barnsley, South Yorkshire to run a series of family reading skills workshops alongside the Key Stages 1 and 2 comprehension skills programme we had already introduced to them. They agreed that the Foundation 'Story Talk' comprehension skills project offered a possible infra-structure for core family learning that would appeal to both parents and children – and might achieve the long-term results we were all looking for.

We explained that the overall aim of the family workshops would be to show parents and children how to use specific comprehension strategies and resources to help them sustain and develop a love of reading and purposeful learning beyond the life of the project. The hope was that the whole school community benefit for the following reasons:

**Reception children** would be shown how to:

- explore books more for pleasure with parents/carers,
- talk in greater depth about the stories,
- use strategies to delve more deeply for answers to their own questions about stories,
- better understand why we read,
- improve vocabulary, communication, and reasoning skills, build self-esteem and confidence (inside and out of the classroom), and
- increase achievement of age-related expectations.

**Parents/carers** would have:

- a better understanding of all the processes involved in reading,
- a better understanding of how to apply the language of comprehension and questioning techniques,
- increased comprehension skills,
- the confidence to read and engage in greater depth with their children,
- the structure for reading, enquiry, and discussion at home which would foster improved communication skills and bonding with their children,
- the knowledge that they would be offering their children effective learning support whilst improving their own literacy skills, and
- increased self-esteem and aspirations.

**Nursery/foundation teachers/school** could expect:

- an increase in the aspirations of hard-to-reach families,
- more frequent parent/carer attendance at family reading workshops,
- enhanced communication between the families and school, and
- a familiar structure for teaching children early comprehension enquiry skills in school and at home.

# Overview of the projects

Although the Pontypridd primary school serves an area of deprivation, many of the 27 parents and carers who participated in the first session (13 more than expected on the day), were in employment. This included mostly working mothers, a small number of working fathers, and two grandmothers.

FIGURE 5.1 'Parents taking part in picture book activities'. Photograph by Mark Hawkins. Reproduced with permission

The head teacher and head of foundation were delighted with the 31 out of 50 children that this involved. The turnout of participating adults was more than they expected, especially since many of them had to take time off work to attend. Although the number of parent/carers had dropped to 17 by the second session due to illness and work commitments, the enthusiasm and engagement in the workshops remained high (see Figure 5.1).

The Barnsley school, on the other hand, serves one of the most deprived areas in Yorkshire where large numbers of families continue to be hard pressed or unemployed. The initial turnout of 11 parents/carers out of the 15 that signed up for the series of workshops, therefore, was quite unexpected. The school's head commented that 'This level of attendance is extremely encouraging, considering how difficult it usually is to drum up parent enthusiasm for core skills workshops'.

The two-day delivery time allocated for the Welsh school project contrasted sharply with the longer period needed to successfully deliver the Barnsley primary workshops. The family sessions ran over a six-week period at regular weekly intervals which helped to encourage a small but dedicated group of mothers and one grandmother/child-minder to attend frequently. They remarked that they were able to keep up this regular attendance because:

1. the 'talk is about reading for meaning and fun and what we enjoy and can learn about reading skills',
2. 'we are being shown how to help our children with specific reading skills at home', and
3. 'we are learning new strategies and trying them out in the session before using them with our children at home together'.

The teacher leading the workshops reported that this approach was 'opening up new horizons for the families by increasing their confidence, introducing them to the skills they already possess and showing them how they can effectively support their children's learning'.

## Outcome of projects

Most of the families who took part in the Pontypridd and Barnsley 2013 action-research completed the course with their children and reported that their experience was life-changing and aspirational. They all commented on the value of the strategies and how this new knowledge had provided them with the skills and motivation they needed to share books in greater depth with their children. They also remarked on how much more time they spent reading with their children at home since learning how to use the resources with confidence.

The outcome of the projects further demonstrated that families from deprived backgrounds with little experience of sharing books for pleasure together, and talking about stories with their children, responded positively to the reading workshops because:

1.  they were provided with a structure and purpose for reading and given explicit reading skills instruction by trained Early Years staff,
2.  the support they received after the workshops linked home and school learning and helped to consolidate the reading skills the children were learning in the classroom, and
3.  the 'book talk' strategies taught in the workshops increased the confidence of parents and children.

Both schools hoped this success would encourage other families to enrol for further reading skills workshops which would help to sustain the project beyond the life of the pilot.

## General feedback from the Pontypridd and Barnsley projects

Parents and carers told us they had been engaged in the activities from the beginning (see Figure 5.2) because the focus was more on reading for pleasure and meaning, rather than hearing their children read aloud and sound out words (Goodall and Vorhaus 2011).

FIGURE 5.2 'Parents were engaged from the beginning'. Photograph by Mark Hawkins. Reproduced with permission

Both Pontypridd participants and Barnsley parent/carers commented on how their children were 'beginning to play with and use the interactive resources on their own' after family members had modelled using them so frequently. They also noticed that they read with their children more often and that their children's enjoyment of books had increased. Families also noted that they were beginning to search for and buy books that promoted more in-depth exploration of the pictures and text using the strategies they had learned. In addition, most agreed that they felt more confident and skilled about sharing books with their children for meaning. They also felt that there had been more bonding with their children as a result – and more 'book talk' at home.

## Parent reaction to the individual strategies and multisensory aids in the sessions

The project's collaborative approach became an effective way of empowering previously hard-to-reach parents to grasp key reading strategies alongside their child in a fun, non-judgemental, active learning environment.

### Session 1: Introduction

The Barnsley head teacher and Year 2 project leader admitted that they felt anxious about the turnout for the first workshop, as 'previous attempts to work with parents around core learning subjects had failed to be successful due to lack of interest'. However, the parents responded well to the structure, interactive learning aids, and content of the session. They also enjoyed discussions around 'conceptual ideas relating to reading' and learning how to organise their routines at home so they could read more regularly to their children. This led to discussion about the parents' aspirations for their children and the importance of reading at home. Despite the challenges of their deprived community, or perhaps because of it, the parents were ambitious for their children. They saw their children's futures including university and good careers. One mother observed that if they read to their children, this will encourage their children to read to their children… and so on. 'And that will have been a really good thing, won't it?' They were becoming aware that investing in their children's education by supporting their reading and learning at home could change their children's lives and their own prospects as a community.

## Session 2: Predicting

Both schools reported that parents enjoyed the predicting activities with their children because it was a skill they recognised and used often in daily life. They understood the purpose of the Picture Viewer and how it helped their child to frame details and clues on the page which they might normally miss. However, one parent was concerned that their child kept 'changing his prediction as he turned the page'. She perceived this as a negative trait and possibly an issue. So, she was relieved to hear that because he had a good understanding of the book, it meant he was able to amend his prediction as the story unfolded. Another parent told us how her 4-year-old had seen 'a triangle-shape in a sea scene and predicted it was a shark in the water'. Her daughter then told her some fascinating facts about sharks that she had no idea she knew. She was delighted by her knowledge – and her imagination. The 'shark' was in fact just a mark on the page. It helpfully demonstrated how we all use prior knowledge to make predictions as we read. Sometimes our predictions are accurate, and other times we need to revisit the clues and think again.

## Session 3: Clarifying

The parents and children soon realised there were links between predicting and clarifying. Both strategies were about searching for clues on the page to confirm understanding. For example, predicting entails examining a range of information to calculate what might happen next and clarifying involves checking meanings to make sense of the small details to understand the bigger picture. They realised that by using the Picture Viewer to look closer, they were able to work out the unknown images and concepts from parts of the story they already knew. One parent commented that 'when we use the reading aids often enough – well, we won't always need them will we?' It was good to see confidence in their skills building as they supported their children in their reading and learning.

## Session 4: Enquiry/questioning

In this session, the Barnsley teaching team began to work more individually with the parents. They showed them how to overcome specific problems that had previously hindered their child's interest in reading. For example, one parent learned how to use their voice, eye contact, hand signs and literal questioning to engage them in literal 'who, what, where' enquiry. Another parent learned 'how to dig more deeply with their child to unleash their incredible imagination'. This gentle step-by-step approach showed the parents how to begin to tackle communication and concentration problems by supporting their child's speech and language issues. The team reported that overall, the parents and children enjoyed both the literal and inference questioning process. It was exciting to see them growing in confidence and engaging in more thinking, talking, and clue-finding together.

## Session 5: Summarising

Parents quickly understood how summarising and retelling stories linked to enquiry and 'who, what, where, why', questioning to establish the facts and deepen understanding about the characters and events in a story. The families began to see that all the strategies were connected by question asking. They realised that the main role of the interactive reading aids was to prompt the children to ask about the information on the page, help them to find the answers, then retell the story in the correct order using the 'Five-Finger Retelling' prompts to help them. This stimulated further discussion about identifying the main points of a story and how specific questions help children to identify this information and retell the beginning, middle, and end of the narrative. Parents were reminded that solely relying on memory to retell information was too difficult for young readers at first. They were relieved to know that their children could refer to the book if they needed to. This cleared up the misconception about comprehension. It is a thinking process and not a question-and-answer memory test.

## Session 6: Last session – combining the skills

Parents were fascinated about the section on child development and how early children start to develop an interest in books. The discussion turned quickly to the parent's observations of how their children's vocabulary and thinking skills had developed over the sessions. They talked about how sharing picture books at home, using the strategies they had been shown, had started to impact on their child's language and communication skills. The parents commented on their children's growing imagination and use of questioning to solve problems in their daily lives. They spoke about the power of pictures and how confident they now felt about asking questions to prompt their children to think more deeply. Some were impressed with the questions the children had asked to find out more about the characters in a story. One parent commented on her daughter's ability to use the skills she'd learned to discuss films. They all recognised how these strategies for making meaning can transfer to other areas of learning. They were also excited to hear that familiarity with these skills encourages children to use them to make links between words and pictures and later to help them make meaning of text. They were amazed by the skills they could see developing so quickly.

# Impact on the parents' learning

The confidence that the Barnsley parents had gained from mastering new literacy skills and realising their potential to learn had made a significant impact on some of them. For example, two parents from the workshop decided to consider further training. One chose to train as a volunteer reader in school, and the other enrolled to train as a teaching assistant, with a view to studying for a degree. Her experience in the workshops had shown her that she had the potential to make a good career in teaching.

Although the regular turnout of parents for both pilots was relatively small, the head of Barnsley primary school reflected that 'the maxim that quality is better than quantity must always be at the heart of family learning initiatives – even if we would love large numbers to be involved'. The aim for both schools was about how to make a difference to as many families as possible over time. She commented further: 'It requires being in for the long-haul and not expecting instant take-up by parents overnight'.

She went on to say that 'once we can establish an infrastructure that raises family expectations for learning, we can transform lives and encourage more family learning at school in the early years'. The hope is that this becomes normal practice for parents who want to support their children's learning and enhance their own skills.

# References

Department for Education. (2021). *The reading framework: Teaching the foundations of literacy, Section 2: Language comprehension*. DfE.

Goodall, J., and Vorhaus, J. (2011). *Review of best practice in parental engagement*. Research Report DFE-RR156. Institute of Education. https://assets.publishing.service.gov.uk/

Twist, L., Jones, E., and Treleaven, O. (2022). *The impact of Covid-19 on pupil attainment*. NFER. www.nfer.ac.uk/the-impact-of-covid-19-on-pupil-attainment-a-summary-of-research-evidence/

# PART 2

# Putting theory into practice: Teaching and reviewing skills

# CHAPTER 6

# Planning comprehension skills activities using picture books

## Co-construction of meaning – where to start?

In her observation survey of early literacy achievement, Marie Clay (2002) highlights how important it is for teachers to guide the early stages of children's reading, using methods that help them to become more aware of their thinking as they construct meaning. The metacognitive processes she suggests are supported effectively in this book through mindful development of key comprehension strategies, using picture books and multisensory learning.

For example, as Clay observes, learning how to clarify meaning helps young children to check their reading for sense, and become more conscious of what they do or do not understand. This checking-in process encourages them to then take the initiative to self-correct when the text does not make sense to them. In addition, she underlines how the enquiry process shows them how to ask and answer their own questions to help them:

1. clarify what is happening in the narrative,
2. establish the facts about the text,
3. delve deeper to predict what might happen next using prior knowledge to help them make meaning, and
4. to make new discoveries in the text.

Furthermore, the process of learning about story structure and how to summarise and retell narrative in the correct order, supports Clay's view that children begin self-monitoring their reading when they understand how books and stories work. This viewpoint is also widely supported by more recent research. The Education Endowment Foundation (2021), for example, agree that a systematic and metacognitive teaching approach helps young children

DOI: 10.4324/9781003226307-8

to consciously apply comprehension skills and to self-monitor their understanding as they read. Other studies also emphasise how important it is to give pupils practice in applying 'the comprehension strategies independently to other reading tasks, contexts, and subjects' to ensure early self-regulation of reading transfers to other learning areas (Thomson and Nixey 2005, Ness 2011, Al Khaiyali 2013).

The purpose of the pre-planned teaching sequences in the book, therefore, is to provide initial guidance in modelling this metacognitive process, and to show teachers and practitioners how to plan their own strategic comprehension sessions. This will eventually enable pupils to practise combining all four SPEC strategies to make meaning of text in whole class, group, or paired activities. Frequent scaffolding of these skills will then encourage readers to generate and answer their own simple and in-depth questions about pictures and text. Recent evidence demonstrates that this type of pupil self-questioning helps to 'improve reading comprehension performance across a range of diverse learners' (Joseph et al. 2015: 1).

So, what are the specific features of the key question types and strategies for making meaning? How do they help to develop early learners' language, cognition, and understanding?

## Teaching children self-questioning skills using picture books

As already discussed, reading does not need to be a text-only activity. After all, the 'who, what, where, how, why' types of question that help us to make meaning of text, can also be used effectively to support understanding of picture narrative. For example, early modelling of self-questioning through 'picture talk' helps to familiarise young children with the explicit and implicit questioning skills they will need later to make meaning of text for themselves. This includes readers who struggle with decoding and those with English as a second language (Al Khaiyali 2013).

## The fundamental question types

The basic types of question are literal and inference. They graduate in difficulty – beginning with simple literal questions which focus on the direct information on the page. They help the reader to establish the basic facts about the characters, actions, and places in a narrative. Then there are three types of inference question which increase in complexity as the reader begins to think more deeply about what is happening, what might happen next (prediction), what the characters are feeling, and finally, how this affects their behaviour and motives (evaluation) as the narrative unfolds. Although there are differences between these inference questions, they all require the reader to search for clues, make links, reach deductions, and make predictions to identify problems and find solutions for the characters. The different question types are as follows:

**Literal**: Explicit questioning (looking for information 'right there' on the page about characters/objects, actions, places) – Who? What? Where?

**Inference – being a detective (predicting)**: Implicit questioning (searching for author clues and evidence on the page to support predictions) – Who? What? Where? Why? How do you know that? (I know because…).

**Inference (evaluative) questioning**: Implicit questioning about characters' emotions and actions (linked to own experiences and text to explain characters' behaviour and motives) – Who? What? Where? Why? How? Why do you say that?

Effective teaching of questioning begins by showing young children how to identify and re-organise different types of information in pictures, then text:

- first, how to identify literal, then inferred meaning in picture narrative,
- then how to link literal and inferred picture clues with words and similar ideas in a sentence to integrate meanings and gain an overall 'picture',
- next, how to link picture and word clues within an illustrated paragraph of text,
- and finally, by understanding how to link words and clues together to construct meaning within a whole passage of text – until text only is providing the pictures in the reader's head.

(See the question samples that illustrate the differences between question types, Chapter 7 Assessment p. 77 and questioning process Part 2 Units 2–4)

# Questioning skills within the reciprocal reading framework

Experience has also shown me that it is essential to teach literal, inference, and evaluative questioning alongside summarising, predicting, and clarifying strategies (Rosenshein and Meister 1994, Parkin et al. 2002). As discussed, this strategic comprehension approach helps readers to fully understand the complexities of 'sense-making' using a combination of skills (Pressley 2000). In addition, they learn how to build the skills they need to answer a range of questions accurately about text. However, perhaps more importantly, they learn how to generate and answer their own questions as they read, which L. M. Joseph et al (2015: 2) conclude helps students to increase their comprehension by focusing their attention 'on the critical information in the text' (e.g. Crabtree, Alber- Morgan and Konrad 2010).

Furthermore, research, practice, and teacher observation have shown that reading skills and writing and learning in general improve when pupils have been explicitly taught how to ask and answer their own range of questions. Assessment of our children's reading skills prior to our initial 2002 comprehension project (Thomson and Nixey 2005), for example, revealed that their lack of conscious self-questioning during reading may have contributed to their poor understanding of:

- story structure and how it supports accurate retelling of a story in sequence,
- different levels of meaning in text (literal, inference, evaluation – 'who, what, where, when, why and how' information),
- how authors plant clues in text to infer meaning, and how these clues offer links to personal meaning for the reader,
- prior knowledge and how to use it to make links with new information,
- how vocabulary and grammar support comprehension, and
- how to gather a range of information efficiently to ask and answer questions about text accurately.

## Developing comprehension skills through 'book talk'

It is vital, therefore, that young children are shown how to engage in reciprocal 'book talk' and ask and answer their own questions. This dialogic approach helps to enrich language, deepen critical thinking, and improve reading comprehension in preparation for learning in Key Stage 1. In addition, the emphasis on 'student-initiated talk and active participation' helps to increase knowledge of vocabulary (Harrison 2004: 87) and understanding of sentence structure and grammar. Furthermore, the authors of the revised Early Years Foundation Stage Statutory Framework (DfE 2021) agree that 'children's back-and-forth interaction with adults' is crucial in forming 'the foundations for language and cognitive development'. For instance, they suggest that effective teaching includes:

- thinking aloud, modelling new language for children,
- paying close attention to what the children say,
- rephrasing and extending what the children say,
- validating the children's attempts at using vocabulary and grammar by rephrasing what children say, if necessary,
- asking closed and open questions,
- answering the children's questions,
- explaining why things happen,
- deliberately connecting current and past events (Do you remember when..?),
- extending children's vocabulary and explaining new words,
- connecting one idea or action to another, and
- helping children to articulate ideas in well-formed sentences.

The instructional plans in this book build on this good teacher practice by providing:

1. guidelines for effective pupil interaction in Teaching Unit 1 (e.g., the 'Language of Discussion' pages 110–120), and
2. an active reading comprehension structure for meaningful discussion Palincsar (1986) based on the reciprocal reading model (see Figure 6.1).

| | |
|---|---|
| *What does this mean?* | *What do you think might happen next?* |
| **Prior knowledge**<br>What do I already know? | **Exploring the cover of a book**<br>Wondering about the contents |
| **Predicting**<br>What might happen next? | **Using the titles, pictures and text**<br>and experience to make predictions |
| **Clarifying**<br>What does this mean? | **Identifying ideas, words, phrases**<br>that are not understood |
| **Questioning**<br>Who, What, Where, Why? How I know that. | **Asking literal, Inference and Evaluation**<br>Questions about pictures and text |
| **Summarising**<br>Beginning, Middle, End<br>What is happening? | **Summing up what you have just read**.<br>Retelling the main points in order |
| **Predicting**<br>What might happen next? | **Predicting what will happen next...**<br>Using the clues in the text and your own experience. |
| Repeating the process ..... | |

FIGURE 6.1 SPEC reciprocal reading framework (based on Palincsar and Brown's 1984 reading model): Teaching children how to apply core comprehension strategies as they read

The simple comprehension structure in Figure 6.1 demonstrates how the four key strategies work in unison to develop language and cognitive skills. The framework's cyclic reading-for-meaning process offers a systematic guide for collaborative class, group, and paired discussion about pictures and text that young children can easily follow. It also provides an active learning framework for transference of comprehension skills to other learning areas.

As Figure 6.1 indicates, it is helpful to begin the reading-for-meaning process and discussion about text with the front cover of a book. Then, before asking readers to examine the title, pictures, and text on the cover for information, it is important to encourage them to share what they already know about the story topic. This prompts their prior knowledge and encourages them to make links between knowledge of the subject and the direct information and clues on the page.

This initial enquiry compels them to make predictions about the theme and contents of the book. With every turning of the page, the aim is to encourage early readers to identify specific information, clarify meanings together, ask questions, discuss the characters' problems as the story unfolds and make further predictions about what might happen next to the characters. Finally, through discussion and adult modelling children learn how to talk about what they have just read and identify the main points of a narrative. They eventually learn how to retell the beginning, middle, and end of the whole story in their own words, using vocabulary they have learned during the process.

# The power of picture books

> Picture books are like poems in their intensity and power… just like words and sentences, we have to give meaning to the pictures we see. This cannot be done passively… (Murris and Haynes 2000)

Visual texts offer us a universal language for making meaning of the world. They invite us to look closer, go deeper, make personal connections, and create our own narratives. From the richly detailed, colourful, and sumptuous, to the abstract, understated, and funny – the unfolding picture book narrative (with and without words) can be fascinating, emotive, and absorbing to read for all ages.

When we choose a picture book, we are mostly drawn to the topic or the impact of the cover. We are attracted by the style of artwork, the title, the type of font, how the images are presented to us – subtle and mysterious or bold and exciting. We might look at the size and shape of the book, the colours and medium used to create the pictures.

Of course, not all picture books are relatable. But most of them beckon us to explore our feelings and experiences to make sense of them. As Gomez-Reino observes (1996), interpreting pictures can be as easy or difficult as reading printed text.

Picture books also provide the perfect stepping-stone for exploring the processes involved in first making meaning of images and words, and eventually text on its own. Readers learn how to create a pictorial summary of the text in their heads, which is easier for them to recall (Gunning 2005: 301).

# Wordless picture books

However, unlike picture books with text, wordless picture books carry the main meaning of the book exclusively through a sequence of illustrations. Since we generate twice as many words to understand illustrations, because pictures are generally more open to interpretation than written text (Frey and Fisher 2008), this provides a useful foundation for building early vocabulary that benefits all young readers.

The pictures in these books are often presented in panels like a graphic novel, such as *The Snowman* by Raymond Briggs (1982) and *Flotsam* by David Wiesner (2006). The advantage of this for beginner/struggling readers or second language learners is that since no decoding of words is required to construct meaning, much of the anxiety is taken out of the reading process (Wolber 2017, Arizpe 2013, Paris and Paris 2007). Consequently, wordless books allow the early reader to construct meaning and 'create the text for themselves' (Sainsbury and Styles 2012: 97, Crawford and Hade 2000).

However, since wordless picture books have no written storyline that helps to clarify the message of the illustrations, they can be ambiguous in meaning. Therefore, adult expectations of children's responses to non-print texts should allow 'enough time for readers to engage with the text, to read, re-read and reflect before being asked to make sense of it' (Arizpe 2013).

## Selecting picture books for comprehension planning

> In order to give meaning to the pictures we connect our own knowledge, our own lives and ourselves with what we see. (Murris and Haynes 2000)

It is essential to carefully consider our choices of picture book and purpose for using them. For example, the first teaching sequences in this book (Unit 1 Part 2, p. 118) begin by asking the children what they think the purpose is of words and images in picture books. 'Do they find the words or pictures are more interesting? Do they feel they tell the same story in different ways? Would the words still be good without the pictures? Would the pictures still work without the words? Do they read the pictures or words first?' The children will probably tell you that 'the text in picture books is straightforward enough'– it is the pictures that have 'complications' (Sainsbury and Styles 2012: 80).

Selecting picture books for comprehension planning can be time consuming. To shorten this process, this section provides you with a list of quality wordless and picture book titles, including information about the reading age and topic key words to help you select an appropriate and appealing book for teaching and practising specific comprehension strategies and objectives. The wordless picture book titles are suitable for all young readers – however, they are particularly appealing to children who struggle with decoding and comprehension, or readers with English as a second language.

Some of the questions you might ask when selecting wordless books and picture books with words are as follows:

- Is the theme of the book accessible and relevant to the age group?
- Is the theme of the book one which will extend readers' understanding of themselves and their world?
- Does the theme of the book draw on prior knowledge of a familiar topic?
- Does the title and picture on the front cover entice you to explore the contents?
- Are there gaps in the text for the reader to fill in? Are they encouraged to use their imagination, ask questions, make predictions, clarify for sense?
- What is the quality of the language in the book, e.g., vocabulary, sentence structure?
- How does the book encourage interaction between the reader and the text (choice of characters, use of suspense, emotions)? How do the pictures and text interrelate?

The following titles provide examples of rich stimulus for discussion. They also offer opportunities for practising specific skills or combining all the SPEC strategies to make meaning using the reciprocal reading framework (see Figure 6.1, p. 57) to guide the process.

# List of picture books for practising SPEC comprehension strategies and 'book talk'

## Strategy: Predicting (discussing what might happen next)

This strategy involves identifying literal and implied meaning and making links with prior knowledge to make deductions based on clues in the story.

Predicting the contents of a book and calculating what might happen next as the story unfolds is central to reading for meaning and pleasure. When young readers become conscious of how they make predictions, and check their understanding of the author's meaning, they begin to see how all four strategies combine to support their understanding as they read.

To make accurate predictions about story outcomes, readers need to have some prior knowledge of the topic and some understanding of emotions and how actions have consequences for characters. When they then encounter a theme they can relate to, they particularly enjoy anticipating the characters' reactions to events, their problems, and how they might solve them.

The type of picture books that provide great stimulus for making predictions are those that feature 'cause and effect' situations, plenty of action, suspense, adventure, and feelings.

### Key focus for discussing and making predictions

- using titles, pictures on front covers to predict contents of book,
- looking for clues, making links, finding evidence on the page,
- using knowledge of cause-and-effect situations to make predictions about what might happen next, and
- making deductions about actions and consequences using 'because' to explain why…

### Key question words/phrases

What might have happened before? What might happen next? Why? How do you know that? Why do you say that? I know that because….

### Practising prediction skills – wordless picture books

Title: *Journey* by Aaron Becker (key words: adventure, fantasy, family, fathers, friendship, magic). Publisher: Walker Books, 2014. Interest age: 4–8. Reading age 5–7 years.

Title: *Quest* by Aaron Becker (key words: adventure, fantasy, family, fathers, friendship, magic). Publisher: Walker Books, 2015. Reading age 5–7 years.

Title: *Return* by Aaron Becker (key words: adventure, fantasy, family, fathers, friendship, magic). Publisher: Walker Books. Interest age: 4–8. Reading age 5–7 years.

Title: *A Wolf in the Snow* by Matthew Cordell (themes: animals, family, friendship, co-operation, trust, bravery, suspense), Publisher: Andersen Press, 2019. Reading age: 3–5 years.

*Practising prediction skills – picture books with text*

Title: *We're Going on a Bear Hunt* by Michael Rosen and Helen Oxenbury (key words: bear, family, adventure, suspense, nature, chant-aloud and actions). Publisher: Walker Books, 1993. Reading age: 3–5 years.

Title: *Good Little Wolf* by Nadia Shireen (key words: animals, quirky, amusing, playful – ending with a twist). Publisher: Jonathan Cape, 2011. Reading age: 3–5 years.

## Strategy: Clarifying (discussing what it means)

Clarifying involves identifying literal and implied meaning and making links to personal knowledge and text clues to support understanding.

In addition, this strategy, like predicting, encourages children to check for meaning before they turn to the next page. When young readers skip over information they do not understand, their interest and sense of what they are reading is soon lost. So, it is important that they learn how to make sense of unfamiliar concepts and unknown words using their understanding of the world, context clues, and knowledge of other words to check their understanding as they read.

The following picture books are ideal for practising clarifying skills because they are full of intriguing notions which 1) arouse curiosity and spark the imagination, 2) encourage the reader to draw on what they already know to delve deeper for meaning and sense, and 3) extend their vocabulary in the process.

*Key focus for discussion about clarifying meaning*

Making sense of words, pictures, and ideas. For example:

- using what you already know to find out what you don't know,
- searching for contextual clues – looking for the 'bigger picture' to make sense of unknown words, images, ideas,
- using knowledge of emotions and their own experiences to clarify characters' behaviour, and motives, and
- searching for evidence from the story to back up their own ideas.

*Key question words/phrases*

Who? What? Where? When? Why? How? Why do you think that? What does that mean? What is happening here? What do I already know that will help me make sense of this? Why do I think that? Why do I say that?

*Practising clarifying skills – wordless picture books*

Title: *Tuesday* by David Wiesner (key words: adventure, animals, quirky, fun, amusing). Publisher: Andersen Press, 2012. Interest age: 3+ years. Reading age: 5+ years.

Title: *Another* by Christian Robinson (key words: animals, people, adventure, playful, quirky, geometric shapes, similarity, and difference, other-worldly). Publisher: Atheneum Books for Young Readers, 2019. Reading age: 5–8 years.

Title: *Brave Molly* by Brooke-Boynton-Hughes (key words: adventure, monsters, feelings, courage, friendship). Publisher: Chronicle, 2019. Reading age: 5–7 years.

*Clarifying practice – picture book titles with text*

Title: *Farmer Duck* by Martin Waddell and Helen Oxenbury (key words: animals, sharing, manners, friendship, helping, farms). Publisher: Walker Books, 1995. Reading age: 3–7 years.

Title: *Where the Wild Things Are* by Maurice Sendak (key words: Monsters, boy, bedroom, magical, forest, gripping, clever, uplifting). Publisher: Red Fox Books edition, 2000. Interest age: 2–5 years. Reading age: 4+ years.

Title: *Aliens Love Underpants* by Claire Freedman, illustrator Ben Cort (key words: funny, poetry rhyme, monster, space). Publisher: Simon and Schuster. Interest age: 3–5 years. Reading age: 4–5 years.

---

# Strategy: Enquiry/self-questioning (discussing: Who? What? Where? When? Why? How?)

Self-questioning is an essential skill that helps readers to gather direct information from the page and elicit deeper meanings to self-monitor their understanding as they read. These enquiry skills involve knowledge of how to ask and answer literal, inference (and evaluative) questions about narrative. For example: literal questions require explicit answers, whereas inference questions ask about the implicit meaning in pictures and text. To respond to inference questions about texts, the reader needs to combine the information and clues on the page and link this to their prior knowledge of feelings and own experiences to judge events, interpret characters' behaviour and motives, and justify their answers.

The following picture books offer opportunities to practise generating and answering literal questions to first establish the facts about the characters, their actions, and settings, then to ask more in-depth detective questions to find out what the characters might be thinking or feeling about the situations they encounter.

*Key focus for discussion*

**Asking questions:**
to check understanding,

- to find out more…
- to look for clues/links/evidence.

**Answering questions** (to ask yourself):
How do I know? Why do I say that?

*Key question words/phrases*

(Literal) Who? What? Where? Right there! I know because it says…

(Inference) Why? How do you know? I know because it suggests…

(Inference/evaluation) Why do you think…? I think… because… (e.g., predicting character's behaviour, expression, actions; linking text clues to own experience).

### *Practising enquiry/self-questioning skills – wordless book titles*

Title: *Footpath Flowers* by JonArno Lawson and illustrated by Sydney Smith (key words: family, animals, nature, kindness, giving). Publisher: Walker Books, 2016. Reading age: 5–7 years.

Title: *Dog on a Digger* by Kate Prendergast (key words: animals, environment, friendship, humour, drama). Publisher: Old Barn Books, 2017. Interest age: 3–10. Reading age: 5+ years.

Title: *Professional Crocodile* by Giovanna Zoboli and Mariachara Di Giorgio (key words: animals, everyday life, witty). Publisher: Chronicle Books, 2017. Interest age: 4–7. Reading age: 5+ years.

### *Practising enquiry/self-questioning skills – picture books (with text)*

Title: *This is Not My Hat* by Jon Klassen (key words: fish, sea, theft, suspense, emotions, humour). Publisher: Walker Books, 2014. Interest age 4+ years. Reading age: 5 +years.

Title: *This Book Just Ate My Dog!* By Richard Byre (key words: animals, funny, inventive, full of surprises). Publisher: Oxford University Press, 2015. Interest level: 3–5 years. Reading age: 2–4 years.

Title: *Charlotte Barbara Throws a Wobbler* by Nadia Shireen (key words: young animals, every day, playpark, funny, self-regulation, emotions). Publisher: Puffin Books, 2021. Reading age: 3–7 years.

## Strategy: Summarising/retelling (discussing what the story is about)

This strategy asks the reader to identify literal and implied meaning to retell the main points of a story in sequence, from the beginning to the end.

Summarising and retelling are key skills that clearly demonstrate whether a reader has understood the story they have been reading or listening to. They also provide teachers and practitioners with an idea of the reader's understanding of story structure, their knowledge of vocabulary, and whether they can express themselves coherently.

The following picture books involve the reader in the process of summarising and retelling by first engaging them in literal questioning about the characters, their actions, and locations to help them set the scene of the story. The reader is then encouraged to generate and answer their own detective questions to reveal the characters' feelings and problems, and how they solve them in the end.

### *Focus for discussion to support summarising and retelling!*

Literal: Gathering explicit information: *Who? What? Where? – Right there!*

Inference Detective: searching for clues: *Who? What? Where? Why? – How do you know that? Why do you think that?*

*Key questions – words/phrases*

**Main points of story – setting scene:**

Person – who? *Who is involved?*
Action – what? *What are they doing?*
Place – where? *Where are they?*

Identifying and retelling:
Beginning/middle/end

Retelling stems: 'In the beginning… then, next, after that, in the end'. (Who? What? Where? Why? How? Problem/how it is solved.)

*Practising summarising/retelling skills – wordless picture book titles*

Title: *Owl Bat Bat Owl* by Marie-Louise Fitzpatrick (key words: animals, cooperation, friendship, family, integration humour). Publisher: Walker, 2018. Reading age: 2–5 years.

Title: *The Lion and the Mouse* by Jerry Pinkney (key words: animals, traditional moral tale, friendship, co-operation). Publisher: Walker Books, 2011. Reading age: 3–5 years.

Title: *Hike* by Pete Oswald (key words: Father, child, adventure, bonding, outdoor activities and challenges). Publisher: Walker, 2021. Reading age: 4–7 years.

Title: *Here I Am* by Patti Kim and illustrated by Sonia Sachez (key words: graphic novel-style, family, feelings, immigration, moving home, diversity, BAME). Publisher: Curious Fox, 2015. Interest age: 5+ years. Reading age: 5–10 years.

*Practising summarising/retelling skills – picture book titles with text*

Title: *Stuck* by Oliver Jeffers (key words: boy, tree, animals, objects, determination, inventiveness, funny). Publisher: HarperCollins, 2022. Interest age: 3–5 years. Reading age: 4–6 years.

Title: *The Gruffalo's Child* by Julia Donaldson and illustrated by Axel Scheffler (key words: animals, adventure, nature, suspense, rhyme). Publisher: MacMillan Children's Books, 2016. Reading age: 4–7 years.

# References

Al Khaiyali, A.T.S. (2013). ESL elementary teachers' use of children's picture books to initiate explicit instruction of reading comprehension strategies. *English Language Teaching*, 7(2), 90–102.

Arizpe, E. (2013). Meaning-making from wordless (or nearly wordless) picture books: What educational research expects and what readers have to say. *Cambridge Journal of Education*, 43(2), 163–176.

Clay, M.M. (2002). *An observation survey of early literacy achievement*. Heinemann.

Crabtree, T., Alber-Morgan, S. R., & Konrad, M. (2010). The effects of self-monitoring of story elements on the reading comprehension of high school seniors with learning disabilities. *Education & Treatment of Children, 33*(2), 187–203.

Crawford, P.A., and Hade, D.D. (2000). Inside the picture, outside the frame: Semiotics and the reading of wordless picture books. *Journal of Research in Childhood Education*, 15(1), 66–80.

Department for Education. (2021). *Statutory framework for the Early Years Foundation Stage*. Available at: www.gov.uk/government/publications/early-years-foundation-stage-framework--2

Education Endowment Foundation. (2021). *EEF toolkit – reading comprehension strategies*. https://educationendowmentfoundation.org.uk/education-evidence/teaching-learning-toolkit/reading-comprehension-strategies

Frey, N., and Fisher, D. (Eds) (2008). *Teaching visual literacy, using comic books, graphic novels, anime, cartoons, and more to develop comprehension and thinking skills*. Corwin Press.

Gomez-Reino, H. (1996). Reading picture books with an artist's eye. In V. Watson and M. Styles (Eds). *Talking pictures: Pictorial texts and young readers*. Hidden & Stoughton.

Gunning, T.G. (2005). Creating literacy instruction for all students (5th edn). Allyn and Bedford.

Harrison, C. (2004). *Understanding reading development*. Sage Publications.

Joseph, L.M., Alber-Morgan, S., Cullen, J., and Rouse, C. (2015). The effects of self-questioning on reading comprehension: A literature review. *Reading & Writing Quarterly*, 32(2), 152–173.

Murris, K., and Haynes, J. (2000). *Storywise: Thinking Through Stories*. DialogueWorks.

Ness, M. (2011). Explicit reading comprehension instruction in elementary classrooms: Teacher use of reading comprehension strategies. *Journal of Research in Childhood Education*, 25(1), 98–117.

Palincsar, A.S. (1986). The role of dialogue in providing scaffolded instruction. *Educational Psychologist*, 21(1–2), 73–98.

Palincsar, A., and Brown, A. (1984). Reciprocal teaching of comprehension-fostering and comprehension-monitoring activities. *Cognition and Instruction*, 2, 117–175.

Paris, A., and Paris, S.G. (2007). Teaching narrative comprehension strategies to first graders. *Cognition and Instruction*, 25(1), 1–44.

Parkin, C., Parkin, C., and Pool, B. (2002). *PROBE – taxonomy of question types, reading assessment New Zealand*. Triune Initiatives.

Pressley, M. (2000). What should comprehension instruction be instruction of? In M.L. Kamil, P.B. Mosenthal, P.D. Pearson, and R. Barr (Eds), *Handbook of Reading Research, Vol 3*. Lawrence Erlbaum Associates.

Rosenshein, B., and Meister, C. (1994). Reciprocal teaching: A review of nineteen experimental studies. *Review of Educational Research*, 64, 479–530.

Sainsbury, M., and Styles, M. (2012). *Children's picture books: The art of visual storytelling*. Laurence King Publishing.

Thomson, D., and Nixey, R. (2005). Thinking to read, reading to think: Bringing meaning, reasoning and enjoyment to reading. *Literacy Today*, 44, 12–13.

Wolber, D. (2017). Unlocking English oral language with wordless picture books. *Illinois Reading Council Journal*, 46(1), 13–24.

# CHAPTER 7

# Assessment and procedure (baseline, intermediate, final review)

## Understanding the early comprehension review process

Teaching children how to identify and consciously use comprehension strategies provides them with an extremely accurate tool for monitoring their own understanding as they read. Although teacher assessment and analysis of a child's knowledge of these strategies is key, ultimately it is the depth of questions the children generate themselves about the text, the accuracy of their answers from the page, and their retelling skills that determine their ability to fully comprehend a text. We can argue, therefore, that the earlier children realise that reading is about understanding, enquiry, and how to make meaning for themselves, the more their reading confidence and literacy will improve and positively impact on their writing and learning in general.

## Section 1: Planning assessment (EYFS reading goals, Year 1 comprehension objectives)

Before instruction begins, it is useful to gain some idea of the children's comprehension ability, if possible, within the first six weeks of the reception year. Then to review their developing comprehension skills on a regular basis following explicit instruction. This is effectively approached by:

1. first exploring the pages of a picture book with them and asking them what they think the story might be about from the information on the front cover,
2. then inviting them to retell the main points of the story, and
3. finally, by asking them literal, then more in-depth questions about the story (Paris and Paris 2003, 2007, Lysaker and Hopper 2015).

DOI: 10.4324/9781003226307-9

## The three phases of comprehension review: Before, during, and after instruction

The assessment framework is divided into three progressive phases of comprehension review (go to Part 3 Section 2 p. 177 for assessment resources):

1. pre-instruction baseline appraisal of language, communication, and reading-for-meaning skills,
2. intermediate appraisal after each comprehension teaching unit (Units 1–4) including pupil self-assessment (intermediate review of developing skills with adult support), and
3. the end-of-year (post-instruction) comprehension skills assessment.

Each phase is designed to help young readers across the developmental range improve their language, communication, personal learning, social skills, and their understanding of inference as they work towards more formal Year 1 reading comprehension objectives. In addition, practitioners are provided with an overview of reading comprehension progress and skills associated with prime areas of learning such as listening, attention, understanding, speaking, motor skills, self-regulation, executive control, and relationship building (see Figure 7.1 pages 70–72). Frequent reviewing of developing skills helps to inform instruction, end-of-year assessment, and transition from reception to Key Stage 1.

This chapter offers guidance on how and when to conduct these informal oral assessments. The guidance also provides a consistent method for observing, noting down, marking, and analysing the children's spontaneous responses to picture narrative and to specific questions about it. In addition, the assessment procedure encourages teacher–pupil questioning and discussion that helps to highlight any language and communication issues for the children. The review process also indicates how each child is progressing with their knowledge and use of comprehension skills. This includes:

1. identifying, labelling, and gathering information accurately,
2. making predictions about a narrative,
3. summarising and retelling,
4. clarifying meaning (building their vocabulary),
5. identifying and answering literal and inference questions, and
6. asking and answering their own simple and in-depth questions.

The assessment process also includes the use of engaging picture books to stimulate 'book talk' which encourages beginner readers to demonstrate how they make meaning, retell stories, and ask and answer their own literal and in-depth questions about the narrative to support their understanding (Paris and Paris 2001, Murris and Haynes 2000).

## The three stages of informal early comprehension skills assessment

1. Pre-instruction baseline appraisal of reading-for-meaning skills (including language and communication)

The purpose of the baseline picture narrative assessment (Section 2, Unit 1) is to offer an effective non-decoding model for reviewing children's language, communication, and early comprehension skills in line with primary curriculum objectives (Early Years Foundation Stage Statutory Framework, early adopter version, July 2020; DfE 2021) using any picture narrative.

The teacher–pupil conferencing procedure provides an effective method for evaluating children's emerging reading-for-meaning ability. This involves using a visual text, such as an illustration or cover of a picture book, prior to guided comprehension skills instruction.

The initial skills review indicates whether the reader can:

- clarify the meaning of images, concepts, words which present the main points about the characters, their actions, and places in a scene,
- locate literal information to answer questions about the characters, their actions, and places in a scene,
- identify clues to make inferences from the picture narrative and text,
- combine literal information and clues to answer inference questions about pictures,
- predict what might happen next based on what has been read so far (titles, pictures, text clues linked to their own knowledge and experience – cause and effect),
- draw on evidence in pictures and text to justify their answers to inference questions,
- draw on their knowledge of vocabulary to understand texts,
- explain the writer's use of language and the overall effect of the text on the reader,
- ask themselves questions such as: *What might happen next? Who? What? Where? Why?* to check their understanding of the picture narrative and text, and
- think about their responses to questions about the text and check whether their answers make sense (such as: *How do I know that? Why do I think that?*).

2. Intermediate appraisal after each teaching unit (Units 1–4)

A series of pre-planned intermediate reviews consolidates the skills taught as each teaching unit progresses. Each review ensures that previous strategies are embedded before teaching the next skills. The assessment objectives relate to 1) prime areas of early learning and development, such as communication and language skills (listening, attention, speaking and understanding) and 2) specific learning areas, such as literacy (comprehension). As each unit review progresses, children are assessed for their combined knowledge of:

- communication and clarifying skills,
- concept of print and reading-for-meaning skills,
- understanding of literal meaning,
- understanding of inference (predicting, responding to inference questions), and
- retelling a story from beginning to end in the correct sequence.

In addition, the aim of these teaching unit assessments is to encourage more teacher–pupil conferencing and pupil self-assessment to help readers:

- become more aware of their learning aims and achievements, and
- improve on specific reading-for-meaning skills as they move through the teaching units.

The pupil-questioning element of this assessment also promotes child-led enquiry and self-regulation, which recent findings suggest gives children a head-start in their reading, learning, and self-efficacy (Education Endowment Foundation 2021, Joseph et al. 2015, Schunk and Pajares 2009, Bandura 1993).

Alongside an optional marking guide and space for teacher comments and recommendations, the intermediate assessments include scripted guidance to support the 'picture walk and talk' procedure (see Section 2A of this chapter, pages 74 and 75). The aim of this discussion is to encourage the reader to identify the main points of an unfamiliar scene, before they are asked to retell the narrative and answer a range of questions about it. This process provides teachers and practitioners with:

a. a comprehensive record of the readers' ability to make meaning of a new text,
b. an in-depth review of pupil progress throughout the skills-building process, and
c. an ongoing record of pupils' comprehension skills till the end of the Reception Year.

The additional pupil self-assessment (see Section 2C p. 80) supports the metacognitive aspect of the unit sessions and encourages children to become more aware of their learning aims and achievements. The assessment process also allows them to see how they can improve on specific reading-for-meaning skills as they move through the following teaching units.

3. The end-of-year (post-instruction) language comprehension skills assessment and the EYFS Profile

'Each child's level of development must be assessed against the early learning goals. Practitioners must indicate whether children are meeting expected levels of development, or if they are not yet reaching expected levels ('emerging'). This is the EYFS Profile'. (DfE 2021: 20)

The expected level of development for comprehension at the end of the reception year is outlined in simple terms in the DfE (2022) *Early Years Foundation Stage Profile 2022 Handbook*. The emphasis is on the child being able to 'demonstrate understanding of what has been read to them' by:

- retelling stories and narratives using their own words and recently introduced vocabulary (summarising, retelling, clarifying),
- anticipating key events in stories (predicting), and
- using and understanding recently introduced vocabulary during discussions about stories, non-fiction, rhymes, and poems and during role-play (clarifying)

These comprehension skills are directly related to the SPEC strategies (Summarising, Predicting, Enquiry, and Clarifying) and to the Year 1 reading comprehension objectives. The SPEC strategies therefore provide an effective structure for working towards proficient reading for meaning skills in preparation for children's learning in Key Stage 1. Figure 7.1 demonstrates how principles relating to the concept of print (Clay 2000) and the stages of early reading comprehension development are associated with the early learning goals. This provides practitioners with a useful cross-reference to draw on when they are assessing their pupils' reading and learning progress before, during, and at the end of the Reception Year.

| Assessing development of early reading for meaning skills against ELGs | | | |
|---|---|---|---|
| Stages of comprehension development | Early Learning Goals (The EYFS Statutory Framework 2021) | | |
| | **Communication and language**<br>Listening, attention, and understanding, speaking | **Physical development**<br>Gross motor skills<br>Fine motor skills | **Personal, social, emotional development**<br>Self-regulation<br>Managing self<br>Building relationships |
| **Emergent Level**<br>(Concepts of print)<br>Concepts of print refers to the awareness of 'how print works.' This includes:<br>• understanding the concept of books and how they function,<br>• recognising differences between visual and written texts, and<br>• a range of understandings that allow the reading process to take place. | • Can differentiate between text and illustration.<br>• Understands that print conveys meaning.<br>• Understands that books/texts are created by writers.<br>• Recites rhymes and sings songs.<br>• Talks about stories.<br>• Tells a story from the pictures.<br>• Labels and describes pictures.<br>• Is beginning to understand what a letter and a word are.<br>• Names some letters.<br>• Recognises some capitals and lower-case letters.<br>• Recognises own first name. | • Holds a book correctly.<br>• Recognises the front and back cover.<br>• Has established left to right movement, top to bottom.<br>• Turns the pages from front to back.<br>• Knows that print carries meaning and that print in English is read from left to right and top to bottom. | • Enjoys sharing books with an adult, and other children.<br>• Can empathise with characters in stories.<br>• Shows preferences for different books. |

FIGURE 7.1  Stages of comprehension development in relation to early learning goals (based on EYFS and Key Stage 1 Statutory Framework 2021 objectives and research by Clay 2000, reflected in the ECLAS-II by CTB 2003)

**Self-regulation: self-confidence and learning self-awareness**
- 'Children are confident about trying new activities and say why they like some activities more than others.'
- 'They are confident speaking in a familiar group, will talk about their ideas, and will choose the resources they need for their chosen activities.'
- 'They say when they do or do not need help.'

**Managing feelings and behaviour**
- 'Children talk about how they and others show feelings, talk about their own and others' behaviour and its consequences, and know that some behaviour is unacceptable.'
- 'They work as part of a group or class and understand and follow the rules.'
- 'They adjust their behaviour to different situations and take changes of routine in their stride.'

**Making relationships**
- 'Children play co-operatively, taking turns with others.'
- 'They take account of one another's ideas about how to organise their activity.'
- 'They show sensitivity to others' needs and feelings and form positive relationships with adults and other children.'

**Physical development**
'Children are active and interactive, developing their co-ordination, control, and movement (through role play, use of multisensory activites to support their reading for meaning).'

**Moving and handling**
- 'Children show good control and co-ordination in large and small movements.'
- 'They move confidently in a range of ways, safely negotiating space.'
- 'They handle equipment and tools effectively.'

**Listening and attention**
- 'They listen to stories… accurately anticipating key events and respond to what they (see) and hear with relevant comments, questions, or actions.'

**Understanding**
- 'Children follow instructions involving several ideas or actions.'
- 'They answer "how" and "why" questions about their experiences and in response to stories or events.'

**Speaking**
- 'Children express themselves effectively, showing awareness of listeners' needs.'
- 'They use past, present, and future forms accurately when talking about events that have happened or are to happen in the future.'
- 'They develop their own narratives and explanations by connecting ideas or events.'

**Working towards Reception expectations**
Literacy ELG:
Language comprehension…
- Children can 'demonstrate understanding of what has been read to them (or what they understand from picture narrative and simple text) by using the following skills:
1) retelling stories and narratives in sequence, retelling using their own words, retelling by drawing on language patterns of stories (which all involve summarising, retelling, clarifying skills),
2) Anticipating key events in stories (which involves predicting skills), and
3) Appropriate use of recently introduced vocabulary during discussions about stories, non-fiction, rhymes, and poems and during role-play (which involves clarifying skills)

FIGURE 7.1 (Continued)

**End of reception year expectations:**

- Can use language to imagine and recreate roles and experiences (e.g., *Clarifying* – use of appropriate vocabulary, *Retelling* – drawing on familiar stories, *Predicting* – identifying cause and effect),

- Can listen to narratives and retell them in the correct sequence, drawing on language patterns of stories (*Summarising* in sequence, using story structure and language: 'Once upon a time…'),

- Can read a range of familiar and common words and simple sentences independently (*Clarifying* – e.g. making meaning of words using context clues),

- Can show an understanding of the elements of stories, e.g., main character, sequence, of events and openings, and how information can be found to answer questions about where, who, why and how (Literal and Inference *Enquiry*).

**Working towards Year 1 comprehension expectations**… using a range of strategies to read pictures and text for meaning, e.g., understanding, interpreting, describing, selecting, or retrieving information, events, or ideas from texts and using quotations and references from texts.

**Year 1 Content Domains (1a/1b/1c/1d/1e)**

1a: Can draw on knowledge of vocabulary to understand texts (Clarifying skills)

1b: Can identify/explain key aspects of texts, e.g., characters, events, titles, and information (Summarising skills)

1c: Can identify and explain the sequence of events in fiction and non-fiction texts (Retelling skills)

1d: Can make inferences from the text (Predicting, Enquiry, Clarifying skills)

1e: Can predict what might happen based on what has been read so far (Predicting skills)

FIGURE 7.1 (Continued)

## Resources for planning or using ready-prepared assessments

Assessment frameworks in the book help to support your own planning of baseline, intermediate and end-of year evaluations using any picture book (see the list of picture books suggested in Chapter 6 pages 60–62). Alternatively, the explicit pre-planned resources in Part 3 pages 177–218 provide reception teachers with a full set of intermediate and end-of-year assessments for immediate use in the classroom. These plans demonstrate in detail how effective assessment works using this evaluation approach. The assessment materials include a picture booklet designed specifically for this purpose. The title of this picture book is *Little Fly and the Spider Trap* – an age-appropriate story based on the familiar nursery rhyme 'Incy Wincy Spider'.

## Picture narrative

The information on the front cover (Figure 7.2) introduces the characters (Mum Fly, Dad Fly, Little Fly, and Incy Spider) and the setting (a garden fence).

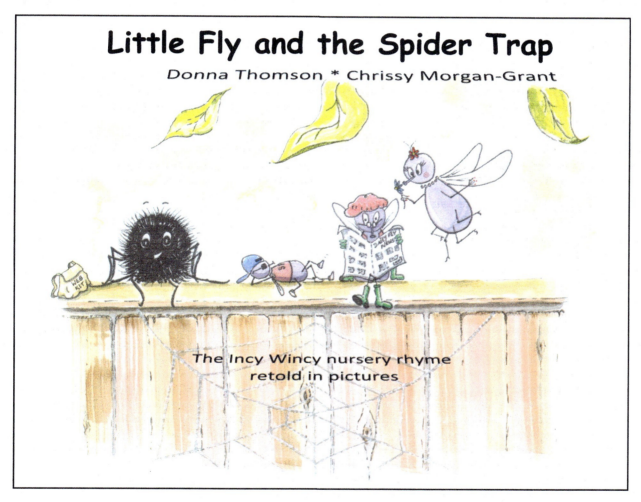

FIGURE 7.2 Front cover of assessment picture booklet *Little Fly and the Spider Trap*. Reproduced with permission from authors Donna Thomson and Chrissy Morgan-Grant

The four inside pages of picture narrative tell a story that is more complex than the simple rhyme. For example, on page one, the picture reveals much more than the words, 'Incy Wincy Spider climbed up the waterspout'. A problem is unfolding that requires the reader to think more deeply.

Little Fly is caught in a web inside the waterspout and the spider is scuttling in… Mum and Dad Fly seem unaware that Little Fly is in danger. These images prompt the reader to wonder what might happen next…

Each page contains a line from the nursery rhyme and a different scene as the story progresses – ending with two lines on the last page. The readers are encouraged to predict what the solution might be for Little Fly and his parents. Will Little Fly escape the spider's web and if so, how?

# Section 2: Guidance on assessment procedure frameworks, marking, and analysis

Although the baseline, intermediate, and end-of-year assessments use the same methods to evaluate reader's responses to narrative, the process becomes slightly longer and more in-depth – and the set of questions more complex – as new skills build on each other and are combined to increase the reader's understanding.

These methods include three assessment stages:

- Section A – comprehending picture narrative,
- Section B – answering and asking questions about picture narrative, and
- Section C – discussing the reader's comprehension strengths and weakness to aid the analysis process.

First the reader is invited to talk about the narrative. Then, they are asked to retell the story in their own words. Next, they are encouraged to answer questions about the narrative before they are given the opportunity to generate and answer their own questions about it. Finally, they are encouraged to talk about their comprehension skills and celebrate their reading progress with their teacher.

All three sections support the planning, and analysis of the baseline, intermediate, and end-of year evaluations. They also provide methods for observing, noting, marking, and analysing the children's spontaneous responses to unfamiliar and familiar text to 1) inform teaching and planning, and 2) to support teacher appraisal of skills before Year 1 transition. Practitioners might also find it helpful to make an audio recording of the readers' comments, retelling of the story, and responses to questions during each stage of the assessments.

## Section A – Comprehending picture narrative

The purpose of this initial section of the assessment is to:

- gather information about the reader's understanding of a narrative, and
- analyse their skills.

The assessment process involves the following three steps:

1. 'Picture walk and talk' procedure – to stimulate the reader's responses to previously unseen narrative.
2. Retelling of the story – to demonstrate the reader's full understanding of the narrative. (The assessor records a transcript of the retelling for analysis).

3. Summarising and retelling analysis – this framework provides the assessor with a method for analysing the reader's ability to identify and retell the main points of a story. These specific elements include: coherence and grasp of the key ideas (who, what, where, problem, solution) sequencing, vocabulary, direct reference to the narrative, ability to make personal connections.

### The 'picture walk' one-to-one assessment procedure

The aim of this teacher–pupil activity (based on Paris and Paris's 2003 'picture walk and talk' model) is to:

1. capture the children's spontaneous reactions to the picture narrative as they explore the pages and talk about the characters, events, and settings, and
2. gain some insight into their comprehension of the narrative before they retell the story.

This type of in-depth discussion helps to activate the reader's background knowledge and encourages them to generate inferences about morals and character's feelings in a similar way to the cognitive efforts required to construct meaning from printed words. Evidence shows that this initial approach to early reading for meaning assessment enables all young readers to engage in the comprehension process (Paris and Paris 2007, Helder et al. 2016, Dooley and Matthews 2009) and provides practitioners with a comprehensive overview of their language, communication, inference skills, and knowledge of story structure. The following steps demonstrate how to help early readers to participate meaningfully in the 'picture walk and talk' (see further examples of these steps in Chapter 9 Section 2 review plans pages 183–212):

- Show the reader the front page of the picture book.
- Invite them to look closely at the picture and talk about what they can see.
- Give them the title of the booklet (unless they can read it out loud for themselves) and ask them to predict what they think the story might be about from the title and clues on the front cover.
- Then encourage them to talk about the characters and picture narrative in greater depth. Give them the names of the characters and ask them to point to who they think each character might be in the illustration. Then encourage them to explain why they think this.
- Next (and only when necessary) prompt them with further questions about the characters, such as: 'What do you think they are doing?' 'What do you think is happening?' Why do you say that?' 'Where do you think they are?' 'How do you think the characters are feeling? Why do you think that?' 'What do they think will happen next? Why do you say that?'
- If they are exploring more than the front cover with you, repeat this process with each page of the picture narrative you are using.

### Retelling story events in order – transcript of retelling

Following discussion about the picture narrative, the reader is invited to retell the key points of the story (who, what, where, problem, solution) using the picture of the story to refer to if necessary. The process of retelling the main events of a story in sequence from beginning to end reveals immediately whether the reader has understood the narrative, has knowledge of story structure, and can draw on their knowledge of vocabulary to summarise the main points in their own words.

*Analysis of retelling and summarising skills*

The following framework provides a completed example of an in-depth analysis of all the elements of early retelling which might otherwise be overlooked. The first section of the analysis table (see Figure 7.3) offers space for a transcript of the reader's retelling of the narrative after the 'picture walk'. Beneath this area there is a list of the six basic elements of retelling and an optional scoring system to record the reader's ability to use each of these elements during the retelling process (on a scale of 0–3 marks for each skill). For example, noting how effectively they can 1) identify the main ideas in the story, 2) summarise these points coherently, 3) retell events and the plot in the correct order, 4) use descriptive vocabulary, 5) make direct references to the picture narrative and title, and 6) make connections with their own experience.

**Transcript of reader's retelling:** of *Gertie the Poorly Gull*
'The bird fell. He was poorly. The boy picked him up. Then daddy got a box and they put him in the cage.'

| Elements of retelling skills<br>Total score poss: 18 points | None<br>0 points | Poor<br>1 point | Average<br>2 points | Good<br>3 points |
|---|---|---|---|---|
| Main ideas – characters, actions, setting, problem, resolution | | | 2 | |
| Coherence – logical | | | 2 | |
| Sequencing of events/plot | | | 2 | |
| Use of descriptive vocab. | 0 | | | |
| Direct reference to title and pictures | | | 2 | |
| Connections with own experience | 0 | | | |
| Total Score: 8/18 | | | | |

Observations (example):
*'C' referred to the pictures to support her retelling – pointing to each one as the story unfolded – but she did not refer to any details. She retold the basic facts she could see on the page, briefly and in very quiet voice.*
*Although she is not a confident storyteller, C's simple narrative included the main elements of the story, such as characters and their actions. The picture prompts helped her to retell the story quite logically and in sequence – but she did not refer to earlier inferences she had made during the 'picture walk', e.g., the characters' feelings (sad). Also, she did not indicate there was a problem for the main character or a possible resolution.*

FIGURE 7.3 Completed example of retelling analysis

## Section B – Answering and asking questions about picture narrative

The assessment procedure is completed by asking the reader a series of different types of question (literal, inference, clarifying, evaluation, and prediction). This review of the reader's explicit and implicit comprehension skills helps the assessor to check whether they have fully understood the images, words, and concepts in the narrative. Following this, the reader is then invited to generate and answer their own questions about the narrative. Figure 7.4's adaptation of Parkin et al.'s (1999) taxonomy of questions provides an overview of the definitions of the different question types and gives the optional scoring for each question.

This methodical teaching approach is based on the principal that teaching children how to first identify literal meaning, then how to generate and answer their own explicit questions, leads them to deeper understanding about what it means to infer. Basaraba et al. (2012: 353) agree that 'without surface-level understanding of a text, deeper interactions with the text are not possible'. They go on to say that when 'designing and providing instruction and developing tests' it is essential to 'recognise that literal understanding is a stepping-stone to more advanced comprehension skills', such as inference, prediction, and evaluation. They also make the important point that these developing skills must be 'examined to continue to see growth in student performance' (Basaraba et al 2012: 353; see also Kintsch and Rawson 2005, Nation 2009).

| Comprehension question types *(hierarchical scoring 1–3 marks) and definitions* | |
| --- | --- |
| **Literal** (*1 mark*)<br><br>(Who, what, where? Right there!) | Explicit enquiry: the reader can locate and retrieve who, what, where information from pictures and text to answer questions. |
| For the following questions: *(Answers will vary – but reader must give evidence suggested in the text)* | |
| Clarification (vocabulary) (*2 marks*) | Explicit and Implicit enquiry: The reader understands the author's meaning and use of language in text. They can link context clues with their own knowledge of words to find the answer. |
| Inference (Prediction) (*2 marks*) | Implicit enquiry: The reader can infer, deduce, and provide evidence for their answers from the text, pictures, and their own background knowledge. |
| Inference (*2 marks*)<br>(Who, what, where? Why? How do you know that?) | Implicit enquiry: The reader uses their prior knowledge and understanding of 'cause and effect' to make connections about direct and inferred clues in the pictures and text. |
| Inference (Evaluation) (*3 marks*) | Implicit enquiry: The reader empathises with the characters using their own life experience and knowledge of emotions to explain the characters' behaviour or possible motives. |
| Generating own questions (*6 marks*) | Explicit and Implicit enquiry: The reader can generate and answer their own literal question (2 *points*), their own inference question (*4 points*) |
| Total score: / points | |

FIGURE 7.4 Analysis guidance – comprehension question types and optional scoring

*Adaptation of Parkin, C., Parkin, C., and Poole, B. 1999 PROBE -Taxonomy of Question Types, PROBE Informal Reading Inventory (emphasising comprehension), New Zealand': Triune Initiatives*

*Features of comprehension question types – working towards Year 1 expectations*

## Literal questions

The scoring system for these question types is based on a graduating scale of difficulty (see Figure 7.4). The simplest questions to answer are 'literal' and they are awarded the lowest score (1 mark) because the information is found directly on the page. The question will ask about either a character (**who** *is involved*?), action (**what** *are they* ***doing***?) or place (**where** *are they*?) and requires the reader to match the same word or similar image on the page with the key word in the question. For example:

**Picture narrative:** Setting shows a bird in a tree in a garden.
**Literal question: Where** is the tree?
**Answer:** The tree is in **the garden**.

## Clarifying questions

The next question-type on the scale is 'clarification'. This is awarded a score of 2 marks. The reason for the higher mark is that 'clarifying' requires the reader to draw on their knowledge of vocabulary to define the meaning of words in context, or to provide a similar word to the key word in the question to demonstrate their understanding. For example:

**Picture narrative:** Same picture as before.
**Clarifying question:** There is a robin in the tree. Suggest another word for 'robin'.
**Answer:** Another word for 'robin' is '**bird**'.

## Inference questions

The score for inference questions differs according to their complexity. For example, readers are awarded either 2 or 3 marks for giving an appropriate answer. There are often two parts to the question, and answers to most inference questions can vary depending on the reader's life-experience or prior knowledge of a topic, but they all require the reader to use 'because' to present evidence from the text.

A straightforward inference question will ask the reader to use clues on the page to explain their answer for 2 marks. For example:

**Picture narrative:** Shows a girl standing **by the door** with her **coat on**. She is **looking out of the nearby window** at the **rain pouring down**.

**Inference question: Why** is the girl **wearing a coat**?

**Answer:** The girl is wearing a coat **because** she is **going out** and she **doesn't want to get wet**. **I know that because** the picture shows that it is **raining outside**.

## Inference – prediction questions

Other inference questions ask the reader to gather the facts and clues on the page and use their knowledge about a topic or event to explain what might happen next in a story and why they think that. For example:

**Picture narrative:** Three boys are **on a beach** in their **swim wear**. The **two oldest boys** are **playing with a ball** and **calling to the youngest to join in**. The **youngest** boy is carrying **a bodyboard** and **pointing to the waves**.

**Inference question: What** do you think **might happen next**? Explain **why** you say that.

**Answer:** I think the youngest boy will **go and play in the waves with his bodyboard**. I say that because he is **pointing towards the sea**, and he doesn't look interested in playing ball.

**Picture narrative:** Shows **a family** by **a tent** in their **pyjamas**. The **lamp** hanging from the tent frame shines on them as **they unpack their sleeping bags**.

**Inference question:** What do you **think the family will do next**? Explain **why** you say that.

**Answer:** I think the **family will sleep in the tent overnight because** it is **getting dark**, and they are **in their pyjamas unpacking their sleeping bags**.

These types of inference questions are also are awarded 2 marks.

### Inference – evaluation questions

Complex inference questions that ask the reader to evaluate a character's motives and behaviour and explain what they are thinking and feeling (and why) are awarded 3 marks, the highest score on the scale. This is because readers need to link facts and clues in pictures and text with their understanding of emotions to present a plausible answer. For example:

**Picture narrative:** The **tallest of the three children** in the night-time seaside scene is **standing by the tent entrance with his arms folded**. The lamp light shows he is **frowning** at the **other two children** who are **taking up all the space inside**. They are **smiling and joking together as if he is not there**.

**Inference (evaluation) question:** Do you think **everyone** is **enjoying camping**? Why do you think that?

**Answer: No,** I do not think everyone is **enjoying camping because** one of the boys is **feeling upset** with the others **for not letting him join in the fun**. I think that **because** he is **frowning and standing with his arms folded outside** the tent while the **other boys are not making room for him** and **joking and laughing without him**.

### Analysis of the participant's responses to the different question types

In the same way that different reading behaviours can indicate whether the child understands or is engaged in a narrative, they can also provide a reliable guide for analysing reasons for the reader's incorrect responses to different types of question. For example, your questions might ask:

- Does the pupil's answer relate to the information in the picture narrative?
- Are they simply guessing or referring to personal experience only to give an answer?
- Has the pupil looked closely enough at the picture detail?
- Is prior knowledge being used in addition to the information in the picture narrative?
- Does the pupil have problems with making links?
- Does the pupil understand the meaning of the vocabulary used in the story title and in the questions?
- Does the pupil have problems with story structure or sequencing?

- Does the pupil have problems expressing themselves?
- Is the pupil engaged in the picture content?

## Section C – Answering questions to support pupil self-assessment

Within the context of a semi-structured interview the children are first read a set of statements and then asked to respond to each with a 'yes' or 'no' answer. The aim of these questions is to gain an insight into their view of reading and perception of their own skills and reading progress throughout the year. In this process they are also asked to explain their negative and positive responses where appropriate. This reflective and insightful conferencing approach helps to improve pupil learning awareness and build self-confidence as their skills develop.

### Marking system

The optional scoring system in the book offers practitioners a progressive structure for evaluating specific comprehension skills over the reception year. The score for each assessment is on a scale of 0–18 marks. The combination of scores for Section A (summarising and retelling skills) and Section B (comprehension questions and answers) provide a final percentage mark. This percentage indicates comprehension skills ability following the intermediate and end-of-year assessments.

### Evaluating comprehension ability

The benchmark for assessing comprehension, therefore, is straightforward for teacher and pupils. There are basically three comprehension outcomes for the reader:

- Easy – 70–100% (13–18 marks): The reader found the assessment easy overall and would benefit from a more challenging text to assess their comprehension strengths and weaknesses moving forward.
- Instructional – 40–65% (7–12 marks): The reader's use of strategies to support their understanding of text is inconsistent. They require more explicit reading comprehension instruction at this level of text.
- Hard – 0–35% (0–6 marks): The reader needs to be given a less challenging text and explicit instruction that shows them how to use comprehension skills in smaller steps to support their understanding.

### Time required for assessment

The reception baseline may take up to 20 minutes per pupil to complete and the intermediate and end-of-year assessments may take up to 30 minutes. However, the procedure can be paused and resumed as appropriate.

### Oral assessment procedure – teacher–pupil conferencing

The assessment must be delivered by a reception teacher, teaching assistant, or appropriately qualified practitioner (e.g., early years lead or SENCO). The procedure requires adults to work with each child on a one-to-one basis. Those conducting the assessment should be fully trained and familiar with the materials (see Chapter 9 Section 2 for pre-planned assessment resources p. 175). It is advised that an audio recording is used during the assessment to record the children's responses to the picture narrative for later analysis.

## Problems that may occur and how to solve them through instruction and assessment

Without explicit instruction to support the question-answering process, some children find it difficult to identify the key word in the question and know how to answer it. For example, some children may avoid revisiting the text to check their answers for sense and accuracy, because they find it difficult to scan the text for specific information. This can lead them to respond evaluatively, giving answers that relate to their personal lives rather than the text and the author's intention. In addition, children are often unsure how to retrieve information from two different sources to answer a question (e.g., text and picture). They may also resort to giving a literal response or rely on memory only without checking for accuracy. All these issues can be resolved through step-by-step modelling of these skills, through regular teacher–pupil review after instruction and by showing pupils how to self-monitor their understanding using specific strategies.

## Reading behaviour and reading comprehension skills analysis

This framework provides a useful tool for understanding the reading behaviour of children who struggle to comprehend texts. This informal method of recording pupils' understanding following the initial picture 'walking and talking' process (Section A, pages 74–75), is based on Clay's Early Print Strategies running record design (cited in Lysaker and Hopper 2015), which was adapted by Lysaker and Hopper (2015) to support their observation of wordless picture book reading. I further modified this research model to create a comprehension assessment tool to support analysis of young children's emerging reading for meaning skills. The Department of Education early adopter reforms (2021) recommend that teachers and practitioners refrain from recording and gathering evidence of children's progress throughout the year. However, since this method highlights specific areas of comprehension difficulty, it provides a useful focus for detecting and solving emerging comprehension problems before they become too entrenched.

The 'reading behaviour' framework helps the assessor to gather information about the reader's comments, body language, and how they make meaning during the 'picture walk' procedure. The process of looking, thinking, and interpreting picture narrative involves talking about the story (what the reader says), physically responding to information on the page (what the reader does) and making sense of the narrative (how the reader makes meaning). On entering reception, young children often rely on body language to express themselves and require frequent prompting and reassurance to encourage them to talk about their ideas. So, it is particularly useful when first assessing their comprehension skills to use a method that helps you to focus on the different aspects of reading behaviour which indicate specific comprehension strengths and weaknesses.

The three sections in Figure 7.5 provide a question checklist for evaluating the reader's spontaneous 'picture walk' responses and space for your comments. For example, in determining whether the reader had a basic understanding of the narrative, you might ask yourself whether the reader's narration of the story was logical. Did they have some knowledge of story structure? Did they use gestures, rather than speech to refer to information on the page? What strategies did they use to make sense of the story?

| Assessing the different aspects of reading behaviour<br>*Tick the following for 'yes' or cross for 'no' in the boxes on the right* | ✓ or X |
|---|---|
| <u>What Reader Says</u> *(their narration skills and knowledge of story structure)*<br>For example, | |
| a)   Did they need to be frequently prompted for responses? | a) ✓ |
| b)   Could they identify who the characters are, their actions, locations, emotions, problems and how difficulties are resolved? | b) ✓ |
| | c) ✓ |
| c)   Was their narration of the story logical? | d) ✓ |
| d)   Could they make predictions? | e) ✓ |
| e)   Could they retell the events in order in their own words? | f) ✓ |
| f)   Could they use descriptive vocabulary? | g) ✓ |
| g)   Could they repeat vocabulary used in story? | h) ✓ |
| h)   Did they refer to their own experiences in relation to the story events?<br><br>Comments: 'C' was able to locate who, what, where information and predict what might happen to the main character from information in the title and picture on the cover with some prompts. | |
| <u>What Reader Does</u> *(gesture, gaze, inflection, pausing)*<br>For example, did they, | ✓ or X |
| a)   scan the pictures for information? | a) ✓ |
| b)   pause for reassurance (to check whether responses are right or wrong)? | b) ✓ |
| c)   point to details in pictures? | c) ✓ |
| d)   shrug in response to your question prompts…? | d) ✓ |
| e)   use other physical responses…..?<br>Comments: Scanned the picture quickly. Pointed at the main character when prompted to say who is in the story. | e) ✓ |
| <u>How the reader makes meaning</u> *(searching, cross-checking, rereading, self- correcting)*.<br>For example, could they, | ✓ or X |
| a)   identify explicit information, | a) ✓ |
| b)   identify clues, | b) ✓ |
| c)   make links using prior knowledge and experience, | c) ✓ |
| d)   check if their ideas make sense, | d) ✓ |
| e)   correct themselves if they do not make sense. | e) X |

Comments Can identify who, what, where information quickly – but only when prompted. She evaluates character's feelings probably from own experience rather than evidence on page. No direct reference to character's expressions or body language in picture. She used limited vocabulary to describe feelings and events in the story. However, her reasoning throughout her interpretation of the pictures is clear and logical (the characters are 'sad because the bird is hurt') – 'because' is used frequently to explain.

Recommendations: She requires knowledge of who, what, where self-questioning prompts to help with story structure and sequencing. This will also support own enquiry about what is happening and help with predictions about what might happen next.

FIGURE 7.5 Figure 7.5 Completed example of a picture walk analysis: Reading Behaviour and Reading Comprehension Skills *Revision of assessment method based on* Lysaker and Hopper (2015) adaptation of *Clay 2005 Early Print Strategies running record design*. See Section 3 for teacher resource.

The frequency of 'yes' or 'no' answers to the questions in Figure 7.5 will indicate the reader's engagement in the story, their initial comprehension strengths and weaknesses, and how to support their reading skills development.

# References

Bandura, A. (1993). *Perceived self-efficiency in cognitive development and functioning*. www.uky.edu/~eushe2/Bandura/Bandura1993EP.pdf

Basaraba, D., Yovanoff, P., Alonzo, J., and Tindal, G. (2012). Examining the structure of reading comprehension: Do literal, inferential, and evaluative comprehension truly exist? *Reading and Writing*, 26, 349–379.

Clay, M.M. (2000). *Concepts about print: What have children learned about printed language?* Heinemann.

CTB. (2003). *ECLAS-II (early childhood learning assessment system, 2nd edition) literacy development checklist*. McGraw-Hill.

Department for Education. (2021). *Statutory framework for the Early Years Foundation Stage*. www.gov.uk/government/publications/early-years-foundation-stage-framework--2

Department for Education. (2022). *Early years foundation stage profile 2022 handbook*. www.gov.uk/government/publications/early-years-foundation-stage-profile-handbook

Dooley, C.M., and Matthews, M.W. (2009). Emergent comprehension: Understanding comprehension development among young literacy learners. *Journal of Early Childhood Literacy*, 9(3), 269–294.

Education Endowment Foundation. (2021). *EEF toolkit – reading comprehension strategies*. https://educationendowmentfoundation.org.uk/education-evidence/teaching-learning-toolkit/reading-comprehension-strategies

Helder, A., van Leijenhorst, L., and van den Broek, P. (2016). Coherence monitoring by good and poor comprehenders in elementary school: Comparing offline and online measures. *Learning and Individual Differences*, 48, 17–23.

Joseph, L.M., Alber-Morgan, S., Cullen, J., and Rouse, C. (2015). The effects of self-questioning on reading comprehension: A literature review. *Reading & Writing Quarterly*, 32(2), 152–173.

Kintsch, W., and Rawson, K.A. (2005). Comprehension. In M.J. Snowling and C. Hulme (Eds), *The science of reading: A handbook*. Malden, MA: Blackwell.

Lysaker, J., and Hopper, E. (2015). A kindergartner's emergent strategy use during wordless picture book reading. *Reading Teacher*, 68(8), 649–657.

Murris, K., and Haynes, J. (2000). *Storywise: Thinking Through Stories*. DialogueWorks.

Nation, I.P. (2009). *Teaching ESL/EF/reading and writing*. Routledge.

Paris, A., and Paris, S.G. (2001). *Children's comprehension of narrative picture books*. CIERA Report 3-012. www.ciera.org/library/reports/inquiry-3/3-012/3-012.html

Paris, A., and Paris, S.G. (2007). Teaching narrative comprehension strategies to first graders. *Cognition and Instruction*, 25(1), 1–44.

Paris, S., and Paris, S.G. (2003). Assessing narrative comprehension in young children. *Reading Research Quarterly*, 38, 36–76.

Parkin, C., Parkin, C., and Pool, B. (1999). *PROBE – taxonomy of question types, reading assessment*. Triune Initiatives.

Schunk, D.H., and Pajares, F. (2009). Self-efficacy theory. In K.R. Wenzel and A. Wigfield (Eds), *Handbook of motivation at school*. Routledge/Taylor & Francis Group.

# PART 3

# Reception resources: Teaching and assessing comprehension skills

# CHAPTER 8

# Foundation teaching and assessment framework (Units 1–4)

A comprehensive summary of the teaching and assessment units in the book is shown in Figure 8.1. It provides an outline of the systematic steps used to teach early communication, strategic reading-for-meaning and self-questioning skills over the reception year in preparation for transition to Year 1. This information includes a profile of the SPEC strategies (Summarising, Predicting, Enquiry, and Clarifying) and list of the multisensory learning tools and techniques used to support the comprehension process.

In addition, the table indicates how the goals of the SPEC comprehension enquiry process correlate with the aims of the Year 1 comprehension learning objectives (content domains 1a–1e). It also indicates how use of picture narrative to embed early reading for meaning and self-questioning prepares young readers for the use of similar skills to develop text comprehension in Key Stage 1. This overview demonstrates how beginner readers can work effectively towards end-of-year Reception reading expectations using this teaching approach.

The teaching sequences involve flexible, discrete daily sessions, which progress from simple elements to the more complex aspects of developing comprehension skills and self-monitoring of understanding. The emphasis of these sessions is to build on existing 'quality first teaching' by increasing playful exploration and conscious thinking supported by teacher–pupil, group, and class discussion about the learning processes involved in developing early comprehension skills and self-monitoring of understanding. This involves a framework for instruction and assessment using picture narrative to:

DOI: 10.4324/9781003226307-11

1. establish an understanding of the four SPEC strategies and multisensory learning techniques,
2. demonstrate how these skills are taught in line with the Early Years Goals in prime learning areas (EYFS Statutory Framework, early adopter version July 2020), and
3. help readers work effectively towards Year 1 comprehension objectives as the sessions progress.

| Pages | SPEC reception teaching and assessment resources | Early years goals (prime learning areas) | SPEC comprehension skills objectives | Working towards Year 1 comprehension objectives |
|---|---|---|---|---|
| | Photocopiable Sections<br>Focusing on:<br>1. Characteristics of effective learning...<br>• Playing and exploring – engagement<br>• Active learning<br>• Creating and thinking critically – thinking<br><br>2. SPEC Comprehension strategies to support understanding and enquiry about picture narrative:<br>• Summarising/*retelling*<br>• Predicting<br>• Enquiry/*questioning*<br>• Clarifying<br><br>3. Working towards Year 1 comprehension objectives (content domains – 1a, 1b, 1c, 1d, 1e)<br><br>4. Consolidation:<br>Teacher planning using a selection of fiction and information picture books to practice literal questioning skills over term. | Focusing on:<br>• Communication and language (book talk and interaction skills)<br>• Physical development (use of multisensory activities to support learning)<br>• Personal, social, and emotional (inference – evaluation skills)<br><br>Multisensory learning: To help children to look more closely, listen more carefully, think more strategically, share ideas with greater confidence. Gradually moving from picture narrative to pictures and simple sentences by modelling how to use:<br>• The Viewer<br>• Questions cards<br>• Role-play<br>• Hand/body signs | Learning how to:<br>Summarise/*retell*<br>• Understand story structure<br>• Build vocabulary (recalling words used in texts)<br>• Gather main points (who, what, where, when, why, how)<br>• Retell simple narratives in sequence<br><br>Predict<br>• Ask questions to gather info (who, what, where, why)<br>• Identify clues and make links<br>• Reason/justify ideas (using 'because')<br>• Anticipate outcomes (cause and effect)<br><br>Enquire/*question*<br>• Literal – identify key words, ask/answer who, what, where?<br>• Inference/evaluation – identifying clues, asking/answering who, what, where, why, (explaining how they know, why they say that)<br>• Presenting evidence from text to justify inference answers<br><br>Clarify<br>• Skim and scan pictures/text to locate clues/key information<br>• Make sense of words, images, and concepts from context<br>• Build knowledge and understanding of vocabulary through 'picture talk' about characters, their actions, and settings<br>• Use appropriate language when retelling in own words<br>• Self-correct for accuracy and sense | Content domains (1a, 1b, 1c, 1d, 1e)<br><br>1a Drawing on knowledge of vocabulary to understand texts. (Clarifying)<br><br>1b Identifying and explaining key aspects of texts, such as characters, events, titles, how items of information are related and organised. (Summarising)<br><br>1c Identifying and explaining the sequence of events in fiction and non-fiction texts, beginning, middle and end – characters, actions, places, problem, resolutions. (Retelling)<br><br>1d Making inferences from the text, predicting events – cause and effect, justify ideas and answers to questions about the text, explain writer's use of language, *and explain the overall effect of the text on the reader.* (Predicting/enquiry/clarifying)<br><br>1e Predict what might happen based on what has been read so far, linking this to own knowledge and experience – cause and effect. (Predicting/enquiry) |

FIGURE 8.1 Overview of foundation framework objectives: Working towards Year 1 expectations

| | | Foundation baseline assessment – prior to picture comprehension instruction | | |
| Pages | Photocopiable sections | Early years goals/prime learning | SPEC comprehension skills objectives | Working towards Year 1 comprehension objectives |
|---|---|---|---|---|
| | Assessment overview<br>Evaluating:<br>1. Communication and language<br>2. Concept of print and early reading for meaning skills | Assessing communication and language<br>• Listening and attention<br>• Understanding<br>• Speaking | Assessing reading-for-meaning skills<br>Evaluating ability to identify key information and answer questions about a story from the cover. | N/A |
| | | Teaching Unit 1 – Communication and reading for meaning skills | | |
| Pages | Photocopiable sections (Units 1–4) | Early years goals/prime learning | SPEC comprehension skills objectives | Working towards Year 1 comprehension objectives |
| | Part 1 – Book talk<br>Communication and language skills instruction<br><br>Part 2 – Reading-for-meaning skills introduction | 1. Book talk<br>Understanding importance of active listening, engagement, and effective discussion<br><br>Introducing Riskometer to encourage participation in discussion, boost self-esteem and learning self-awareness | 2. Reading for meaning (and sense)<br>Introducing reading for meaning, e.g., understanding:<br>• the concept of print (how to approach a book/how picture content and words convey a message)<br>• language comprehension and the importance of key words<br>• why we read<br>• reading pictures for meaning<br>• how to draw on own experience and knowledge of familiar stories to support understanding<br><br>Clarifying skills (checking meaning):<br>• Increasing understanding of vocabulary through 'picture book talk' (setting, character, and general vocabulary)<br>• Discussing how to clarify meanings using own experience of the world, knowledge of words and contextual understanding<br>• Modelling how to make corrections when necessary<br><br>Plenary example: Asking the children to feedback what they have found out about reading. | (Content domains 1a, 1b, 1c, 1d, 1e)<br>1a (Clarifying)<br>1b (Summarising)<br>1c (Retelling)<br>1d (Predicting/clarifying)<br>1e (Predicting/questioning) |

FIGURE 8.1  (Continued)

| Pages | End of Unit 1 skills assessment (Parts 1 and 2) 1. Communication and language 2. Concept of print and early reading for meaning skills | Reviewing skills (Unit 1, Part 1) • Listening and attention • Understanding • Speaking | Reviewing skills (Unit 1, Part 2) Ability to: • identify key information • answer questions about a story from the cover | N/A |
|---|---|---|---|---|

Teaching Unit 2 – Literal enquiry (and clarifying)
Being a Literal Patroller: (*Who, what, where – right there!*) Practicing gathering explicit information to ask and answer who, what, and where questions about what is right there on the page.

| Photocopiable sections (Units 1–4) | Early years goals/ prime learning | SPEC comprehension skills objectives | Working towards Year 1 comprehension objectives (content domains 1a, 1b, 1c, 1d, 1e) |
|---|---|---|---|
| **Pages** Unit 2 Literal enquiry-focusing on comprehension self-questioning skills: Part 1 'Who' questioning Part 2 'What' questioning Part 3 'Where' questioning Part 4 'Who, what, where' questioning Simple enquiry – Literal Patroller Showing pupils how to: • Identify and name explicit information on the page • Identify and organise key words (character, action, place) • Consciously build vocabulary by repeating words they hear or see on the page • Create full verbal or written questions and statements using author's vocabulary | • Literal enquiry focus • Communication and language skills • Physical development (using multisensory learning tools to support learning self-awareness and literal self-questioning activities) Multisensory learning: modelling how to use the Viewer, questions cards, role-play, hand/body signs to help children to: • look more closely • listen more carefully • think more strategically • share ideas with greater confidence | Literal enquiry focus Part 1 – 'Who' enquiry • To identify literal information about characters in pictures • To gather, organise and categorise this information to help reader generate and answer own and other's questions Part 2 – 'What' enquiry • To identify literal information about what the characters are doing in pictures • To gather, organise and categorise this information to help generate and answer own/others questions Part 3 – 'Where' enquiry To identify literal information about settings and where characters are in relation to each other/ objects in pictures. To gather, organise and categorise this information to help generate and answer own/others questions. | Literal enquiry focusing on: **1a** Drawing on knowledge of vocabulary to understand texts. (Clarifying) **1b** Identifying and explaining key aspects of texts, such as characters, events, titles, how items of information are related and organised. (Summarising) |

FIGURE 8.1 (Continued)

| | | | |
|---|---|---|---|
| | Clarifying skills – modelling how to consciously:<br>• clarify meanings drawing on knowledge of words and contextual understanding<br>• check that their questions make sense<br>• make corrections when necessary<br>• extend their knowledge of vocabulary (synonyms/antonyms) and grammar to support their understanding of spoken and written language<br>• skim and scan accurately for same, similar images, words, and ideas to support the literal questioning process | Gradually moving from picture narrative to pictures and simple sentences.<br><br>Consolidation: Teachers own planning using real picture books across a range of subjects and specific prime areas to practice literal questioning and clarifying skills. | Part 4 – 'Who, what, where' enquiry<br>• To identify literal key word information about characters, actions and places in pictures and text<br>• To gather, organise and categorise this information to help generate and answer own/others questions<br><br>Plenary after each session – Encouraging them to reflect on and share their thoughts about being a Literal Patroller (to encourage self-assessment).<br><br>For example:<br>• What have they found out about gathering literal information from pictures (and text).<br>• Do they like asking and answering their own questions about picture information? Why?<br>• Which questions do they enjoy asking most? 'Who?' 'What?' or 'Where?' Can they explain why? | ✓ ✓ |
| Pages | Assessing end of Unit 2 literal skills | Reviewing 'Who, what, where' literal self-questioning skills (Part 4) | |
| | Teaching Unit 3 – Inference enquiry<br>Being Detective Clooze: (*Who, what, where, when? Explaining how and why I think that*) Practicing searching for clues, making links, and generating and answering inference questions. | | |
| **Photocopiable sections (Units 1–4)** | **Early years goals/ prime learning** | **SPEC comprehension skills objectives** | **Working towards Year 1 comprehension objectives (content domains 1a, 1b, 1c, 1d, 1e)** |

FIGURE 8.1 (Continued)

| Pages | | Inference enquiry focus | Inference enquiry focus | Inference enquiry focus |
|---|---|---|---|---|
| | Unit 3<br><br>Part 1 – Making predictions and clarifying meanings.<br>Part 2 – Understanding cause and effect<br>Part 3 – Deductions and predictions<br>Predicting (introducing Detective Clooze) – modelling how to consciously:<br>• identify clues<br>• make links using clues and own knowledge to ask questions and make logical predictions about a story<br>• use simple past, present, future tenses, and general vocabulary to explain what is happening and what might happen next<br>• use 'because' to justify their ideas<br><br>More complex enquiry (inference questioning) modelling how to consciously:<br>• seek and link clues on the page with their own knowledge to answer simple inference questions about narratives accurately<br>• generate and answer own inference questions about pictures and text with confidence<br><br>Checking meaning:<br>• Increasing understanding of vocabulary through 'picture book talk' (setting, character, and general vocabulary)<br>• Extending knowledge of synonyms and antonyms to support inference questioning (*nurturing literal questioning, clarifying, retelling, inference, and evaluation questioning skills*) | - Communication and language<br>- Physical development (using multisensory learning tools to support learning self-awareness and detective self-questioning activities)<br>- Personal, social, and emotional (inference – evaluation skills)<br><br>Multisensory learning<br>Modelling how to use the Viewer, questions cards, role-play, hand/body signs to help children to:<br>• look more closely<br>• listen more carefully<br>• think more strategically<br>• share ideas with greater confidence<br><br>Gradually moving from picture narrative to pictures and simple sentences.<br><br>Consolidation: Teacher's own planning using real picture books across a range of subjects and specific prime areas to practice literal and inference questioning, predicting and/or clarifying skills. | Part 1 – Predicting and clarifying<br>• To identify the difference between literal 'who, what, where' information and clues<br>• To use prior knowledge, literal information, and clues to make logical predictions about what might happen next<br>• To give reasons for predictions that link to text and own experience<br>Part 2 – Cause and effect<br>• To consciously draw on prior experience and text clues to explain what might happen next in text<br>• To justify predictions using picture and text clues<br>• To understand the reasons for making predictions<br><br>Part 3 – Deductions and predictions<br>• To draw on knowledge of cause and effect to link picture and word clues, make deductions and predict story outcomes<br>• To draw on knowledge of personal emotions to identify character's feelings and actions from picture clues<br>• To link picture and word clues to ask and answer simple inference questions and make predictions about characters problems<br>• To look for clues from book cover, pictures, and titles to predict story contents or information<br><br>Example of plenary – Ask the class which they would rather be – a Literal Patroller or an Inference Detective? Why? What is the difference between them?<br>• What have they found out today about asking detective questions?<br>• Have they noticed how answers to 'why' questions require them to use 'because' to explain how they know the answer from the pictures or text? | 1a Drawing on knowledge of vocabulary to understand texts. (Clarifying)<br><br>1b Identifying and explaining key aspects of texts, such as characters, events, titles, how items of information are related and organised. (Summarising)<br><br>1c Identifying and explaining the sequence of events in fiction and non-fiction texts, beginning, middle and end - characters, actions, places, problem, resolutions. (Retelling)<br><br>1d Making inferences from the text, predicting events - cause and effect, justify ideas and answers to questions about the text, explain writer's use of language and b) to explain the overall effect of the text on the reader. (Predicting/enquiry/ clarifying)<br><br>1e Predict what might happen based on what has been read so far, linking this to own knowledge and experience – cause and effect. (Predicting/enquiry) |

FIGURE 8.1 (Continued)

| pages | End of Unit 3 inference assessment | Reviewing inference self-questioning skills (Parts 1–3)<br>Part 1 – Making predictions and clarifying meanings.<br>Part 2 – Understanding cause and effect<br>Part 3 – Deductions and predictions | ✓ ✓ ✓ ✓ |
|---|---|---|---|
| | | **Unit 4 – Summarising and retelling skills** | |
| | **Photocopiable sections (Units 1–4)** | **Early years goals/ prime learning** | **SPEC comprehension skills objectives** | **Working towards Year 1 comprehension objectives (content domains 1a, 1b, 1c, 1d, 1e)** |

| Pages | Unit 4<br>Part 1 – Retelling (summarising) – sequencing<br>Part 2 – Retelling picture narrative – beginning, problem and solution<br>Retelling: Teaching class, groups, pairs how to identify the beginning, middle, end of narrative.<br><br>Modelling how to:<br>• build and use vocabulary that relates to characters, actions, places, problem, and resolution in the story<br>• increase children's understanding of story structure to help them retell the main points of narrative in sequence<br>• build their knowledge of story stems (Once upon a time.. Once there was… the problem was… etc.) to support coherent retelling<br><br>Checking meaning:<br>Increasing understanding of vocabulary through 'picture book talk' (setting, character, and general vocabulary)<br>(Nurturing literal questioning, clarifying, retelling, inference, and evaluation questioning skills) | Summarising and retelling focus:<br>• Communication and language<br>• Physical development (using multisensory learning tools to support learning self-awareness and literal self-questioning activities)<br>• Personal, social, and emotional (inference – evaluation skills)<br><br>Multisensory learning Using Viewer/hand and body signs (who, what, where?).<br>Question cues and retelling prompts (beginning, middle, end), question cards/actions, retelling role-play.<br><br>Consolidation: Teacher's own planning using real picture books across a range of subjects and specific prime areas to practice literal and inference questioning, predicting, and/or clarifying skills. | Summarising and retelling focusing on:<br>Part 1 – Sequencing<br>• To gather literal key words and ask and answer 'who' 'what' 'where' questions from this information to retell stories<br>• To retell a story in the order the events happen in own words using Three-Finger or Five-Finger sequencing prompts<br><br>Part 2 – Beginning, problem and solution<br>• To identify the theme (central, recurring idea) in a familiar text<br>• To ask and answer literal questions about the characters, their actions, and where they are in a story<br>• To help identify the main ideas in a story<br>• To make inferences and draw on knowledge of 'cause and effect' to identify the characters' problems, and solutions<br>• To summarise the main ideas of a picture narrative in their own words drawing on knowledge of vocabulary and information they have gathered<br>• To retell a story in sequence using finger prompts (In the beginning, Then, Next, After that, In the end) | 1a Drawing on knowledge of vocabulary to understand texts. (Clarifying)<br><br>1b Identifying and explaining key aspects of texts, such as characters, events, titles, *how items of information are related and organised.* (Summarising)<br><br>1c Identifying and explaining the sequence of events in fiction and non-fiction texts, *beginning, middle and end – characters, actions, places, problem, resolutions.* (Retelling)<br><br>1d Making inferences from the text, *predicting events – cause and effect, justify ideas and answers to questions about the text, explain writer's use of language and explain the overall effect of the text on the reader.* (Predicting/enquiry/clarifying)<br><br>1e Predict what might happen based on what has been read so far, *linking this to own knowledge and experience – cause and effect.* (Predicting/enquiry) |

FIGURE 8.1  (Continued)

| Pages | | | |
|---|---|---|---|
| | Assessing end of Unit 4 summarising and retelling skills | Evaluating summarising and retelling, literal and inference self-questioning skills (Parts 1–2) | ✓ ✓ ✓ ✓ |
| | END OF RECEPTION YEAR COMPREHENSION ASSESSMENT | Evaluating summarising, retelling, predicting, clarifying skills, plus literal and inference self-questioning ability | Same as above |

FIGURE 8.1 (Continued)

# CHAPTER 9

# Teaching and assessment plans, guidance, and resources (Units 1–4)

Sections 1–3 in this chapter provide practitioners with pre-planned teaching and assessment lessons and activities for Units 1–4, including a range of resources to support comprehension activities and multisensory learning. The step-by-step multisensory comprehension teaching sequences and activities offer practitioners a scripted example of how to:

- use a metacognitive instructional approach,
- teach the various elements of the SPEC reading comprehension strategies, (Summarising/ retelling, Predicting, Enquiry and Clarifying),
- use the multisensory learning aids,
- use graphic organisers,
- support independent, paired, and small group learning of these skills, and
- assess readers' conscious use of specific comprehension skills following instruction.

## Section 1: Pre-planned photocopiable teaching sequences and activities (Units 1-4)

The practical resources for Teaching Units 1–4 include in-depth plans with an outline of the learning objectives, teaching progression, and activities for each session. These resources include two colour picture booklets featuring adaptations of familiar nursery rhyme themes which have been specifically created for the teaching and assessment activities in the book.

DOI: 10.4324/9781003226307-12

The teaching methods used in these units are based on Palincsar and Brown's (1984) strategic reading approach (see Chapters 4 and 6) and Kintsch's construction-integration comprehension model (1998, 2004; see pages 11 and 12). The reciprocal reading process provides a useful structure for engaging young readers in active meaning-making during reading. Kintsch's theory helps them to think about the mental processes involved in making sense of information they read and hear. Indeed, many cognitive psychologists view Kintsch's model as being 'the most complete and fully developed' explanation of the comprehension process (Duke et al. 2011: 53). In essence, this is because it describes how skilled readers construct meaning and make sense of the main ideas in text by:

1.  integrating the information on the page with their prior knowledge,
2.  creating mental representations of word meanings, such as concrete words (e.g., dog) and abstract words (e.g., freedom), and
3.  developing a 'situation model' at the point of reading which provides an overall mental picture of the objects, characters, actions, events, and places in the text (Helder et al. 2016).

Unit 1 instruction begins by modelling listening and discussion skills to encourage readers to share ideas and 'talk' about picture books more confidently. This progresses to more explicit teaching of comprehension skills in Units 2–4. These sessions model strategies, and self-questioning techniques to support understanding of picture narrative and simple text in preparation for developing the strategies further in Key Stages 1 and 2.

The detailed skills assessment at the end of each unit provides teachers with a useful evaluation tool for appraising individual comprehension skills development. This opportunity to review the children's knowledge of the newly acquired skills offers a focus for further instruction, if necessary, before moving to the next unit.

## SPEC comprehension strategies (Units 1–4)

Although all the SPEC skills support the reading for meaning process, the key strategy that underpins early teaching of comprehension and learning self-awareness is 'clarifying'. When young children learn how to check for meaning and sense as they read, the other strategies can work together in greater harmony (Clay 2002, Oczkus 2003).

**Clarifying skills** (checking meaning – continuous use of this strategy through units)

Focus of lesson – modelling how to:

- build vocabulary through 'picture book talk' (the setting, characters, and general vocabulary),
- clarify meanings using their knowledge of words and contextual understanding,
- check that their story retelling and answers to questions make sense,
- make corrections, when necessary,
- extend knowledge of vocabulary and grammar through 'picture book talk' to support understanding of spoken and written language, and
- skim and scan accurately for same, similar, and opposite images, words, and ideas to support the questioning process.

Multisensory learning: Demonstrating how to use Viewer, question cards, role-play, hand and body signs to help readers to:

- look, listen, think, share ideas about language, grammar, spellings, word meanings in context, and
- move gradually from understanding picture narrative to clarifying meanings in pictures and text.

## Clarifying (throughout teaching units)

For children to gain contextual understanding of language they must be taught explicitly how to interpret pictures and words in context. Throughout the teaching units, the reader is encouraged to monitor their understanding as they read, by focusing on how the meanings of words and images come together to form the 'bigger picture' ('the context'). In other words, readers are shown how to make sense of images and words on the page as if they were jigsaw pieces. With this understanding, they realise that when the pieces fit together and make sense, they present the 'whole picture' of the narrative (like a completed jigsaw puzzle).

This is further demonstrated in Unit 3. When children are shown how to make sense of new ideas or words in context, they learn how to use their prior knowledge and reasoning skills to help them draw meaning from surrounding words or images in the text to increase their understanding of narrative.

Good text detective work relies on these vital skills and the other SPEC strategies to help the reader make links, elicit meanings from context, and combine prior knowledge, prediction, and interpretation skills to create sense out of confusion as they read. When they learn how to combine the following strategies to accurately generate and answer their own in-depth questions about texts, they can self-monitor their understanding more effectively as they read.

Picture comprehension enquiry is further supported with the use of multisensory learning aids and techniques, such as: the Picture Viewer, question cards, role-play, hand and body signs. The combined use of these sensory activities encourages all young readers (developmental ages 3–6 years) to look more closely, listen more carefully, think more strategically, and share ideas with greater confidence. Readers progress gradually from skimming and scanning picture narrative for meaning, to investigating pictures and simple sentences to gain a deeper understanding of the author's message. These activities are essential for building early comprehension skills and help to promote greater recall, metacognition, and understanding of new concepts which in turn boosts personal learning and self-esteem.

**Outline of teaching sequences in Units 1–4** for teaching and assessment plans, using accompanying picture booklets (see Section 3, p. 219 for accompanying learning support resources).

The following unit headings provide an overview of the teaching progression. These plans can be divided into shorter teaching sequences to suit the needs of the teacher. Each unit contains extension activities and comprehension skills practice which help to embed the strategies.

**Unit 1 (Part 1) – Book talk: Communication skills** (listening, responding, engaging)

Focus of lesson – modelling how to:

- listen actively,
- interact with others effectively, and
- participate in meaningful and respectful discussion.

Multisensory learning: Introduction of Riskometer to encourage participation in discussion and boost self-esteem and learning self-awareness.

**Unit 1 (Part 2) – Reading for meaning** (introduction to concept of print and clarifying meaning)

Focus of lesson – modelling how to:

- identify specific features of a book and picture content,
- talk about making meaning as we read (how key words paint a picture in your head), and
- ask questions about reading, such as… Do we understand pictures before we understand words? How and why do we read pictures?

**Unit 2 (Parts 1–3) – Literal enquiry** (Literal Patroller questioning steps: who, what, where – right there! *Nurturing clarifying, enquiry and retelling skills*)

Focus of sessions – modelling how to:

- identify and name explicit information on the page,
- gather and categorise key words (character, action, place),
- build vocabulary by repeating words they hear or see on the page, and
- create full verbal or written questions, answers (statements) using this vocabulary.

Multisensory learning (see Section 3 for resources): Demonstrating how to use sensory aids: Viewer, question cards, role-play, hand and body signs to help readers:

- look more closely, listen more carefully, think more strategically, share ideas with greater confidence, and
- gradually move from picture narrative to exploring pictures and simple sentences for information.

**Unit 3 (Parts 1 and 2) – Predicting/inference skills** (introducing Detective Clooze: Who, what, where, when – why do you think that? *Nurturing literal questioning, clarifying, retelling, inference, and evaluation skills*)

Focus of sessions – modelling how to:

- identify and consciously seek clues,
- make links with literal information and clues,
- use own knowledge and prior experience to ask 'why' questions and make logical predictions about a story ('cause and effect'),
- use own experience of emotions to make predictions about characters' feelings and thoughts,
- use simple past, present, future tenses,
- build general vocabulary to explain what may have happened, is happening and what might happen next, and
- use 'because' to justify ideas.

Multisensory learning: Modelling how to use Viewer, question cards, role-play, hand and body signs to help readers:

- to look and listen more closely for clues,
- think more strategically to make links, share ideas, and make plausible predictions, and
- gradually move from searching for clues in picture narrative to thinking more deeply about connections between pictures and text.

**Unit 3 (Part 3) – More complex enquiry** (Detective Clooze steps: Inference questioning – why, who, what, where, how I know that. *Nurturing literal questioning, clarifying, retelling, inference, and evaluation skills*)

Focus of session – modelling how to:

- consciously seek and link clues on the page with their own knowledge or experience,
- ask and answer simple inference questions about narratives,
- identify and use synonyms to help them generate inference questions, and
- use 'because' to explain ideas and give full answers to inference questions.

Multisensory learning: Modelling how to use Viewer, question cards, role-play, hand and body signs to:

- help children to look and listen more closely for clues,
- think more strategically to reason, make links, evaluate, and make deductions, and
- move gradually from seeking visual clues in narrative to making links between picture and text clues.

**Unit 4 (Parts 1 and 2) – Summarising/retelling** (beginning, middle, end, problem, solution. *Nurturing literal questioning, clarifying, retelling, inference, and evaluation skills*)

Focus of sessions – modelling how to:

- identify the beginning, middle, end of narrative,
- build and use vocabulary that relates to characters, actions, places, problem, and resolution in the story,
- increase children's understanding of story structure to help them retell the main points of narrative in sequence, and
- build on their knowledge of sequencing story stems (In the beginning... Then... Next... After that... In the end... The problem was... etc.) to support coherent retelling.

Multisensory learning: Demonstrating how to use hand and body signs to:

- support recall and re-order information to retell accurately,
- use role-play to re-enact stories and share ideas, and
- help readers gradually move from summarising picture information to retelling picture narrative and simple sentences in sequence.

# Section 2: End-of-unit skills review plans (Units 1-4)

Section 2 provides reception teachers with a full set of explicit, intermediate, and end-of-year assessment plans for immediate use in the classroom. The aim of these reviews is to assess readers' conscious use of specific comprehension skills following instruction. Frequent reviewing of developing skills helps to inform:

- instruction,
- provide end-of-year assessment,
- support transition from reception to Key Stage 1.

These resources demonstrate in detail how effective assessment works using this evaluation approach and include a picture booklet designed specifically for this purpose (p. 248). For further information about the assessment procedure, scoring, and analysis, see Chapter 7, p. 80.

## The three phases of comprehension review

The assessment framework is divided into three progressive phases of comprehension review (see Chapter 7, p. 67 for further details about each review phase):

**Phase 1: The baseline assessment** – to evaluate initial listening, speaking, communication, and early meaning-making skills prior to and after instruction.

**Phase 2: The intermediate assessments** – to 1) check the children's progress following specific stages of instruction (literal questioning, inference skills, clarifying, and retelling), 2) check that new strategies are established before moving to the next teaching unit (1–4), 3) provide a pupil self-assessment option which gives young readers an opportunity to think and talk about their comprehension strengths and weaknesses before they move to the next stage of learning.

**Phase 3: The end-of-year (post-instruction) assessment** – to gain an overall picture of the reader's comprehension skills before they progress to Year 1 (some of the assessment questions offer an optional written response).

## Teacher–pupil assessment aims

The one-to-one assessment process combines cognitive and multisensory activities (see Chapters 3 and 4), such as thinking, questioning, reasoning, viewing, listening, and discussion in line with the learning aims of the new Early Years Foundation Stage framework (early adopter guidelines, DfE 2021). The purpose of this teacher–pupil interaction is to encourage deeper enquiry and understanding of the narrative before the children respond to questions about the text. The combination of an interactive approach and pupil self-assessment also helps to foster children's reading self-regulation (Schunk and Zimmerman 2007, Pascal et al. 2018, Schunk and Pajares 2009).

## Phase 2 – Outline of intermediate assessment aims for each teaching unit (1–4)

The following unit headings provide an overview of the focus for each assessment and the skills being reviewed after instruction.

### Unit 1 (Part 1 – Reviewing book talk skills (*listening, responding, discussing*)

For assessment plans and accompanying picture book resources, go to pages 176–228

Assessing communication and language skills – focusing on:

- pupil's understanding of the importance of active listening and responding, and
- pupil's understanding of the purpose of discussion and how to participate in small group and class discussion effectively.

**Unit 1 (Part 2) – Reviewing reading for meaning skills** (*picture book comprehension*)

Assessing concept of print, literal, prediction, and clarification skills – focusing on:

- identifying key information about a story from the front cover of a picture book,
- understanding how picture comprehension supports the reading process, and
- understanding why authors write and the purpose of reading for meaning.

**Unit 2 (Parts 1–4) – Reviewing literal enquiry skills** (*asking and answering literal questions*)

For assessment plans and accompanying picture book resources, go to pages 188–228.

Assessing pupil's literal understanding and 'who, what, where' self-questioning skills – focusing on (being a 'Literal Patroller') who can:

- identify the characters in stories and gather literal information about what they are doing and where they are in each scene,
- ask and answer own 'who, what, where' questions from the literal information gathered, and
- clarify meaning of explicit information on the page using knowledge of vocabulary, other stories, and picture narrative.

**Unit 3 (Parts 1–3) – Reviewing inference enquiry skills** (*asking and answering inference questions*)

For assessment plans and accompanying picture book resources, go to Pages 196–228.
Assessing pupil's understanding of inference: 'Why, who, what, where, how do you know?' – focusing on (being a detective who can):

- draw on knowledge of who, what, where literal skills to begin deeper enquiry,
- identify clues and make links with literal information to make accurate predictions,
- use prior knowledge of 'cause and effect' to identify problems and possible solutions for characters,
- justify predictions using picture and text clues,
- understand the reasons for making predictions,
- predict outcomes using knowledge of emotions and motives,
- ask and answer in-depth questions to check understanding of text and author's intention, and
- Clarify understanding or words, images, concepts using knowledge of vocabulary, other stories/rhymes, and own experiences of the world.

**Unit 4 (Parts 1–2) – Reviewing summarising and retelling skills** (*who, what, where, problem, solution*) and assessing end-of-year comprehension skills

For assessment plans and accompanying picture book resources, go to Pages 209–228.
Assessing the reader's understanding of the whole story – focusing on (being a Literal Patroller and Detective) who can:

- select key information about a simple story, e.g., nursery rhyme (*who the story is about, what they do in the story and what happens in the end*),
- identify the beginning, middle, and end of a simple story,
- retell events in the correct order using sequencing words,
- identify the theme in a familiar text,

- make inferences and draw on knowledge of 'cause and effect' to identify the characters' problems, and solutions to these,
- generate and answer their own questions about characters, actions, places, problem, and solution to identify main points to support retelling of stories,
- use Five-Finger prompts to retell the beginning, middle, and end of stories in sequence, and
- draw on knowledge of vocabulary and other texts to retell coherently.

# Section 3: Learning support resources

Contains the following frameworks, graphic organisers, posters, picture booklets, and graphic multisensory tools to support Teaching and Assessment Units 1–4.

1. **two print-out colour picture booklets** created specially to engage the children and support the teaching and assessment activities in the book,
2. **graphic organisers** to help children record their ideas, understand how information is connected and organise their thinking in a logical way,
3. **cut-out multisensory graphic templates** to encourage children's independent learning,
4. **posters** to reinforce learning in the classroom, and
5. **assessment frameworks** to support the review process.

## Purpose of the multisensory learning aids and how to use them

1. **Two full colour picture booklets** tell age-related contemporary stories in pictures based on the familiar nursery rhymes ('Humpty Dumpty' and 'Incy Wincy Spider'). The print-out pages of picture narrative can be used separately for teaching and assessment activities or joined together to form a picture book. The two picture booklets are:
   - *The Book Day Parade* by Donna Thomson, illustrated by Jake Biggin, which contains eight specially commissioned picture book pages for the teaching unit activities.
   - *Little Fly and the Spider Trap* by Donna Thomson, illustrated by Chrissy Morgan-Grant, contains five specially commissioned picture book pages for the assessment (baseline, interim and end of Reception year teacher appraisal and pupil self-assessment).

2. **Graphic organisers** – these visual learning tools contain space for children to draw or write down their ideas. The recording process helps to deepen their thinking and understanding, whilst showing them how to organise their ideas in a way that is easy for them to internalise. Graphic organisers also provide an interactive method for practitioners to demonstrate learning steps or create a running record of children's comments and ideas during lessons. For example:
   - **WWW (Who, What, Where) Literal Key Word Organiser** helps children to identify, organise, and record key information to generate their own who, what, where literal questions about pictures and text.
   - **The Three- and Five-Finger Retelling Organiser Maps** are linked to finger actions that support independent retelling. The series of boxes in the template are designed to help children gather and record key information to support their retelling of a story in sequence from beginning to end.

- **The SPEC 'Brilliant Book Talk' Chart** provides practitioners (and parents at home) with a means of recording and celebrating their children's strategic use of reading skills during book talk activities.
- **Characters Feelings in a Story** – the aim of this graphic organiser is to help young readers to make links between the character's feelings, their problems in the story, and how they solve their difficulties in the end. The columns provide space to draw and label the characters' body language and facial expressions the children have identified in the picture narrative, then link their drawings to a range of emoji faces and labelled emotions displayed on the sheet.

3. **Multisensory graphic templates** – the following cut-out graphic paper tools support sensory learning associated with developing comprehension thinking skills and early learning goals. These are:
   - **'The Riskometer'** is a well-tried and effective paper device for boosting reluctant speakers' self-confidence during class discussion. The graphic template provides teachers with the outline of a scale and arrow. When the parts are cut out and pinned together, the moveable arrow can be used on the scale to show an increase in courage and risk-taking during discussion. The aim is to acknowledge individual children's thinking and talking about their learning to encourage positive self-awareness of new skills.
   - **'The Picture Viewer'** is a simple and effective graphic design which encourages young children to frame specific information and examine picture details more closely for clues through a peephole that can be moved around the page.
   - **The 'Q cards' (questioning cards)** remind the children of the hand-sign symbols associated with specific question types. The purpose of the different question cards is to prompt them to ask and answer their own 'who, what, where, why, how do you know?' questions about a story.

4. **Posters** – supporting teaching and learning in the classroom:
   - **Language of Discussion** (and cue cards) – this poster provides a scaffold for purposeful and meaningful 'talk' and respectful listening. The starter phrases can be photocopied and cut up to use as cue cards to provide a guide for speakers during class discussion or working together in groups and pairs. The children learn through experience that there are rules for debate – that during discussion there are no 'right' or 'wrong' points of view. Everyone's opinion is valid – provided it is expressed with respect and consideration for others.
   - **Author poster** (reading for meaning – pictures in your head) – this poster reminds the children that authors write to share the same ideas and information they have in their heads. They do this by choosing words carefully to describe what they are thinking. These key words paint the picture for the reader. The children are reminded that if you do not have a picture in your head that makes sense – you do not understand the author's meaning.
   - **Using Our Senses to Learn poster** – reminds the children of the variety of senses we use to help us learn and how multisensory learning aids such as the Picture Viewer, hand signs, question cards, and Five-Finger Retelling Map help us to make meaning of pictures and words.
   - **The Literal Patroller poster** ('who, what, where – right there!') reminds the children that the Patroller's job is to look closely at the images and sentences on a page and write down

everything they see. On patrol he notes down what is happening 'right there' in front of him —who is involved, what they are doing, and where they are. Once children are familiar with gathering literal key words, they are ready to be shown how to ask and answer 'who, what, where' literal questions from the information they see right there on the page.

- **The Inference Detective poster** (searching for clues and evidence) reminds young readers of Detective Clooze's role and the concept of 'predicting'. They understand that the Detective's job is to find clues on the page to add to the Literal Patroller's 'who, what, where' information. When they join the clues and information together with their own knowledge and experience it helps them to guess what may have happened and to predict what may happen next in a story.

5. **Assessment frameworks** (retelling and reading behaviour) – these frameworks help to support the review process by providing practitioners with a consistent method for recording and analysing 1) specific elements of children's retelling skills, and 2) comprehension skills development following their spontaneous responses to picture narrative. See Chapter 7 p. 76 for a completed example of how to use the retelling analysis record.

# References

Clay, M.M. (2002). *An observation survey of early literacy achievement.* Heinemann.

Department for Education. (2021). *Statutory framework for the Early Years Foundation Stage.* www.gov.uk/government/publications/early-years-foundation-stage-framework--2

Duke, N.K., Pearson, P.D., Strachan, S.L., and Biullman, A.K. (2011). *What research has to say about reading instruction* (4th edn) (S.J. Samuels and A.E. Farstrup, Eds). International Reading Association.

Helder, A., van Leijenhorst, L., and van den Broek, P. (2016). Coherence monitoring by good and poor comprehenders in elementary school: Comparing offline and online measures. *Learning and Individual Differences,* 48, 17–23.

Kintsch, W. (1998). *Comprehension: A paradigm for cognition.* Cambridge University Press.

Kintsch, W. (2004) The construction-integration of text comprehension and its implications for instruction. In R. Rundell and N. Unrau (Eds), *Theoretical models and processes of reading* (5th edn). International Reading Association.

Oczkus, L. (2003). *Reciprocal teaching strategies at work.* International Reading Association.

Palincsar, A., and Brown, A. (1984). Reciprocal teaching of comprehension-fostering and comprehension-monitoring activities. *Cognition and Instruction,* 1, 117–175.

Pascal, C., Bertram, T., and Rouse, L. (2018). *Getting it right in the Early Years Foundation Stage.* The British Association for Early Childhood Education.

Schunk, D.H., and Pajares, F. (2009). Self-efficacy theory. In K.R. Wenzel and A. Wigfield (Eds), *Handbook of motivation at school.* Routledge/Taylor & Francis Group.

Schunk, D.H., and Zimmerman, B.J. (2007). Influencing children's self-efficacy and self-regulation of reading and writing through modelling. *Reading & Writing Quarterly,* 23, 7–25.

# Section 1: Pre-planned photocopiable teaching sequences and activities (Units 1–4)

# Unit 1 (Part 1): Overview of Sessions 1–5

## Book talk: Learning how to listen, respond, and discuss

**Learning objectives** – to be able to:

- recognise the difference between poor and effective listening,
- understand and begin to use the language of effective discussion, and
- reason with others, accept their views, and make links to others' ideas.

**What you need (see resources p. 219–253):**

Flipchart/pens, 'Show and Tell' – *The Book Day Parade* (photocopiable picture book, Language of Discussion Poster and cue cards, Riskometer

**Picture Books:**

*Quiet Please*, Owen McPhee! By Trudy Ludwig and Patrice Barton (Session 2, p. 110)
*The Rainy Day* by Anna Milbourne and Sarah Gill. (Session 3, p. 112)
*Where the Wild Things Are* by Maurice Sendak or *Not Now Bernard* by David McKee (Session 4, p. 113)
*Max and the Won't Go to Bed Show* by Mark Sperring or *I Am Not Sleepy and I Will Not Go to Bed* by Lauren Child (Session 5, p. 114)

**Summary of Sessions 1–5** (teacher/class, groups, and pairs):

**Session 1** – Listening and responding (whole class discussion)
**Session 2** – Active listening – thinking about listening skills (whole class discussion)
**Session 3** – Modelling the 'Language of Discussion' (whole class and group discussion)
**Session 4** – Discussion using Riskometer (whole class and group discussion)
**Session 5** – Practising the Language of Discussion (child-led small group/pairs discussion)

# Teacher notes

## Book talk: Learning how to listen, respond and discuss

*(Sessions can be divided into small teaching sequences as required.)*

Unit 1, Part 1 focuses on the important role that discussion plays in the reading for meaning process. It is vital that children understand how listening respectfully to others using a framework that encourages mindful 'talk' about texts helps them to enjoy a deeper understanding of books and each other.

The children are shown how there is no right or wrong view in discussion. Everyone is entitled to their opinion. However, they must be polite and always consider others' feelings. Discussion ('book talk') involves listening and sharing thinking in a caring way with others by agreeing with, disagreeing with, or adding to their point guided by the language and rules of debate. For example, 'good' listeners follow the rules of discussion by:

- looking at the person who is speaking,
- thinking about what they are saying,
- listening rather than waiting to talk, and
- asking the person speaking to explain if you do not understand what they are saying.

---

### Session 1: Listening and responding

**Learning objectives** – to be able to:
a. explain the meaning and purpose of discussion.
b. draw on their own experience to reflect on the importance of other's feelings during discussion.

Explain to the children that over the next sessions they will discover more about each other's thinking, ideas, and experiences of life through discussion, careful listening, and good teamwork. They will be shown how to:
- use the 'Language of Discussion' to help them talk about ideas and solve problems together,
- work effectively together as a team and in pairs, and
- complete a variety of fun and challenging tasks that will help them to think about and explore stories and information more deeply for meaning.

### Activity 1 - The meaning of 'discussion'

Begin by asking the class to explain the meaning of 'discussion'? (*Record the children's responses on a flipchart/whiteboard for you to refer to later.*)
- How is discussion different from talking? (e.g., *talking is about telling others something. Discussion is about listening and sharing ideas*).
- What is the purpose of discussion? (e.g., *discussion helps you come to a decision, plan, and solve a problem with others*).
- How does discussing a problem help us find an answer? (e.g., *it helps us to see things from a different point of view. To question something further. To understand something or someone else better or learn something new*).

Ask them to discuss the following questions with their partners then feed back their ideas: Why it is important to think of others' feelings during discussion? What do they think might happen if they are unkind or rude to others when sharing their thoughts with them?

**Plenary:** Ask the children to tell you what they have learned about discussion and why they think it is important. (*You might find it helpful to refer to the children's comments recorded on the flipchart during the session.*)

## Session 2: Active listening

**Learning objectives** – to be able to:
a. explain the importance of being a 'good listener'.
b. recognise the difference between 'good' and 'poor' listening skills.

Revisit the main points of the last session.
- Ask the children if they can tell you what the word 'discussion' means and why it is important (e.g., *sharing our thinking with others helps us to see things from a different point of view. To question something further. To understand something or someone else better or learn something new*).
- Explain that in this session the children will learn why careful 'listening' is important when discussing ideas with others.

## Activity 2 – Being a 'good' listener
- Begin by reading a story about 'poor listening' (e.g., Quiet Please, Owen McPhee! *about a boy who loves talking rather than listening*).
- Ask the children to tell you what the story was about and what they liked or did not like about the main character's behaviour and why.

Then ask (*It might be helpful to record the children's responses on a flipchart to refer to later*):
- Why do you think it is important to be a 'good' listener during discussion?
- Are you a 'good' listener? Why do you say that? What are you doing when you are listening well? Why is it helpful to listen carefully to others?

Next ask: Why are you a 'good' listener if you...
- look at the person who is speaking?
- think about what they are saying?
- listen rather than waiting to talk?
- ask the person speaking to explain what they mean if you do not understand what they are saying?

## Activity 3 – 'Poor' listening – 'Show and Tell'

Read page 1 of The Book Day Parade. (*Throughout the session ensure that the children who are actively engaged in 'good listening', especially those that find it tricky, are given plenty of praise and positive feedback.*)

- Invite the class to look at the picture 'Show and Tell'. Ask them to discuss in pairs or as a class what they think is happening in the scene. How do they think the picture shows poor listening? (*It's Rabbit's turn to 'show and tell'. He is talking about 'sticky tape' and how to use it. However, no-one is listening. Mouse is reading, Bear and Pig are whispering, and Wolf, Turtle, and Crocodile are playing together.*)
- What do they think will happen because no-one is listening to Rabbit?
- Give them a further example of poor listening. Have a conversation with another adult in the room using 'bad listening' skills such as: interrupting each other, random change of the subject in response to a question, fidgeting, poor eye contact, and talking to someone else and so on.

Ask the children if they thought this was a 'good' discussion and why? (*Record the children's responses on a flipchart to refer to later.*)
- Were we listening to each other?
- What were we doing when not listening?
- How do you think the person was feeling when the other was not listening to them?
- What do think makes a discussion enjoyable? What rules should the class have for discussion?

**Plenary:** Discuss the rules of effective discussion: (e.g., *good listening, consideration, and respect for others*)
- Did any of these things happen in this session?
- How did it affect the discussion?
- Ask the children what they have learned from this session today and to explain why.

### Session 3: Modelling the 'Language of Discussion'

**Learning objectives** – to be able to:
a. draw on their own experience to talk about the rules for discussion.
b. use the language of effective discussion to support thinking and learning.

Begin by asking the class if they can remember what the rules of discussion are (e.g., *good listening, consideration, and respect for others*).
- Ask the children why it is important to pay attention to others' ideas, reasons, and points of view during discussion.
- Talk again about how it feels to be ignored or 'talked over' by others.

**Introduce: The 'Language of Discussion' poster on the flipchart.**

Talk about how this approach helps you to...
- think about what you want to say before you speak,
- respond to the last speaker politely, and
- show you have heard what they have said by saying why you agree, disagree, or want to add to it.

Explain that they are going to practise using this language from now on – whenever they are in discussion as a class, in groups, or in pairs till it becomes normal practice.

**Activity 4 – Practising the 'Language of Discussion' as a class** (*What would happen if it never rained?*)
- Read *The Rainy Day* by Anna Milbourne and Sarah Gill or a similar book about rainfall.
- Follow this with a discussion about rain – what do they like and dislike about rainy days? Why is rainfall important?
- Then ask a question about the topic that might encourage a lively discussion.
  For example: *'What would happen if it never rained?'* (To encourage less teacher-led and more child-led discussion it is important to play the role of facilitator and step back as much as possible whilst modelling 'good listening' and the discussion process.)
- Remind the class of the rules for 'good listening' (*to listen and not interupt the speaker, give each other plenty of time to speak, put hands up to speak when the speaker has finished, take other's feelings into account during discussion*).
- Tell them that the 'Language of Discussion' poster is there to guide them as they share ideas. (Support this by gently re-wording the way they present their views. You can re-enforce this further by showing them when and how to use the actions displayed on the poster to help them indicate whether they agree with the speaker, want to make a link, or add a further point.)
- Record their views on the flipchart (reasons for their opinions and links they have made with each other's views). When you feel that they have all had a chance to speak, read out the views you have recorded to give the children time to reconsider their opinions.

**Plenary:** Discuss whether the language used by the speakers has changed the way everyone listened to each other…
- Did they find that it made them feel safer to express themselves? Why?
- Did the discussion become more interesting? How?
- Did they make links with each other's thoughts and ideas? Examples?
- Did they feel they had learned something new from the discussion? Examples?
- How did that feel before, during, and after the discussion?

**Session 4: Using the Riskometer to encourage participation**

**Learning objectives** – to begin to:
a. draw on knowledge of the language and rules for discussion to share views confidently with others.
b. use the language of effective discussion to value and acknowledge other's views.

Ask the children what they thought was good or disappointing about the discussion in the last session and why. For example:
- Did everyone listen to what the speaker was saying?
- Did they wait for them to finish before putting their hands up to speak?
- Did they remember to acknowledge others or add to the points that were being made?

Discuss the fears that some children have about participating in debate.
- Do they fear that the other children will laugh at their views and ideas?
- Do they worry that what they want to say might be 'wrong' in some way?

Revisit the 'Language of Discussion' poster (it might be helpful to make cue cards of the symbols on the poster to support group and paired discussion). Agree as a class that the more they use this language in class:
- the safer they will feel about sharing their ideas in front of each other,
- the more they will value other's views, and
- the more confident they will be about expressing an opinion.

**Introduce the 'Riskometer'.** Show the children how it works and tell them that you will use it during discussion sometimes to encourage everyone to join in. (*It might be helpful for another adult to operate the 'Riskometer' during the discussion to allow the teacher to record the children's ideas on the flipchart*). Explain that...
- Every time someone has the courage to say what they feel or think in discussion (particularly those who may not often speak up in class) the dial on the Riskometer will go up a level.
- At the end of the session the Riskometer will show the level of 'risk-taking' that has helped the discussion to grow and reach a conclusion.
- The children will soon discover that far from joining in being 'risky', the greatest 'risk' to them will be missing a chance to say what they think and to add to the discussion.
- They will see that instead of being judged for their opinions and ideas, they will gain respect for coming up with a different point of view.
- They will see that there is no 'right' or 'wrong' in discussion – everyone is entitled to their opinion – provided they are aware of other children's feelings in the room.

**Activity 5 - 'Teacher-led discussion'**

Read *Where the Wild Things Are* by Maurice Sendak or *Not Now Bernard* by David McKee, or similar book with theme about children and parents/adults.
- Ask the children for their thoughts about the story and the characters' behaviour.
- Ask them an intriguing question to stimulate discussion: *'Is it better to be a child or an adult?'* (Explain that it will only be a short discussion of 10-15 minutes - use a timer).
- Record the children's views and links to each other's ideas.
- Display the 'Language of Discussion' poster (or cards) somewhere that can be seen by all.
- Help them to re-phrase if they forget to use this language in the heat of the moment.

**Plenary:** Ask the class if they felt it was a good discussion and why. (*Did the 'Language of Discussion' help the flow when sharing ideas?*)

**Session 5: Practising the Language of Discussion**

**Learning objectives** - to be able to:
a. reason with others, accept their views, and make links to others' ideas in pairs and small groups.

b.  use the language of effective discussion to debate a question meaningfully together.
   •  Ask the children how different they think discussion is in pairs or small groups compared to class discussion? (*What could they do to make sharing ideas in a small group 'a good discussion'?*)
   •  Discuss the importance of thoughtful listening and responding. Ask them to think about what happens normally during a group task. (*Remind them of the rules of discussion and how important it is that other's ideas and points of view are respected whether they agree or disagree with what has been said.*)

**Activity 6 – 'Child-led discussion'**

Read *Max and the Won't Go to Bed Show* by Mark Sperring and Sarah Warburton or *I Am Not Sleepy and I Will Not Go to Bed* by Lauren Child to the class.
   •  Talk about the theme of the book with the children. Then to stimulate their discussion ask: '*Should children be made to go to bed when they're not tired?*'
   •  Organise the class into pairs or threes and ask them to discuss the above question. Explain that this will give them a chance to practise 'good discussion' on their own for 5-10 minutes.
   •  Remind them to think carefully about what they want to say before they speak and to listen closely to each other using the 'language of debate' prompt cards to guide them.

**Plenary:** Ask the groups or pairs to feed back their thoughts from the discussion (stating 'Yes' or 'No' to the question and explaining why) before talking about 'co-operative listening and responding' in the groups. Invite them to share what they have learned from this session today and why.

# Unit 1 (Part 2): Reading for meaning – overview of Sessions 6–8

**Lesson objectives** – to be able to:

- understand that reading requires you to decode words – but also to make meaning and sense of pictures and text,
- understand how pictures without words have meaning, and
- draw on knowledge of vocabulary to demonstrate understanding of picture narrative.

**What you will need (see resources p. 219–253):**

**Stationery**: Flipchart, pen, blue tack, envelopes for jigsaw pieces
**Posters**: Authors – why they write, Learning through senses, Language of discussion
**Pictures**: 'Show and tell' p. 1 of *The Book Day Parade* (cut-out 3 jigsaw pieces of picture) (Session 7)
'Playing in the Water' scene (Session 8)

**Summary of Sessions 6–8** (teacher/class, groups, and pairs):

**Session 6** – Discussing why authors write (teacher/whole class, pairs, or group)
**Session 7** – Making sense of pictures and words (teacher/whole class pairs or group)
**Session 8** – Reading pictures and words for meaning (teacher/pairs, group, whole class)

# Teacher notes

*(Teaching sequences can be divided into smaller sessions as required.)*

The second part of Unit 1 begins by asking the children to think about *why* we read. They are encouraged to realise for themselves that reading is an essential skill in the world today. For example, we read to help us learn, for pleasure, and to be able to carry out everyday tasks.

The following teaching sequences also demonstrate how authors write to share their ideas with their readers. The sessions explain how writers choose words carefully to describe what they are thinking. These key words paint the picture for the reader. The children discover that if they do not have a picture of the story in their minds which makes sense, it indicates that they do not understand the author's meaning.

The emerging reader also learns that pictures can present more information about the characters and events in a story than the text to begin with. They discover that just as key words on the page create pictures in your head, the process of labelling and explaining images creates new words and vocabulary. Pictures have layers of meaning – like text. They provide a good foundation for developing early comprehension skills. They begin the comprehension process for young readers by inviting them 1) to gather the information they see on the page, 2) dig deeper for clues, 3) draw on their experience of the world, and 4) draw on their knowledge of characters, events, and ideas from other picture narratives to help them understand the author's meaning.

## Session 6: Discussing why authors write

*(It might be helpful throughout the sessions to record the children's discussion on the flipchart to revisit in the plenary.)*

**Lesson objectives** - to be able to:
a. understand how author's words create pictures for the reader,
b. recognise what 'good' readers do when they read for meaning and sense.
- Ask: Why do authors write? (*Allow time for the children to think and discuss this as a class*).
- Guide their ideas by referring to the Language of Discussion and by showing them how their thoughts link together. (*Make notes of their comments, you might like to refer to them in the plenary*).
- Agree with the children that authors write with a purpose in mind.
- They write to entertain and share ideas, feelings, and information with us.
- Their aim is to connect with the reader.
- An author has a picture in their head (their message). They want the reader to have the same picture in their heads as they read. To make sure of this, they carefully choose words that will paint the picture for the reader.

**Reading for sense** – Ask the children if pictures come into their heads when they read or listen to a story.

**Activity 1 'Pictures in your head'** (Picture 1 and Author poster)
- Read the sentence aloud: 'The huge dinosaur towered over the trees'.
- Ask: Did a picture pop into your heads when you heard that sentence? (*Give the class time to respond to this - they might like to draw the picture they have imagined*).
- Then show them the Author poster and the text. Was the image in their minds like the one on the poster? (*If the answer is 'Yes' - tell them they have understood the author's words*).
- Explain that if you do not have a picture in your head as you read or listen to a story, it is because you may not understand what the author is saying.
- Tell them that 'good' readers go back and re-read so they can make changes to the picture in their heads to make sense of the text.

**Ask: What do good readers do when they read?**

Prompt discussion by showing the children the front cover of a book. Give them time to talk about reading and how they approach books, before summing up the following points.
- We look at the pictures (to get an idea of *what the story is about*).
- We try to decode (work out *what the words say*).
- We try to comprehend (work out *what the words mean*).

## Session 7: Making sense of pictures and words

**Lesson objectives** – to be able to:
a. demonstrate understanding of pictures without words using knowledge of the surrounding world, and observation skills,
b. understand how pictures and text link together to present the full meaning.

Explain that good readers do more than 'say' the words on the page, they read to understand and enjoy the author's words.
- They do this by clarifying (checking they understand) the meanings in pictures and text.
- They use what they already know about language and the world around them to help them make meaning of information they hear or read.

**Activity 2 'Seeing the whole picture' - 'Show and tell'**

*First create three large 'jigsaw pieces' using images from the first picture of* The Book Day Parade *(e.g., Image 1: Rabbit, Image 2: Characters in the class, Image 3: Rabbit's paw holding the sticky tape).*

*Stick each 'jigsaw piece' randomly on the flipchart.*

Explain that when we read pictures, they help us to create words in our heads. The words authors select are like parts of a jigsaw puzzle.

- Give the children an example of this process. Say the sentence: 'Rabbit shows the class his sticky tape'. Ask them to tell you if they can see a 'picture in their heads' when they hear or say these words.
- Then piece together the jigsaw cut-outs of the 'Show and Tell' scene on the flipchart to show the whole picture. Ask them if the 'picture in their heads' looks something like this scene.
- Explain that each jigsaw shape on the flipchart links to the other pieces in the jigsaw (the 'context') to form a complete picture of the words and meaning in the sentence.
- Hand out an envelope to pairs that contains 'jigsaw shapes' of the same or another picture for them to piece together. (*If you choose another picture, give them a simple sentence that helps them visualise the picture in their minds before they piece it together.*)
- Ask them if they can show or explain how they put the pieces together.
- Agree as a class that good readers put words and images together as they read to create full meaning and understanding.
- When the pieces fit together, they can 'see the whole picture'.
- However, if they don't know how to put the jigsaw pieces (words and images) together – the picture will be jumbled in their heads, and they will not understand the author's meaning.
- So, to fully understand what they are reading, they need to clarify (make sense of) meanings as they go along to create a whole picture that makes sense.

Tell them that over the next sessions they will learn more about how we make meaning when we listen to or read a story.


## Session 8: Reading pictures and words for meaning

**Lesson objectives** – to be able to:
a. discuss details in pictures,
b. draw on knowledge of vocabulary to demonstrate understanding of picture narrative,
c. draw on characters from familiar stories to demonstrate their understanding,
d. recognise how we use our senses to help us make meaning of pictures and text.

**Activity 3 - Discussion about picture books**

Ask them if they now have 'pictures in their heads' when they listen to stories. Does this help them to understand and enjoy the story more? Ask them to explain why.

Ask:
- Why do books have pictures?
- Do you read the pictures before the words on a page?
- Discuss why readers often look at the pictures first to 'see' what the author is saying before reading the words.

**Activity 4 (Picture/Text 2) – 'Playing in the Water'**

Pair/class discussion:
- Read out the sentence: 'Sam, Jo, Benji, and Digger are playing in the water'.
- Ask them if the text gives them a clear picture of 'Sam, Jo, Benji, and Digger' and where they are? Perhaps these characters are people? Or maybe they are animals? It says they are playing in 'water'.
- Maybe they are in a paddling pool in their back garden or perhaps they are playing in the sea?
- Hold up the picture and explain how sometimes illustrations tell us more about the story than the words do on their own.
- Hand out Picture 2 to pairs and give them a couple of minutes to look at the picture and talk about what they think is happening.
- Then discuss the picture as a class – asking pairs to talk about the story in the picture.
- Then ask the children to think about the information they see in pictures, e.g., What helps us to make meaning of images? Perhaps the characters remind us of other story characters? Maybe the setting looks familiar to us?
- What do good readers do when they read pictures? How do we read pictures that have no words?
- Explain that reading pictures for meaning is like reading words for meaning.
- We use our eyes, ears, mouths, heart, mind, and memory to help us understand the author's message. For example, we use our... (*point to each in turn – and mime looking, listening, speaking, feeling, thinking*). Then invite the children to join in as you repeat the words and actions...
  - *eyes* to look closely for information and to focus on the details on the page,
  - *ears* to listen to what others are saying about the story to support our own understanding,
  - *mouths* to talk about what we think is happening in the story – sharing our ideas with others,
  - *hearts* to connect with the character's feelings in the story (to empathise and anticipate what they might do next in the story),
  - *mind* to imagine and wonder more deeply about what is happening in the story from the information we have gathered, and
  - *memory* to link what we remember about storytelling, and our own experiences of the world to identify themes and information on the page.

Tell them that when we read for meaning... we use what we know about the world. We put this with what we see on the page – and check that the pictures we have in our heads make sense.

**Plenary:** Ask the children if they now think that pictures have meaning without words? What have they found out about reading today? Has anything surprised them? Why do they say that?

# Unit 2 (Part 1): Literal enquiry – overview of Sessions 9–12

## Being a Literal Patroller: How to ask and answer 'who' questions

**Lesson objectives** – to be able to:

- identify the characters in stories and gather literal information about them,
- ask and answer own 'Who' questions from the literal information they have gathered,
- ask literal questions about words, images, concepts on the page to clarify information about story characters.

**What you need (see resources pages 219–253):**

**Items:** Flipchart, pen, blue tack, demo 'Question' mark and 'Who' label, red pens (for class), Literal Patroller puppet

**Pictures:** 'Playing in the water', (Unit 1, Session 8 recap), 'In the Park' p. 2 of *The Book Day Parade*, (copies for class and flipchart recap, Session 7 Unit 1)

**Posters:** Discussion, Author, Literal Patroller, Using Our Senses poster (hand and body signs)

**Multisensory aids:** Picture Viewer, hand sign for 'who' questions (circling face), Riskometer, discussion cue cards, 'Brilliant Book Talk' chart

**Summary of Sessions 9–12** (teacher/class, groups, and pairs):

**Session 9** – Identifying literal 'Who' information in pairs (photocopiable picture: 'In the Park')
**Session 10** – Learning how to ask and answer literal questions
**Sessions 11 and 12** – Practising asking and answering 'who' literal questions
*Extension and consolidation included at the end of these lesson plan sessions*

# Teacher notes

(3 x 30-minute teaching sequences can be divided into smaller sessions as required)

*Encourage the children to use their picture reading strategies in other learning areas to build their comprehension skills and thoughts about the process of making meaning.*

## Being a Literal Patroller *('who, what, where – right there!')*

Literal questions are the simplest and most direct of the three question types to answer because the meaning is obvious and does not require interpretation. Literal information can be seen directly on the page and refers to the characters ('who'), actions ('what'), and locations of the characters ('where') in the story. The sessions in Unit 2 teach children how to systematically identify and understand these different types of literal meaning ('who, what, where') as they read. Literal questions ask the reader to link the key words in the questions with the same words and meanings in the text and pictures to answer questions about the characters. Once children understand this, they can formulate and answer their own literal questions with ease.

The sessions in Part 1 focus on asking and answering literal 'Who' questions. First readers are shown how to identify characters in picture narrative and a line or two of familiar text. Then how to locate and organise key information about their identities (names, gender, what they look like) to help them generate and answer their own literal questions about them.

## Recap Unit 1 (Reading for Meaning)

Ask the children the following questions to prepare them for the next sessions:

- What do good readers do when they read? *They look at the pictures (to get an idea of what the story is about); decode (to work out what the words say); comprehend (to work out what the words mean).*
- How do authors pass on their message? *They choose words that create a picture in the reader's head.*
- What happens if you do not understand the author's meaning? *You do not have a picture in your head – or the picture in your head does not make sense.*
- What senses do we use to help us to read pictures and words for meaning? *We use our eyes, ears, mouths, heart, mind, and memory to help us understand the author's message.*

Pictures have meaning, the same as words do. Explain that just like words and sentences, we give meaning to the pictures we see. To make meaning of pictures, we use what we know about the world and our knowledge of language to identify, name, and think about what we see on the page. We then check that the ideas we have in our head make sense.

## Recap Unit 1 – Playing in the Water: Reading pictures for meaning

Hold up the picture 'Playing in the water' and remind the children that last session they looked at a picture of a boy (Sam) and his two dogs (Benji and Digger) who were playing in the sea. They were shown how pictures can sometimes tell you more than words do. They learned that key words are the main information that tell you about the characters, their actions, and places ('who, what, where'). Without it we do not have an accurate picture of the author's message in our heads. Explain that the author gives the reader this literal information first to set the scene of a story.

**Session 9: Identifying literal information – 'who' (characters)**

**Learning objectives** - to be able to:
a. understand that the information you can see directly on the page is known as 'literal' information,
b. recognise how literal information is used to set the scene of a story,
c. recognise the meaning of literal sign language and colour codes,
d. identify literal information about the characters and demonstrate this understanding by using a Picture Viewer and circling the information correctly in red.

**Introducing the Literal Patroller** - Explain that over the next few weeks the children will learn how to be Literal Patrollers. They will be shown how to identify key words to help them ask and answer questions about the characters, what they are doing, and where they are in a story. Remind them that they will need to practise looking for and gathering 'who, what, where' information as often as possible to become super Literal Patrollers.

**Being a Literal Patroller** (Patroller poster, puppet). Present the Literal Patroller and talk about their role. Explain that they are always first at the scene of a story. It is their job to note down everything they see happening 'right there' on the page. They ask themselves – *'Who is in the story?' 'What are they doing?' 'What is happening? 'Where is it happening?'*

Now hold up the Literal Patroller poster and read out the words. Ask the children to look closely at the picture book pages in the poster and answer the following Patroller questions about the story:

> Q: *Who is in the story?*
> A: *Goldilocks*
> Q: *What is she doing?*
> A: *Eating from a bowl.*
> Q: *Where is this happening?*
> A: *In her/someone's house/kitchen, at the table.*

When Patrollers answer these questions, they are receiving the author's literal message. This is information the author wants us to have immediately by putting it *right there* in the picture or text for us to see. These facts tell us about the *characters*, their *actions*, and *places* in the story. Explain that the children will be able to practise this further in the next activity (see Activity 1 example).

## Multisensory activities to support enquiry

**Riskometer** – This is useful device for encouraging reluctant speakers to join in and share ideas with their groups or class. The adult moves the dial to indicate the level of 'risk-taking' involved for the participating speaker and to prompt the other children to acknowledge this with supportive clapping.

**'Brilliant Book Talk' - Smiley Chart -** It might be helpful to introduce team points at this stage to encourage participation in class discussion and group activities.

**Literal hand and body signs** (*who, what, where - right there!*):

- Tell them that you will use a special sign when you ask each of the literal questions: *Who, what, where?*
- Hold up the Using Our Senses poster and discuss the three different hand and body signs they can see on the poster.
- Explain the hand and body signs will help them to identify the different types of literal question you will ask them over the next sessions.
- With practice, they will soon learn how to use these signs themselves when they ask and answer their own literal questions.

**Model each sign for them and encourage the children to repeat your actions:**

- Who? – circle your face (indicating a 'who' question about story characters).
- What? – jog on the spot (indication a 'what' question about the character's actions).
- Where? – hold your hand above your eyes in a searching pose (indicating a 'where' question about places and the character's whereabouts).

Encourage them to repeat the phrase 'who, what, where - right there!' when they are searching for literal information. This will remind them that the answers to literal questions are directly on the page. In other words, the information they see 'right there' is obvious (they do not need to search for clues to find literal answers).

**The Picture Viewer** - gathering information to ask literal questions:

- Tell them that Literal Patrollers ask 'who, what, where' questions about information they see 'right there' on the page.
- However, before they can ask questions about these basic facts, they need to look carefully to see who the characters are, what they are doing, and where they are in a story. They use a Picture Viewer to help them do this.
- Hold up the Picture Viewer and show the children the hole they will look through to search for the information.
- Tell them that to be Super Literal Patrollers they will need their own Picture Viewers to help them to look for key facts about the characters in the story. (*Maybe the puppet could look through the hole at the children and ask them to help him look for information during the next activity.*)

**Activity 1 'Who is in the Park?'** (gathering 'who' information).

*Hand out a copy of the picture on your flipchart and a Picture Viewer to each child.*

- Ask them look carefully at this picture using the Viewer to help them. Ask: '*Who can you see... right there on the page?*'
- Demonstrate how to use the Picture Viewer. Place it on the photocopied picture and move it around to look more closely at the characters. Show them how the hole can be used to frame the details of the characters' faces so the information can be gathered more easily.
- Then ask pairs of children to circle the story characters they have found with a red pencil (e.g., *Turtle, Bear, Pig, Wolf, Crocodile, Mouse, and Rabbit*).
- Invite them to share this information with the class. Demonstrate they have identified the information correctly by circling each character in red on your flipchart copy.

**Session 10: How to ask and answer 'who' questions**

**Learning objectives** - to be able to:

a. explain the difference between a question and an answer,
b. understand that literal 'who' information refers to facts you see directly on the page about the characters,
c. use literal hand sign language for 'who' questions (circling their faces),
d. identify a literal 'who' question and understand that it is about a person,
e. use part of the 'who' question to answer in a full sentence.

**Activity 2** (using same Activity 1 picture: 'In the Park')
- Ask them what they think the difference is between a statement (making a comment) and asking a question. Allow them time to think this through and offer ideas.
- Clarify that you make a statement when you *know something*, e.g., 'Piglet is hiding in the bushes'. You ask a question when you are unsure or *do not know* something. For example you may not know the identity (name) of the person or character involved. For example, *'Who is hiding in the bushes?'*
- 'Who' questions are about people and characters. Explain that you ask a 'who' question to identify characters and find out more about them in a story. When you ask a 'who' question - you put the word 'who' at the beginning and add a question mark at the end.
- Model asking 'who' questions using a sign (circling your face) to indicate you are asking about the character's identity. For example, **Who** *is in the bushes?*
- Show them how to use part of the question to answer in a full sentence. Point to Piglet in the picture and encourage them to join in the answer: **'Piglet** *is in the bushes' (using the same sign).*
- Explain that when answering a 'who' question, they will notice that the person's name replaces the 'who' word, and a full stop replaces the question mark at the end of the question. For example (circling your face): Point to the picture. Q. **Who** *is on the bike?* Circle the information in red pen. A. **Rabbit** *is on the bike.*

**Session 11: Practising asking and answering 'who' questions**

**Learning objectives** - to be able to:
a. identify literal 'who' information (about other children in the classroom),
b. ask their own 'who' questions and give answers in full sentences.

**Activity 3 - Asking and answering 'who' questions about each other** (names and what they are wearing)
- Model further examples of 'who' questions and answers by asking the class what they are wearing: **'Who** *is wearing a red top?'* **'Joe** *is wearing a red top'*, and so on.
- Invite pairs to take it in turns to ask and answer their own 'who' questions about the type of clothing they or other children are wearing.

## Session 12: Practising asking and answering 'who' questions

**Learning objectives** – to be able to:

a. identify the characters in a story and gather literal information about their appearance,

b. ask and answer their own 'who' questions in full sentences from the literal information gathered.

**Activity 4 - Further Literal Patroller practice** (using Activity 1 picture 'In the Park')

- Remind them that as they are Literal Patrollers, it is their job to look for key facts about the characters in a story.
- Tell them to look at the information they have already circled in red.
- Then ask them to use their Picture Viewer to look even closer at the details on the characters' faces and bodies. For example, *Bear has golden curly hair, Wolf is fluffy and brown, Mouse is small and has big ears, Piglet is pink with a big snout, Turtle is large and round, and Crocodile is tall and scaly. What are they are wearing? Wolf is wearing a red cloak, Turtle is wearing a Humpty Dumpty costume, Crocodile is wearing a pirate's hat, eye patch, and a hook on his hand, Mouse is wearing a clock costume, Piglet is wearing an Incy Wincy Spider costume, Bear is wearing a dress, Rabbit is wearing a blue jacket.*
- Share this information as a class.
- Then invite pairs or the whole class to practise answering *your* literal questions.
- Next ask them to think of their own literal questions and to ask and answer each other's questions about who is in the picture and what they look like (circling their faces as they do this), e.g., Q. **'Who** *is in the bushes?'* A. **'Piglet** *is in the bushes'*. Q. **Who** *is pink with a big snout? A.* **Piglet** *is pink with a big snout. Q.* **Who** *is small with big ears? A.* **Mouse** *is small with big ears.* And so on. Use of the Riskometer at this stage (for class points) encourages participation!

**Extension:** You may wish to further demonstrate how 'who' questions are formed by modelling how to write them on the board and using sticky notes for the 'who' word and the 'question mark'. The two sticky notes can then be removed by children in turn – to reveal how the answer to each question has the name at the beginning and a full stop at the end of the sentence.

Children practice writing answers to 'who' questions and generating their own 'who' questions about characters they have identified and circled in a different picture or text.

**Consolidation:** Snap or Happy Family card games – matching information/identifying different characters (encouraging players to look more closely for information). Generating and answering their own 'who' questions about what the characters are wearing and their general appearance in the cards.

**Plenary:** Finally encourage them to share their thoughts about being a Literal Patroller. What have they found out about asking and answering their own questions about pictures?

# Unit 2 (Part 2): Literal enquiry – 'what' questions – overview of Sessions 13–16

**Lesson objectives** – to be able to:

- identify literal key words about characters and their actions in picture narrative,
- ask and answer their own 'who' and 'what' questions from the literal information gathered.

**What you need (see resources pages 219–253)**

**Items:** Flipchart, pen, blue tack, blue pencils for class, Literal Patroller puppet
**Pictures:** 'Goldilocks images' (on Literal Patroller poster), Revisiting photocopiable pages 1 and 2
 (from *The Book Day Parade*) picture booklet
**Posters:** Language of Discussion, Author, Literal Patroller, Use of Senses
**Multisensory learning aids:** Picture Viewer, hand signs (circling face – 'who'; jogging – 'what'),
 Riskometer, discussion cue cards, 'Brilliant Book Talk' chart

**Summary of Sessions 13–16** (activities modelled by teacher, children, and puppet):

**Session 13** – Identifying literal information to ask what characters are doing
**Session 14** – Learning how to ask literal 'what' questions about characters' actions
**Session 15** – Practising asking and answering 'what' questions about each other's actions
**Session 16** – Asking and answering 'who' and 'what' questions about story characters
**Extension** – Practising writing own 'what' literal questions and answers
**Consolidation** – Happy Family card game, role-play, and own questions

## How to ask and answer 'what' questions

(3 x 30-minute teaching sequences which can be divided into smaller sessions as required)

Part 2 of the Literal Unit focuses on 'what' questions and demonstrates how this type of literal question is slightly more involved than asking and answering 'who' and 'where' questions. This is because in addition to asking about actions, this sort of question can also ask what is happening in a story. For example, when the reader asks literal questions about the 'actions' of characters, they only require a verb or the addition of a noun to answer them, e.g., **'What is Rio doing?** Rio is **eating an apple'**. Whereas, when the reader asks 'what is happening?' the answer usually requires a combination of 'who, what, where' information about a greater chunk of the story to give a full response (see the 'Retelling Story Map' p. 240).

Also, questions beginning with the word 'what' offer only part of a guide for a response. The words need to be rearranged to make a statement. For example: *What is Ella **doing in the pool**? Ella is* **swimming** *in the pool.*

### Recap – Literal 'who' enquiry

*(Maybe the Literal Patroller puppet could ask the questions and Riskometer could be used to encourage participation.)*

- What is the Literal Patroller's job? (*They note down everything they see that is happening 'right there' on the page. They ask themselves – 'Who is in the story?' 'What are they doing?' 'What is happening?' 'Where is it happening?'*).
- What type of literal question asks the reader to name the character in a story? (*A 'who' question asks for the name or identity of the character in a story.*)
- How do you ask a 'who' question? For example: I want to find out if any of you have a pet rabbit. How would I ask this question? (Circle your face to indicate a 'who' question to remind them: *Who has a pet rabbit?*)
- Ask: If you have a pet rabbit – how do you answer this question? (*I have a pet rabbit*).

### Practising hand and body signs for 'who', 'what', 'where' – right there!

Remind them that Literal Patrollers use hand and body signs for 'who', 'what', 'where' – right there! They use three different signs to help them remember each type of key word and literal question. Ask the puppet to show the class the sign that asks who the characters are in the story (circling face). *Maybe the puppet cannot remember and needs the children's help here!* Then tell them that since they will be looking for information today about what the characters are doing in stories, they will be using another sign. Model the 'what' sign (jogging on the spot) that refers to the characters' actions.

---

**Session 13: Identifying literal information to ask what characters are doing**

Learning objectives - to be able to:
a. understand literal 'what' information refers to what you see characters doing on the page,
b. understand the difference between 'who' and what' information,
c. recognise the different hand and body signs for 'who' and 'what' questioning,

---

d.  skim and scan for information using the Picture Viewer,

e.  correctly locate and circle the characters' actions in blue pencil on the page.

Emphasise that 'what' information in a story is different to 'who' information.

- When you look for 'what' information on a page you are looking for details about the characters' actions (what they are doing) in the story, e.g., *'What is the man doing?' 'The man is running' (mime jogging on the spot)*.

- Tell them that 'what' questions and answers involve 'doing' words, e.g., **'What** is the dog **doing?' 'The dog is barking'**.
  (*Perhaps the children could join in as you model this further with a series of actions e.g., waving, hopping, reading etc.*). **'What** is the puppet **doing?' 'The puppet is waving'**. And so on.

**The Picture Viewer** - gathering information to ask literal questions

- Remind them that Literal Patrollers ask three types of question: 'who, what, where' about information they see 'right there' on the page.

- Point to the 'Goldilocks' illustration on the Literal Patroller poster. For example: Who has a spoon and bowl? (*Goldilocks has a spoon and bowl.*) What is she doing? (*She is eating from the bowl.*) Where is she? (*She is in the kitchen/three bears house/at the table.*)

- However, before they can ask questions about a more unfamiliar story, they need to look carefully to see who the characters are, what they are doing, and where they are in a story. They use a Picture Viewer to help them do this.

- In this session they will use their Picture Viewers again to gather information about characters in stories.

- This time they will use the Viewer to find information about what the characters *are doing*.

- Remodel how to use the Viewer. Remind the children that they need to place the Viewer on the page and move the hole around the page to find the characters. Explain that the hole in the Viewer will frame the character's actions and highlight what they are doing in the scene.

- To help them search for this information more easily, explain that they will learn how to skim and scan for picture details using the Viewer.

**Activity - Skimming and scanning to answer and ask what characters are doing**

Tell the class that today and in following sessions they will be learning how to skim and scan for 'who' and 'what' key words and images to help them ask and answer 'what' questions.

Explain that skimming and scanning are essential tools that help you to answer literal questions with accuracy, confidence, and speed. These skills also prepare you for trickier detective questions later.

Tell the children that to answer a literal question that asks what a character is doing successfully, they need to learn how to skim and scan to match the key word in the question. 'What' key words refer to the image or word that describes the character's actions on the page. They can do this quickly if they learn to skim pictures and text from left to right and scan up and down to find the information. *Some children might find it easier to use their eyes only. Others might find the Viewer helps them to do this successfully.*

## Activity 3 – Revisit 'Show and Tell' picture Unit 1

Hand out copies and Picture Viewer to pairs. Again, this activity might be more practical at the children's tables rather than on the carpet.

- Ask the children to look at the picture with you.
- Then remind them that as Literal Patrollers it is their job to gather information they can see about the characters on the page and what they are doing. Literal information is always right there on the page – it is never hidden (*'who', 'what', and 'where' - right there!*).
- Explain that they will use their Picture Viewer and skim and scan to look more closely for information about the characters and their actions in the picture. (*Maybe the puppet could look through the hole at the children and ask them to explain or show him how to skim and scan for information on the page.*)
- Remind the children that skimming and scanning involves moving around the page and zooming in on details to look more closely at the characters and what is happening. Using the Viewer, demonstrate how to *skim* left to right and *scan* up and down to find then frame the characters on the page.
- Ask them to circle the characters they see in red pencil on the sheet.
- Then circle the actions and objects linked to **what they are doing** in blue.

Finally ask pairs or the whole class to take it in turns to ask literal questions about the characters and what they are doing. Remind them to use the 'who' and 'what' information they have circled on the sheet. For example:

Q: *Who is sitting in the book corner?* A: *Mouse is sitting in the book corner.*

Q: *What is Mouse doing?* A: *Mouse is reading*. And so on.

*Perhaps Literal Patroller puppet can remind them to:*
- answer questions in full sentences (for team points or stickers),
- circle their faces when they ask 'who' questions,
- jog on the spot or swing their arms when they ask 'What' questions.

**Plenary:** Ask the class if they enjoy being Literal Patrollers. Do they like asking and answering their own questions? Do they find the questioning easy or difficult? What sort of question do they like asking and answering the most? 'Who' questions or 'What' questions – why?

**Extension:** Practising writing their own 'what' literal questions and answers.
- Writing answers to 'who' and 'what' questions (see photocopiable guidance and activities).
- Writing their own 'who' and 'what' questions about characters they have identified and circled in a different picture or text (see photocopiable activities).

**Consolidation:** Happy Family card game – matching information/identifying different characters, their occupations, and what they are doing (encouraging players to look more closely for information). Generating and answering their own 'what' questions about the characters' actions in the cards.

# Unit 2 (Part 3): Literal enquiry – 'where' questions – overview of Sessions 17–20

**Lesson objectives** – to be able to:

- identify literal key words about characters/objects, their actions, and places,
- identify and use positional words to provide accurate answers to 'where' questions,
- ask and answer 'who', 'what', and 'where' questions from key literal information gathered.

**What you need (see resources pages 219–253)**

**Items**: Flipchart, pen, blue tack, paper, pencils/pens for class drawing (Session 17), green pencils (Session 19), Literal Patroller puppet
**Pictures:** 'In the Park', p. 2 of *The Book Day Parade* picture booklet (Sessions 19 and 20)
**Posters:** Language of Discussion, Author, Literal Patroller, Use of Senses, 'Brilliant Book Talk' chart
**Multisensory learning aids:** Picture Viewer, hand signs, Riskometer, discussion cue cards, question cards (who, what, where?)

**Summary of Sessions 17–20** (teacher/class, groups, and pairs):

**Session 17** – Identifying literal information and how to use positional words and phrases, e.g., 'in', 'out', 'on', 'next to' – to state where characters and objects are in a story (teacher models – pairs and class join in)
**Session 18** – Structure of literal question types: comparing 'who', 'what', 'where' questions and answers (teacher modelling/class practice)
**Session 19** – Gathering 'where' information about the scene of a story and asking 'where' questions (teacher modelling and pairs/groups/class activity)

- *Skim* left to right and *scan* up and down to find the characters on the page.
- Identify each character you find (e.g., Rabbit, Crocodile, Bear etc.), then ask 'What are they doing?'

## Activity 1 - 'What are they doing?'

Hand out picture 2, 'In the Park', blue pencils and Picture Viewers to pairs. *This activity might be more practical for the children to do at their tables rather than on the carpet.*
- Ask pairs of children to take it in turns to skim and scan the scene using the Viewer (you may prefer to give children their own Viewer and copy of the picture).
- Then ask them to identify each character and discuss what the characters are doing.
- Next tell them to circle the characters' actions in blue pencil.
- Finally ask the pairs to share this information with the class (e.g., Rabbit is riding his bike, Crocodile is kicking a ball, Bear is jumping over a puddle, and so on).
- Explain that in the next session they will be shown how to use this information to ask and answer 'what' questions about the character's actions.

## Session 14: Question structure - asking 'what' questions about characters' actions

**Learning objectives** - to be able to:
a. ask your own literal question about characters' actions using the information gathered,
b. respond to and use the jogging sign for a 'what' literal question appropriately.

**Asking** 'who' and 'what' questions - what is the difference?
- Remind the class that 'who' asks *about a person*. When you ask this type of question you use the word 'who' at the front of the sentence. Q. '**Who** is smiling?' (Circle face).
- However, 'what' asks about a person's *actions*. When you ask a 'what' question, you put the words 'what' at the front and 'doing' at the end of the sentence. Q. '**What** is Rabbit **doing**?' (Jog on spot).

## Activity 2 - 'What are they doing in the park?'

Revisit Activity 1 picture 2 and hand out a blue colour pencil to pairs.
- Explain that you are going to show the children how to ask their own 'what' questions using the key information they gathered in the last session.
- Ask them to look together at this information in the park scene. They will see that they circled what the characters are doing in blue, e.g., Rabbit is riding his bike.
- Ask them to take it in turns to point to a character and ask what they are doing (prompting them to jog on the spot when they ask these questions to indicate that they are asking about the character's actions), e.g., *What is Crocodile doing? What is Bear doing? What is Piglet doing?* And so on.
- Then to reinforce how to ask a 'what' question (model jogging on spot) and repeat the activity as a class – pointing at character's actions in a different picture narrative as you and the class ask: 'What are they doing?' Or 'What is she/he or the character (name) doing?'

## Session 15: Question structure - asking and answering 'what' questions

**Learning objectives** - to be able to:
a. understand the difference between asking and answering 'who' and 'what' questions,
b. ask your own literal 'what' question using the correct hands/body sign,
c. answer literal 'what' questions correctly in full sentences.

### Answering 'who' and 'what' questions - what is the difference?
- Explain that it is also important that Literal Patrollers know the difference between answering a 'who' question and responding to a 'what' question.
- First model a 'who' question about a child or adult in the class, e.g., 'Who has dark brown hair?' Then invite the children to *ask a 'who' question* about someone in the class (circling their faces) and encourage others in the class to answer in a full sentence (for team points).
- Remind them that when *you answer 'who' questions* you put the character or name in front, e.g., Q. *'Who is dancing?'* A. *'Ellie is dancing'*.
- But when you ask answer a 'what' question - you put the 'doing word' at the end, e.g., Q. *'What is Ellie doing?'* A. *'Ellie is dancing'*.

Remind them that when you ask 'who' questions you circle your face to indicate you are asking about a character. When you ask 'what' questions you jog on the spot or swing your arms to show you are asking about the character's actions (what they are doing).

### Activity sheet 3 (pairs) - 'What are you doing?'

Asking and answering literal 'what' questions about each other's actions - images from Activity 1 picture 'In the Park':
- Invite the children to take it in turns to mime these actions for each other, e.g., running, jumping, hiding, skipping etc.
- Encourage them to ask and answer each other's questions in full sentences: e.g, *'What are you doing?'* *'I am jumping'*. This helps them see how 'what' questions and answers are formed. They will quickly see that 'what' comes at the beginning of the question and the answer has the 'action (doing)' at the end.

Remind them that when you ask 'what' questions you *jog on the spot or swing your arms* to show you are asking about the character's actions (what they are doing).

## Session 16: Asking and answering 'who' and 'what' questions about characters' actions

**Learning objectives** - to be able to:
a. use the Viewer effectively to skim and scan for information,
b. identify and gather information about the character's actions,
c. ask and answer own 'who' and 'what' questions in full sentences using the information gathered.

**Session 20** – Practising asking and answering 'where' questions about places, characters, and objects in a story scene (teacher guidance/pairs/group/class activity)

**Extension** – Practising writing own questions and answers to 'who, what, where' questions

# Teacher notes

### Literal Patroller – How to ask and answer 'where' questions

(3 x 30-minute teaching sequences which can be divided into smaller sessions as required)

Part 3 demonstrates how literal 'where questions' are straightforward for children to generate and respond to. They ask the reader to either locate the whereabouts of characters and objects or to identify places and settings. The children need to know that the subject of a 'where' enquiry is usually at the end of a question, for example *'Where is **Hannah**?'* or *'Where is Penzance?'* or *'Where is the box?'* To respond they simply need to begin their answer with the person's name, the place, object, and add the 'where' information at the end, for example: *Hannah is outside, Penzance is in Cornwall, The box is on the table.*

Positional vocabulary for 'where' questions helps readers to explain the location of characters and objects in relation to where other things are: 'next to', 'beside', 'opposite to', 'outside', 'inside' and 'near'.

### Recap – literal 'what' enquiry

*(Maybe the Literal Patroller puppet could ask the questions and Riskometer could be used to encourage participation.)*

- What is the Literal Patroller's job? (*They note down everything they see is happening 'right there' on the page. They ask themselves – 'Who is in the story?' 'What are they doing?' 'What is happening?' 'Where is it happening?'*).
- What type of literal question might I ask if I want to know what a character is doing in a story? (*I ask a 'what' question: 'What is she/he/it doing?'*).
- What is the difference between 'who' and 'what' questions? (*'Who' questions ask about characters in a story. 'What' questions ask about the characters' actions – what they are doing.*)

### Practising hand signs for 'who, what, where' questions

Remind them that Literal Patrollers use hand and body signs for 'who', 'what' 'where' – right there!

- They use three different actions to help them remember each type of key word and literal question.
- Ask the puppet to show the class the 'who' question sign that asks about the characters in a story (*circling face*). Then the sign for 'what' questions that asks what the characters are doing (*jogging on the spot/swinging arms*). *Maybe the puppet cannot remember both signs and needs the children's help here.*
- Tell them that since they will be looking for information today about *where* the characters or things are in story settings, they will be using another sign. Model the 'where' sign (*hand over eyes – searching*), e.g., *'Where are the children in the story?'*

## Session 17: Identifying literal information to ask 'where' characters are in a story

**Learning objectives** – to be able to:

a. respond to and use the hand sign for 'where' questions correctly,
b. identify information relating to characters' whereabouts and places in text,
c. identify and use vocabulary to describe the position of a character or object in a scene,
d. answer a 'where' question using the correct positional words in a full sentence.

Emphasise that 'where' information in a story is different to 'who' and 'what' information.

- When you look for 'where' information on a page you are looking for details about places, settings, and where the characters or things are in pictures and text, e.g., *(mime searching)* Q. *'Where is the dog?'* A. *'The dog is **under the table**'*.
- Tell them that 'where' questions and answers involve the 'positional' words and phrases they will recognise from their maths lessons.
- Ask the children to give some examples of words and phrases that describe the position of a person or object and where they are in relation to other things, e.g., 'in', 'on', 'under', behind and 'over', or 'on top of', 'next to'.
- Ask them to give you an example (for team points) of a sentence containing positional words, such as, *'The cat is **on the bed**'*, *'The bird flew **over the roof**'*. Ask the children if they can think of any other 'position' words and phrases that describe where people or things are (*inside, outside, in between, beneath, besides, around, forwards, backwards, sideways, left, right*).

### Activity 1 – Positional 'where' picture

Hand out a piece of paper and pencil to each child. Ensure their names are on the sheet.

- Explain that you want the children to draw a picture that shows where the following people and things are as you describe them (you can use a nursery rhyme theme, or the example below).
- Tell them that they will need to listen carefully as you describe where to position the character or object in their picture.
- **First ask them to draw a house.**
- Then put a sun *in* the sky.
- Then draw a tree *next* to the house.
- Put a bird flying *over* the roof of the house.
- Draw a dog *outside* the front door.
- Draw a man *under* the tree.
- Put a hat *on* the man.
- Draw a little girl *beside* the man.

### Activity 2 – 'Where' pictures – locating the positions of objects and characters

(Using the children's Activity 1 drawings and Picture Viewers.)

- Tell pairs to use their Picture Viewers to look carefully at each other's pictures. Ask them to discuss *where* the characters and objects are in the picture.
- Explain that the Literal Patroller (puppet) would like to draw his own picture using the same details. Could they help him by telling him what is in their pictures…

- Model how to use the sentence stem 'There is... in my picture' to help them share this information with the puppet in full sentences, e.g., *'There is **a house** in my picture'*, *'There is **a tree** in my picture'*, *'There is **a man** in my picture'* and so on... The puppet begins to draw this information on the flipchart but says he does not know where to put the characters and objects... He asks them: *'Where is the tree?'* (*At this point the puppet might make silly errors for the children to comment on*).
- Model the answer: *'The tree is next to the house'* and encourage the class to answer the puppet's following questions using the positional words 'in', 'over', 'next to', 'under', 'beside' etc. Q. *'**Where** is the man? A. 'The man is **under the tree**'. Q. '**Where** is the girl?'* A. *'The girl **is next to the man**'*. And so on. (*Maybe the puppet could give team points or stickers as an award.*)

## Session 18: Structure of literal question types

**Learning objectives** – to be able to:
a. identify the difference between 'who, what, where' questions,
b. ask their own 'where' questions about people and objects in the classroom,
c. answer other's 'where' questions correctly in a full sentence.

Asking and answering 'who', 'what', and 'where' questions – what is the difference? (Re-model use of hand and body signs for each question type.) Remind the children that:
- Who' questions *ask about a person*.
- When you ask this type of question you use the word 'who' at the front of the sentence. e.g., (Circle face) Q. *'**Who** is smiling?'*
- You answer 'who' questions by simply replacing the word 'who' with the person's name.
- A. *'**Alice** is smiling'*.
- 'What' questions ask about a person's *actions*.
- When you ask a 'what' question, you put the word 'what' at the front of the question and add the word 'doing' at the end. e.g., (Jog on spot) Q. *'**What** is Alice **doing**?'*
- You answer by putting the person's actions at the end of the sentence, e.g., A. *'Alice **is smiling**'*.
- 'Where' questions ask about a place or where a character or object is in the story.
- When you ask a 'where' question you put the word 'where' at the front of the question, e.g., (Hand over brow – searching) Q. *'**Where** is Alice?'*
- You answer by adding the person or object at the beginning of the sentence, e.g., A. *'Alice is **in the classroom**'*.

## Activity 3 – Practising asking and answering where questions
- Model 'where' questioning further (using the searching sign) by asking where individuals or objects are in the classroom, e.g., *'Where is **Clara**?' 'Where is the **puppet**?'*
- Repeat that to reply to a 'where' question you say *where the character or object is* at the end of your answer, e.g., A. *'Clara is **on the carpet**'* or *'The puppet is **in the box**'*.
- Invite the children to answer other 'where' questions with you in full sentences, e.g., Q. *'**Where** is Joe?' A. 'Joe is **next to Clara**'* or *'Joe is **in front of Sam**'. Q. '**Where** is the whiteboard?' A. 'The whiteboard **is behind the desk**'*. And so on...

- You may wish to extend this by asking the class, groups, or pairs to ask and answer each other's 'where' questions about objects in the classroom, e.g., Q. *'Where are the books?'* A. *'The books are on the shelf'*.

## Session 19: Gathering 'where' information about the scene of a story

**Learning objectives** - to be able to:
a. use the Viewer to locate characters and objects on the page,
b. gather 'who, what, where' information about characters and objects in a scene.

### Activity 4 - 'Playing in the Park'

Hand out Activity 4 picture narrative 'In the Park' and Picture Viewers to pairs - ensuring their names are on the sheets.
- Remind them that Literal Patrollers use the Viewer to find information about who is in a story scene, what they are doing, and where the characters, objects, and places *are* in the story (e.g., *Turtle is walking on the path behind the others, Croc is playing with a ball on the grass, Mouse is jumping over a puddle on the path, Wolf is throwing an apple core into a bin, Bear and Piglet are playing hide and seek ahead of them all, Rabbit is riding a bike*).
- Demonstrate again how to skim left and right and scan up and down to move the hole of the Viewer around the page. Show them how you can then zoom in on details to find out more about the characters and objects and where they are (in relation to each other).
- Ask pairs of children to take it in turns to look carefully at the scene using the Viewer to locate these details and discuss what they can see.
- Next tell them to circle where the characters and things are in **green** pencil.
- Finally ask the pairs to share this information with the class (using the puppet and Riskometer might be helpful).
- Explain that they will be shown again how to use this information to ask and answer 'where' questions about the characters, objects, and places in the scene.

## Session 20: Practising asking and answering 'where' questions about a story scene

**Learning objectives** - to be able to:
a. ask their own 'where' questions using the information gathered,
b. answer their own 'where' questions accurately in a full sentence.

### Activity 5 - Where in the park?

Revisit Activity 4 hand-outs 'Playing in the park'. Tell the children that you are going to show them how to ask and answer their own 'where' questions using the key information they gathered about children playing the park in the last session.
- Ask them to look together at the 'where' information they circled in green on the activity sheet. This shows where the characters, objects, and places are in the picture, e.g., *Rabbit is **on his bike**. Piglet is **in the bushes**. The Park is **near some houses**.*

- To reinforce how to ask a 'where' question (model the searching sign), point to some of the characters or objects in the pictures and ask where they are in the scene, e.g., *'Where is Rabbit? Where is Piglet? Where is the park?* And so on.
- Ask the class to take it in turns in their pairs to point to a character, object, or place and ask where they are (prompting them to use the 'where' searching sign) – then answer their questions, e.g., *Q. 'Where is Wolf? A. Wolf is **next to the bin**. Q. Where is Turtle? A. Turtle is **on the path**. Q. Where is Crocodile? A. Crocodile is **on the grass***. (Encourage them to find as many 'where' questions and answers as possible for team points.)

**Plenary:**
- Bring the pairs together to share their questions and answers with each other as a class. (Scoring team points for good questions and answers, e.g., one point awarded for each literal 'where' question and for each answer).
- Ask the children what they have learned in the last few sessions about being Literal Patrollers.
- Ask the class if they enjoy being Literal Patrollers. Do they like asking and answering their own questions? Do they find the questioning easy or difficult? Which sort of question do they like asking and answering most? 'Who', 'What', or 'Where' questions – why?

**Consolidation:** Use the question cards as prompts to generate and answer their own 'who, what, where' questions about familiar pictures and text (class, group, or paired activity).

**Extension:** Practising writing answers to 'where' questions (see guidance and activities).

- Ask the children to practise writing their own 'where' questions and answers about characters, objects, and places they have identified and circled in a different picture or text (see photocopiable activities). *Remind the children that written **questions** must always have a question mark at the end of the query and written **answers** must have a full stop at the end of the sentence.*

# Unit 3 (Part 1): Inference enquiry – making predictions – overview of Sessions 21–24

**Lesson objectives** – to be able to:

- identify the difference between literal 'who, what, where' information and clues,
- use prior knowledge, literal information, and clues to make logical predictions about what might happen next in a story,
- give reasons for their predictions that link to their own experience and the text.

**What you need (see resources pages 219–253)**

**Items:** Flipchart, pen, paper blue tack, red/blue/green felt tip pens, pass the parcel packages
**Puppets:** Literal Patroller, Detective Clooze
**Pictures:** 'The Photo' p. 3 of *The Book Day Parade* photocopiable picture booklet for Sessions 21, 22, and p. 4 'Sitting on the Wall' for Session 24
**Posters:** Literal Patroller, Detective Clooze, Use of Senses, Language of Discussion, 'Brilliant Book Talk' chart
**Graphic organiser:** WWW (Who, What, Where) Key Words
**Multisensory aids:** Picture Viewer, Riskometer, discussion cards

**Summary of Sessions 21–24** (teacher/class, groups, and pairs):

**Session 21 –** Practising literal 'who', 'what', 'where' questions and answers
**Session 23 –** Being a detective: Finding clues and making predictions
**Session 24 –** Gathering facts to make predictions
**Extension –** Predicting what might happen through drawing and writing the next story scene
**Consolidation –** Practising writing own literal questions and answers about next story scene

# Teacher notes

(3 x 30-minute teaching sequences which can be divided into smaller sessions as required)

## Being a Detective (searching for clues): in-depth reading for meaning

Unit 3 prepares the children for the important rank of the Inference Detective. It makes them aware of possible outcomes and how small clues on the page are vital. Like fingerprints left at the scene of a crime – they point to who is involved, what characters have been doing, and where they have been. This information can help them to anticipate what may happen next and explain why from the evidence found in the pictures and text.

When children make predictions, it engages them more deeply in the story and prompts them to ask what might happen next. It invites them to think about what is plausible and draws them into clue-searching to support their hunches about likely outcomes. This process requires them to activate their prior knowledge, ask themselves questions, recall facts, re-read, skim and scan, and infer to enable them to fully comprehend the author's meaning.

The purpose of this unit is to help the children to identify context clues, make logical links and connections with the author's intention and refer to their own personal world to justify their deductions.

Children can understand and predict story and non-fiction outcomes when they can explain how actions produce consequences and how a series of incidents can be created from one act. This is an invaluable investigative skill that relies on making links through a process of thinking, questioning, and reasoning to calculate what may have happened before or what may happen next.

## Recap (answering in pairs) – Units 1 and 2 (reading for meaning, literal enquiry)

To encourage participation throughout the sessions you could:

a. ask the children to discuss the answers in pairs and use the Literal Patroller puppet to ask the questions,
b. include the Riskometer and team points to reward answers.

- What do good readers do when they read? *They look at the pictures (to get an idea of what the story is about); decode (to work out what the words say); comprehend (to work out what the words mean).*
- How do authors pass on their message? *They choose words that create a picture in your head.*
- What happens if you do not understand the author's meaning? *You do not have a picture in your head – or the picture in your head does not make sense.*
- Can you read picture books that have no words? *Yes, pictures have meaning – the same way words do.*
- Do our senses help us to read pictures and words for meaning? *Yes – we use a combination of looking, listening, thinking, speaking, and feeling to help us make sense of pictures and text.*
  *When we read for meaning we use what we know about the world… We put this with what we see on the page… and check that the pictures we have in our heads make sense.*

- What type of information do Literal Patrollers look for when they first arrive at the scene of a story? (*'Who, what, where' information about the characters, their actions and where they are – that is right there on the page*).
- Show the different hand and body signs Literal Patrollers use when they ask 'who, what, where' questions. (*'Who?' – circling face, 'What?' – jogging on spot, 'Where?' – hand over eyes, searching action*).

## Session 21: Practising literal 'who', 'what', 'where' questions and answers

**Learning objectives** - to be able to:
a. draw on 'who, what, where' skills to gather information about a scene,
b. generate and answer own range of literal questions about the information gathered.

### Activity 1 - 'The Photo'

Using a copy of the picture and large copy of the WWW graphic organiser on the flipchart:
- Ask the children to look closely at the picture on your flipchart.
- Invite them to be Literal Patrollers and discuss what they can see 'right there' in the picture. Scribe their ideas on the board.
- Agree that Mouse (*Hickory Clock*), Bear (*Goldilocks*) and Piglet (*Incy Spider*) are leaning against the wall, and that Turtle (*Humpty Dumpty*) and Wolf (*Red Riding Hood*) are sitting on the wall. Crocodile (*Captain Hook*) is standing behind Turtle with his arm around him. Near them is a huge puddle in the road. We can see in the corner of the picture that Rabbit is coming towards the puddle on his bike.
- Write the following sentence on the flipchart, 'The friends are standing in their costumes by the wall'. Then invite the children to read the line of text with you out loud.
- Ask the children *'Who is in the picture?'* (circling faces). *'What are they doing?'* (Jogging) *'Where are they?'* (Hands over eyebrows - searching).
- As they answer these questions – circle the 'who, what, where' images in the picture and underline the following words in the line of text on the flipchart: 'The friends' ('who' in red), 'are standing in their costumes' ('what' in blue), 'by the wall' ('where' in green).

*An enlarged copy of the WWW graphic organiser might be useful for organising this information on the flipchart. Simply enter the 'who, what, where' key words in the boxes, e.g., ('Who') **'The friends'**, ('What') **'are standing in their costumes'** (Where) **'by the wall'**. Then ask the children to read across the boxes with you. They will see how this information joins together to form a sentence.*
- Next invite them to ask and answer a range of literal questions about the information they see in the picture, e.g., Q. **Who** *is in the picture? A.* Bear, Mouse, Croc, Wolf, Piglet, Turtle, and Rabbit *are in the picture. Q.* **What** *is Piglet* **doing**? A. Piglet is **looking up** at the tree. Q. **Where** is Turtle? A. Turtle is sitting **on the wall**. (This can be done in small groups, pairs of as a class).
- Then ask questions about the key words in the WWW graphic organiser on the flipchart: Q: **Who** is standing by the wall? A: **The friends** are standing by the wall. Q: **What** are they **doing** by the wall? A: They are **standing in their costumes** by the wall.

## Session 22: Making predictions

**Learning objectives** - to be able to:
a.  understand the difference between literal information and clues,
b.  identify clues and explain their meaning in context.

### Activity 2 - Introducing Detective Clooze

Explain that in the following sessions they will use their super literal skills to become Detectives. They will learn how to gather information from pictures and text to help them delve deeper for information about what is happening to the characters and why. This further information will help them to make predictions about the story.

- Show the Prediction poster, then introduce Detective Clooze (using different hats or puppets to demonstrate the difference between the Literal Patroller and Detective roles).
- Explain that Detectives and Literal Patrollers have different jobs. The Literal Patroller helps the Detective by patrolling the scene of a story and telling them the facts they *can see right there*!
- Detective Clooze uses this 'who, what, where' information and their special inference powers to search for clues that will help them to unravel the author's hidden meaning.
- Ask the children if they can explain what a 'clue' is. (A clue helps you to solve a problem, mystery, or puzzle or to understand something better). Explain that *clues, for example, help you find ideas that are not right there on the page (like literal information). Instead, clues suggest ideas that help you to work out what is happening or might happen next.*
- Demonstrate this by showing them the picture of a cake and footprints in the Detective Poster. Can they explain what might be happening from these clues?
- Explain that to make predictions about what might happen next in a story, you also need to know 'who, what, where' facts about the characters and events that you can link to your own experiences and knowledge of the world. You can then join this information together with the ideas suggested by the clues to solve the mystery.
- Tell the children that the next activity will help them to understand how they make predictions using their senses and what they already know about the world.

### Activity 3 - 'Pass the parcel' (making predictions)
- Invite a volunteer to come to the front of the class to help you investigate an unwrapped parcel (or adults can guide this activity in small groups).
- Explain that you and the helper will take it in turns to look at, feel, listen to, and smell the parcel for clues that reveal the contents.
- Tell the class that you want them to guess the contents of the parcel from these clues.
- Before the parcel is unwrapped, ask the children to predict what they think is in it.
- Whose prediction is correct? Ask the children how and why they made their predictions. Ask them to identify the clues that helped them to guess correctly.
- Explain that when you make a prediction - you use what you know to work out the clues (e.g., object shape, sound, smell etc.) to help you guess what you do not know (the hidden information).

## Session 23: Being a detective - finding clues and making predictions

**Learning objectives** - to be able to:
a. understand the meaning of 'cause and effect',
b. draw on knowledge of consequences to make accurate predictions about stories,
c. provide reasons for ideas and predictions using 'because' to explain.

Tell the children that before they can be Super Detectives, they need to practise finding clues and making accurate predictions about picture information and text.
- Explain that to help them do this, they need to join in as much 'think-aloud' talk as possible to predict logical consequences for characters and events in stories. When they talk through possibilities that may happen it will help them to make the links that explain how 'cause and effect' works.
- Tell them that they will start thinking and talking about what the story characters are doing and what might happen to them because of their actions in the next activity.

### Activity 4 'Watch out!' - Predicting what might happen next in a story

Revisit the copy of 'The Photo' picture on the flipchart.
- Draw the children's attention to the Activity 1 picture and text ('The Photo') on the flipchart.
- Remind them that when they were Literal Patrollers in an earlier session, they gathered information about this picture. They discussed who they could see in the picture, what the characters were doing, and where they were.
- Invite them to look at the picture again and give you the key 'who, what, and where' information they found 'right there' on the page.
- Explain that when we use this key information together with clues that link to our own experiences and knowledge of the world, it helps us to make predictions about what might happen next in a story.
- Ask them to begin thinking like Detectives about information they *cannot see right there* on the page. Can they find clues that suggest what might be happening or is about to happen in the picture? For example: Why do they think the friends are standing in a huddle? Why is Piglet looking up at the tree branch?
- Emphasise that good Detectives must also give reasons for their predictions that link to the information and clues on the page.
- Tell them that they use the word '*because*' to help them explain their reasons, e.g., *Turtle's friends might be wearing costumes* **because** *they want to dress as their favourite story characters for the Book Day Parade.*
- Then further model how to make a prediction using a full sentence. Encourage them to give their reasons using '*because*'... e.g., *I think... the friends are standing in a huddle* **because** *they are having a photo taken of them in their costumes. I say that* **because**... *they are all facing one way and smiling or making faces. Also, there is someone's extended arm with a phone pointing at the group.*
  *I think...* **because**...
- Draw their attention to further details in the picture, such as the puddle, Rabbit coming towards them on his bike, and the words in the speech bubble, 'Watch out!'

- Ask them to think about these clues. Can they link this information to their own experiences of playing or riding a bike near water? (e.g., *Riding a bike through water can cause splashing*).
- Ask why them why they think someone is saying 'Watch out!' (e.g., *There is a puddle in the road near them. Someone is warning the group that Rabbit is approaching the puddle on his bike*).
- What do they think might happen next? (e.g., *Rabbit might ride through the puddle and splash them all*). What does it feel like to be splashed when you are not expecting it?
- Invite them to predict what the friends might do next and why? (e.g., *They might try to climb the wall and sit with Turtle to get out of the way or climb the tree, or stop Rabbit...*)
- Explain that authors do not tell you everything at the scene of a story. They usually leave gaps in the information (clues that suggest what is happening or may happen next) to make the story more interesting. They encourage you to use your own experiences of life to fill in the gaps in the information to help you predict what might happen next in the story.
- So, you need to be a Literal Patroller (asking who, what, where?) and an Inference Detective (asking why and how do you know?) to make predictions.
- When you link the facts on the page with the picture and word clues it helps you to think more deeply about the characters' behaviour, feelings, and events in a story.

## Session 24: First gathering facts to make predictions

**Learning objectives** – to be able to:
a. ask 'How do I know?' and 'Why?' questions to identify clues,
b. draw on prior knowledge, facts, and clues on the page to make logical predictions,
c. give reasons for predictions using 'because' to explain.

Hand out the Picture Viewers. Tell the children that they will need the Picture Viewer to help them patrol for key facts about the characters in the next picture activity before looking for clues about the story. Explain that there are two holes in the Picture Viewer. The larger hole can be used to frame bigger areas on the page and the smaller hole is useful for focusing on tiny details.

*Remind them that they need to place the Viewer on the page and move the holes in the Viewer across the page and skim from left to right and scan up and down to find clues.*

## Activity 5 – 'Sitting on the Wall'

You might prefer pairs to sit at their tables for this activity. Hand out 1) copies of Picture 3 that you have on your flipchart, 2) Viewers, and 3) red, blue, green colour pencils.
- First read the line of text at the bottom of the picture together ('Humpty Dumpty sat on a wall').
- Explain that their knowledge of nursery rhymes may help them to guess what might happen next in this version of the story. But first they need to gather the facts...
- Ask the children to look carefully at the picture using the Viewer to help them. Who can they see right there? What are the characters doing? Where are they?
- Remind them how to use the Picture Viewer by placing it on the picture and moving it around to look more closely at the characters, their actions, and the setting (place). Show

them how the hole can be used to frame the details, so the information can be gathered more easily.

- Then ask pairs of children to circle the story characters they can see with a red pencil, then circle 'what they are doing' in blue pencil, and finally 'where they are' in green.
- Finally read the line of text again as a class. Then ask them to underline the key words that refer to the character (in red), their actions (in blue), and place (in green).
- To help them find these key words in the sentence remind them to ask themselves, 'Who is the sentence about?' (Humpty Dumpty), then ask 'What did he do?' (sat), 'Where?' (on a wall).

## Activity 6 - What might happen next?

Revisit 'Sitting on the Wall'. Pairs and class can move to the carpet for this activity to stimulate more discussion.

- Ask the pairs to share the literal information they have circled in the picture and line of text.
- Agree that Humpty and his friends are getting ready to watch the Parade. The picture shows:
    a. Turtle and Wolf are sitting on a low garden wall.
    b. Mouse is helping Bear to climb on the wall.
    c. Crocodile is standing behind Turtle, leaning against him.
    d. Piglet is climbing along a branch that is hanging over Turtle's head.
    e. Rabbit is on a bike riding towards a puddle in the road.
    f. The wall is in front of leafy terraced street houses near the park and the street and houses are decorated with festive flags.

- Encourage them to ask each other literal questions about the characters' actions and where they are (using the literal 'who', 'what', 'where' signing to remind them of the different question types).
- These simple questions will lead them to think beyond the obvious information to seek answers to more in-depth detective questions such as 'how do you know?' and 'why?'
- Remind them that Inference Detective answers to questions are different to Literal Patroller answers. Detectives need to give reasons for their answers that link to clues in the pictures and text (using 'because' to explain).
- Model how to answer inference questions that require them to give reasons for their answers using clues in the picture and text. (*Remind them to use part of the question to help them to answer in a full sentence*). For example:

Q: **Who is dressed as Humpty Dumpty?** A: **Turtle** is dressed as Humpty Dumpty.
Q: **How do you know?** A: **I know because** Turtle is wearing **an egg-shaped costume**.
Q: **Why is Wolf dressed in a red cloak and hood?** A: Wolf is dressed in a red cloak and hood **because** he wants **to look like Red Riding Hood**.

- Can they guess which nursery rhyme and fairy story characters the other friends are dressed as? Why do they say that? How do they know that?
- Can they find clues that suggest what might happen next to Turtle and the other characters?

What might happen, for example, when you are climbing or sitting on a wall? (The clues are there in the characters' actions). For example, have they noticed that Turtle is sitting on the wall and has lots of activity around him and he is looking rather wobbly? What do they think will happen next to Turtle and the other characters and why? (*Will they all fall off the wall? Why do you think that?*)

- Ask the class to share the information they have gathered, their predictions about what will happen next and reasons for their predictions.
- Explain that they will see the picture of what happens next in the next sessions and will see if their predictions were correct.

**Plenary:** Ask the class if they can explain what a 'clue' is in their own words and what they know now about making predictions. Ask them which they would rather be and why - a Literal Patroller or an Inference Detective? What is the difference between their jobs? Do they agree that Detective Clooze can delve deeper for meaning to make predictions - but the Literal Patroller can only ask about what he sees 'right there?'

**Extension:** Drawing or writing what might happen next in a story. Then practising writing their own 'who, what, where' literal questions and answers about this next stage in the story.

**Consolidation:** Ideas for predicting might include physical activities such as hide and seek, role-play and use of question cards to prompt questioning about familiar stories and a range of unseen picture books.

# Unit 3 (Part 2): Inference enquiry – cause and effect – overview of Sessions 25–26

**Lesson objectives** – to be able to:

- understand the meaning of 'cause and effect' to make predictions about story outcomes,
- consciously draw on prior experience and text clues to explain what might happen next,
- justify predictions using picture and text clues,
- understand the reasons for making predictions.

**What you need (see resources p. 219–253)**

**Items:** Flipchart, pen, paper, blue tack, red, blue, green felt tip pens
**Puppets:** Literal Patroller, Detective Clooze
**Pictures:** 'Sitting on the Wall' p. 4 of *The Book Day Parade* photocopiable picture booklet (Session 26), and 'The Fall' (Session 26)
**Graphic organiser:** Who, What, Where(WWW) Key Information
**Posters:** Literal Patroller, Detective Clooze, Use of senses, Language of Discussion
**Multisensory aids:** Picture Viewer, Riskometer, hand signs, discussion cue cards, 'Brilliant Book Talk' chart

**Summary of Sessions 25–26** (teacher/class, groups, and pairs):

**Session 25** – Prediction – understanding cause and effect
**Session 26** – What caused the problem? What might happen next?
**Extension** – Writing, drawing, small world play/role-play to encourage discussion
**Consolidation** – See list of picture books that encourage the predicting process

# Teacher notes

(2 x 30-minute teaching sequences which can be divided into smaller sessions as required)

**Being a detective: Understanding cause and effect**

Part 2 of this unit engages the children in the process of thinking, questioning, and reasoning about 'cause and effect' situations to help them understand how personal experiences influence how we make predictions about stories. They learn, for example, that character's actions cause story outcomes in much the same way as our actions have consequences in real life. Sessions 25 and 26 demonstrate how readers link their prior knowledge and the author's clues to identify problems for the characters and make predictions about likely outcomes.

To achieve the most from this process the children learn to make predictions before, during, and after reading – checking and modifying their ideas as they read to gain a full understanding of the author's meaning and intention.

**Recap Unit 3** (Being a detective – learning how to predict)

Detective Clooze puppet could ask the questions and Riskometer and team points could be used to encourage participation.

- How did you predict what was inside the parcels in the last session? (*By looking for clues – shape, size, smell, feel of parcel to help you guess what was inside*).
- How did you predict what might happen next to Turtle and the other characters in the story? (*By looking for 'who', 'what', 'where' information on the page – then searching for clues to explain the characters' actions.*)
- What does Detective Clooze do at the scene of a story? (*Detective Clooze makes predictions about what might happen next in a story.*)

---

### Session 25: Activity 1 (class discussion) - predicting - cause and effect

**Lesson objectives** - to be able to:
a. understand the meaning of 'cause and effect' in everyday life,
b. consciously draw on prior experience to explain an action and what might happen next,
c. give reasons why specific actions have consequences using 'because' to explain why.

**Being an Inference Detective - making predictions**

Detectives use their personal knowledge and experience to help them make predictions about stories and they always check to see if their predictions are correct.
- Show the Prediction poster. Remind the children that Detective Clooze looks for clues on the page to find out...
- what might have happened before a story scene (for example: *Q. Why was Goldilocks on her own in the Bear's house? A. Goldilocks was on her own in the Bear's house because the Bear family had gone out for a walk*).
  - what might happen next (for example: *The Bears might return from their walk and catch Goldilocks in their house*).

---

- Explain that we make predictions in many situations. Sometimes we know what will happen next because we have experienced it before. For example, if I jump up - I know I will come down!
- Our actions usually cause things to happen. The cause is the reason something has happened. This is known as **'cause and effect'**. We use the word 'be**cause**' to help us explain why something happened. (This happened – *because* I did that!)
- Talk about everyday '*cause* and **effect**' situations with the class - modelling how to use simple past, present and future tenses, and general vocabulary. For example:

**'My clothes are dirty** be*cause I fell in the mud'*.
I **do not like bananas** be*cause I ate too many* and they **made me sick.**
I **will not play with my friend** Joel be*cause **he is mean to me.***

- Ask the children for examples of things that have happened to them because of their actions.
- Discuss whether their personal experiences might help them to accurately predict story outcomes and why.

**Activity 2 (Class discussion) When I did that... this happened!**
- Look at the examples on the flipchart that explain cause and effect (an action that causes something to happen).
- Ask the children to predict what might have happened before or what might happen next because of these actions. For example:
  a. Pricking the balloon (*might **cause** it to pop*),
  b. Leaving an ice-cream in the sun (*will **cause** it to melt*),
  c. Going out in the snow without a warm coat (*might make you cold*).

**Session 26: What caused the problem? What might happen next?**

Revisit Picture 4 'Sitting on the Wall'.

**Lesson objectives** - to be able to:
a. identify the clues on the page that suggest what may have happened before this narrative,
b. consciously draw on prior experience and text clues to explain what might happen next in text,
c. justify predictions using picture and text clues,
d. understand the reasons for making predictions.

Remind the children that in the last session they learned how being Super Literal Patrollers helps readers to become great questioning Detectives. Draw their attention to the circled and underlined information on Picture 4 'Sitting on the Wall' (from the previous Prediction sessions).
- Tell them that first they looked for literal information they could see on the page about Turtle and his friends (remodel the signing actions to remind them of the literal question they asked: 'who' – circling your face, 'what' – jogging, and 'where' – searching).
- Then they thought about their own experiences of climbing and playing on and around walls with friends. They used this knowledge and searched for clues that suggested what might happen to the characters because of their actions, e.g., What can happen if you are not careful?

- Ask pairs to identify the clues in the text and pictures that suggest what may have happened before this scene.
- Tell them to repeat their predictions about the story and to give their reasons for them. Encourage them to use the word 'because' to help them explain. (For example, did they predict that the characters actions may have caused Turtle's fall and led to their own problems? What are the clues in the story that suggest this?)

**For example:** some of the characters may have knocked Turtle off the wall and fallen off the wall themselves *because*:

a. they were scrambling for a place to watch the Book Day parade on or around the wall and bumped into Turtle and each other, or

b. they were trying to avoid Rabbit splashing them as the bike went through the puddle.

**Possible clues:**
- Bear (Goldilocks) and Mouse (Clock) were having difficulty climbing up on the wall (because of their costumes).
- Croc (Hook) was standing behind Turtle. He was leaning on him and stretching forward to see the first float coming.
- Pig (Incy Spider) had climbed on an overhanging branch above Turtle to get a better view.
- Turtle (Humpty Dumpty) was not holding on to the wall. He was reaching over for Wolf's crisps with one hand, while looking in the other direction and pointing at the float in the distance with the other.

**Activity 3 – 'The Fall': Being a Literal Patroller and gathering key information**

Attach Picture 5 next to Picture 4 on the flipchart. Hand out Viewers and copies of Picture 4 to pairs.
- Explain to the children that they are now going to explore what happened to Turtle and the other characters in the next picture.
- Hand out copies of Picture 5 to pairs and ask them to read the line of text with you at the bottom of the picture ('Humpty Dumpty had a great fall').
- Then (hand out red, blue, and green pencils) invite them to be Literal Patrollers again. When they look through their Viewers remind them to skim from left to right and scan up and down for the 'who, what, where' information they can see right there in the picture, and in the line of text.
- Then ask them to take it in turns to circle the information in the picture using red, blue, green pencils.
- Finally tell them to underline the 'who, what, and where' key words in the sentence.
- Then as they share this literal information with the class, record the information in 'who, what, where' (WWW Organiser) columns on the flipchart and read the sentences back together as a class. You could then ask volunteers to come to the front of the class and show or put the key information in the correct column for you. For example:

*(Who) Turtle, Bear, Mouse, and Pig (What) are getting up or lying on the pavement (Where) near the wall.*
*(Who) Wolf (What) is still sitting (Where) on the wall.*

*(Who) Crocodile (What) is flopped over (Where) the wall.*

*(Who) Crocodile (What) has half of Turtle's costume (Where) on the end of his hook.*

*(Who) The Queen of Hearts, the pantomime horse, and soldiers (What) are standing looking upset (Where) on the pavement (Who) Rabbit (What) is riding away from the scene (Where) on his bike.*

## Activity 4 – 'The Fall': being a detective, finding clues that explain what has happened

- Ask pairs to be Detectives and look for clues in the picture and text that might explain what has happened to the characters in this scene.
- Were their predictions correct? What caused the characters to fall off the wall? Was it Turtle's fault that he fell or was he knocked of the wall? Why do they think that?
- Next display Picture 4 on the flipchart. Invite pairs to share the clues they have found with the class.
- Discuss how these clues link to the previous scene in Picture 4 (on the flipchart). Encourage the children to explain what they think caused the various problems in Picture 5. For example:

*Why do they think Turtle fell off the wall? How do they think it happened?*

*Why was Crocodile flopped over the wall? How did that happen?*

*Why do they think Mouse and Bear landed on top of each other?*

*Why do they think Pig was lying on the ground?*

*Why do they think Turtle, Mouse, and Bear were wet?*

*Why do they think Turtle's costume was torn?*

- Remind them to answer in full using part of the question to help them using 'because' to give their reasons. Allow the children 'to have a go' before you give them the clues. This will give you a chance to see how they are thinking.

Clues to consider: Maybe...
- Pig fell out of the tree and knocked Humpty off the wall.
- Humpty fell because he was reaching for Wolf's bag of crisps and lost his balance.
- Crocodile was leaning on Turtle and knocked him off the wall – hooking Turtle's costume as he fell.
- Rabbit splashed Humpty and some of the others when he rode through the puddle. This may have caused Bear and Mouse to grab Humpty and knock him off the wall. Or maybe the splash gave Humpty a surprise and made him wobble and fall off the wall.

## Activity 5 – 'The Fall': being a detective, finding clues that explain what might happen next

Discuss as a class how the following clues might suggest what happens next:
- Ask them to discuss what Turtle may be feeling or thinking – and what the problem may be for him. (His costume has been torn in half and he is wet.)
- Then read out the word clues together and ask them to circle the clues in the picture that link to what is happening in the story and what may have happened before. (**'Humpty Dumpty had a great fall'**... and... *image of Turtle getting up from the pavement, upset with a torn wet costume.*)

- Then ask the pairs to discuss what they think might happen next and why. (*Can Turtle's costume be put together again? How might that be possible?*)
- Invite the pairs to feed back their ideas and to give reasons for them.

Discuss why we make predictions.
- How does predicting help us in life? Ask them to give examples and explain their ideas. (Predictions can help us to prepare so we can make plans, e.g., based on the weather; predictions might keep us safe, e.g., if I do that... this might happen; make decisions each day.)
- Why does predicting make a story more enjoyable? (*When our predictions about the story are correct it shows we understand what is happening and we are connecting with the author. Making predictions about what might happen next is fun. Anything else?*)
- What other things do we make predictions about and why?

**Plenary discussion:** what have the children found out today about making predictions? Have they noticed how often they make predictions in a day?! Perhaps they could make a prediction about what is going to happen to them next, e.g., What will they have for lunch? What games might they play during breaktime? Will it rain this afternoon? etc.

Tell them that in the last session they will think about how Inference Detectives make predictions about stories from book covers.

**Extension:** Writing, drawing, small world play/role-play opportunities that encourage discussion about clues, 'cause and effect' situations, and how and why we make predictions.

**Consolidation:** See list of picture books that encourage the predicting process (p...) and use of past, present, and future tenses in discussion about what may have happened in a story, what is happening, or what might happen next and why.

# Unit 3 (Part 3): Inference enquiry – overview of Sessions 27–29

**Lesson objectives** – to be able to:

- draw on knowledge of cause and effect to link picture and word clues, identify characters' problems, and predict story outcomes,
- draw on knowledge of personal emotions to identify characters' feelings and actions from picture clues,
- link picture and word clues and knowledge of vocabulary to ask and answer simple inference questions,
- link picture and word clues on book covers to predict story contents or information.

**What you need (see resources p. 219–253)**

**Items:** Flipchart, pen, paper blue tack, red, blue, green felt tip pens, Detective Clooze puppet
**Pictures:** 'The rescue' p. 6 of *The Book Day Parade* (Session 27 & 28), selection of fiction and information picture books (Session 29)
**Graphic organiser:** Who, What, Where (WWW) Key Information
**Posters:** Literal Patroller, Detective Clooze
**Multisensory aids:** Picture Viewer, Riskometer, hand signs, discussion cue cards, 'Brilliant Book Talk' chart

**Summary of Sessions 27–29** (teacher/class, groups, and pairs):

**Session 27** – Making deductions and predictions (flipchart)
**Session 28** – Predicting how the story might end – word and picture clues – giving reasons for deductions
**Session 29** – Predicting contents of books from clues on the cover
**Extension** – Finding key information in an unfamiliar book title to draw their own book cover. Writing or drawing what they think the book is about. Giving reasons for their ideas

# Teacher notes

Link images and word clues to answer inference questions about pictures and text.

The last of the Unit 3 sessions explains how the children can build on their prediction skills to delve deeper for meaning. Part 3 extends their understanding of 'who', what', and 'where' to include 'how' and 'why'. They are shown how to search for clues using prediction skills to understand the author's hidden and implied meaning to answer and generate their own detective questions.

They are shown how authors use inference to give readers extra details. This process significantly improves their vocabulary, helps them to make key links, and encourages independent reasoning and deduction. Like a detective, they learn how to delve deeper for evidence to back up what they have inferred from pictures and text. This procedure also helps them to identify the difference between being literal and using inference to ask and answer questions.

A particularly effective way to encourage children to make predictions is to discuss the cover of a book with them. Children enjoy making predictions about the contents of a book from the visual clues on the cover. It offers them an opportunity to use their investigative and interpretative skills and personal knowledge. The cover tells them whether the contents are fiction or non-fiction, and enables them to figure out from the title and pictures whether it is a theme or subject they like, or they already know about. It also tells them what sort of vocabulary they may need to know. The book title often provides key word clues about the contents and theme of the book, whereas the cover picture tends to offer more inferred information about the characters and events inside. Importantly, when the cover grabs a child's interest, they are more inclined to make predictions about the contents.

## Recap (answering in pairs) – Unit 3 Being a detective

*(Maybe the detective puppet could ask the questions and Riskometer and team points could be used to encourage participation.)*

- What do you call information that is right there on the page? (*Literal information – who, what, where key words. Refer to these words displayed somewhere in the classroom or write them on the board.*)
- What does Detective Clooze do at the scene of a story? (*Detective Clooze 'searches for clues and makes predictions' – encourage the children to say this in rhythm while tapping on knees to help them remember it.*)
- How do you make 'predictions' about stories? *1) We use what we know, 2) We use 'who, what, where' information, 3) We use clues on the page.*
- How does predicting help you to think ahead? (*Predicting is about 'cause and effect', e.g., I know if this happens... then this might happen next because...*).

## Session 27: Making deductions and predictions from clues in pictures and text

**Lesson objectives** - to be able to:
a. gather literal information to gather the facts and set the scene,
b. draw on knowledge of cause and effect to link picture and word clues, identify characters' problems and predict story outcomes.

Explain to the children that Detectives link pictures and word clues to help them understand what is happening and to make predictions as they read. Tell them that in this session they will use their knowledge of the world and their detective skills to help them think more deeply about what is happening in the story and how the characters are feeling in the pictures and text.

### Activity 1 - 'The Rescue': What is happening?

Picture 6 on flipchart. *You may choose to do the following activity as a class, one section at a time so the children can show their pictures each time and you can make a visual assessment to see who has been able to process and follow the instruction correctly.*

- Hand out copies of Picture 6 with Viewers and red, blue, and green pencils to pairs (mixed reading ability). *Ensure that the children put their names on the back of the pictures for the next session.*
- Ask the children to read the line of text at the bottom of the picture out loud with you: 'All the King's horses and all the King's men couldn't put Humpty together again'.
- Then, ask them to patrol the page with their Viewers and circle the literal who, what, where information in the picture (using the red pencil for 'who' is in the story, blue pencil for 'what the characters are doing' and 'green' pencil for where they are positioned in the picture). This is a good opportunity for you to see whether they can successfully identify the correct information and select the right colour pencil for the purpose. (Only offer your help once they have 'given it a go').
  a. First ask them to find the 'who' information in this picture and circle this in red. Then ask them to show you where they have drawn their circle on the page.
  b. Next ask them to look at 'what the characters are doing' and circle this information in blue.
  c. Finally, ask them to find the 'where' information and circle it green, to show you that they understand the difference between actions and 'positional' information.

### Activity 2 - 'The Rescue': What is happening (continued)

*If you feel confident that most of the children can manage this first stage, move onto the next instruction.*
- Next ask the pairs to underline the 'who' information (*'Kings men, Kings horses'*) in the line of text in red pencil and show you where they have drawn this line.
- Then circle the image and underline the 'who' key words in red on your copy of this picture on the flipchart.

- Next, ask them to underline the 'what' information in the line of text in blue pencil ('*couldn't put Humpty together again*'). Remind them again that 'what' key words refer to the characters' actions – what they are doing. Ask the pairs to show you the words they have underlined in the text or ask the children to share this as a class.
- Finally, circle and underline the 'what' information on your copy of the picture.
- Then show the class how the information in the picture and text are linked by drawing a line from the underlined words to the images you have circled in the picture: '*Kings men, Kings horses*' (who) and '*Couldn't put Humpty together again*' (what).
- Ask them if the problems in the 'Humpty Dumpty' nursery rhyme are similar to the problems Turtle experiences in this *Book Day Parade* picture and to explain why they think that.
- Discuss the information they have gathered and whether their predictions were correct.
- (*Turtle is standing near a small puddle on the pavement. His costume is torn. His friends, the Queen, Guards, and pantomime horse are around him. They are not able to help Turtle. Rabbit is cycling towards them holding something in the air.*)
- Encourage pairs to ask each other simple literal questions about the scene using the circled information they can see right there on the page, e.g., *Q. Who is wearing a torn costume? A. Turtle is wearing a torn costume. Q. What is Rabbit doing? A. Rabbit is cycling towards everyone. Q. Where are the Queens men? A. The Queen's men are standing around Turtle.*

## Session 28: Being a detective: Linking clues about feelings to the problem

**Lesson objectives** - to be able to:
a. draw on knowledge of personal emotions to identify character's feelings and actions from picture clues,
b. link picture and word clues and knowledge of vocabulary to ask and answer simple inference questions.

## Activity 3 - 'The Rescue': What might happen next?

*The discussion and predictions in this activity might offer links to role-play after the lesson and provide a good opportunity for creating a vocabulary word bank on the flipchart, which the children can refer to when writing.*
- Hand out the picture used 'by pairs' in the last activity.
- Explain that today they will be Inference Detectives. They will learn how to link clues in the pictures and text to ask and answer more in-depth 'who, what, where' questions. For example, they will be asking 'How do you know that?' and 'Why?' to help them find out more about the characters' feelings and make predictions about what might happen next.
- Revisit the information they have circled in the Activity 1 picture and invite them to share their literal questions and answers with the class.
- Next ask pairs to use their Viewers to search for clues that might explain what the characters are thinking and feeling. Ask them what sort of clues might help them? (*Expressions on the characters' faces and their body language*).

- Demonstrate how to successfully find clues about characters feelings. Explain that they need to place their Viewers on the bodies and faces of each character in the scene. Show them how the hole can be used to frame the character's individual expressions and their movements.
- Ask pairs to discuss what they think the characters are feeling or thinking and reasons why, based on their own experiences.
- Ask pairs to share the clues they have found with the class. For example:

*Turtle looks unhappy. He is showing everyone the front of his torn costume.*
*Crocodile is holding the other piece of the egg costume and looking guilty.*
*One of the Queen's Guards look puzzled, is scratching his head and looking puzzled.*
*The other guard is kneeling down to see if he can help.*
*The Queen and Turtle's friends look on sympathetically. They can't put his costume together again - it looks like a lost cause.*
*Rabbit is cycling towards Turtle looking excited. He is holding some sticky tape up high.*

- Using the clues they have gathered about the scene, ask the children what they think the problem is for the characters. (*No-one can help Turtle to put his costume together again.*) Do they think the problem can be solved? How?
- Ask pairs to search for a clue in the picture that links a character and an object in this scene with an event that happened earlier in the story. (*Rabbit talking about sticky tape in class.*) Can they predict how the problem might be solved? (*Rabbit uses his sticky tape to put Turtle's costume back together again because he wants to make friends after splashing Turtle.*)
- Then ask them to discuss why Rabbit might have deliberately splashed Turtle and his friends (e.g., *They were not listening when he was trying to tell them about 'sticky tape' in Show and Tell time. Or he felt left out because they had not asked him to join them on Book Day*). Can they explain why they think that? Are there clues that suggest he was upset with them?
- Then ask them to discuss what they think might happen next and why. (*After Rabbit mends Turtle's costume, they are all friends again. They have forgiven Rabbit for splashing them **because** they are grateful for his help.*)
- Finally invite the pairs to feed back their ideas and to give reasons for them. (For example: *Maybe Rabbit joins the friends, and they might all watch the parade together because they are friends again. Or maybe they are all invited to join the Queen and guards on the float **because** they are also wearing costumes with a nursery rhyme and fairy tale theme*).

## Session 29: Activity 3 - predicting - clues on a cover

*Use a varied and intriguing range of fiction and non-fiction covers - class discussion.*

**Lesson objectives -** to be able to:
a. link picture and word clues on book covers to predict story contents or information.

Show covers one by one of a selection of books from a range of fiction and non-fiction titles known to you.

- Ask the children if they think the book covers offer information about the contents inside? Can they explain the purpose of the title and picture on a cover? (*To offer clues about the book's contents*).
- Discuss how information and story book titles are different. For example:
  a. Covers of information books give key facts about the contents and often have drawings or photographs about the subject on the cover.
  b. Storybook covers usually rely on the illustrations and key word clues in the title to suggest the main theme of the story.

- Discuss each book in turn: ask the class to see if they can correctly predict what the contents of the books might be about from the clues in the pictures and the key words in the titles. Can they tell you whether the book is a story or factual from these clues?

**Plenary:** Ask the children if they now notice when they are making predictions. How do they know when they are predicting? How often do they predict correctly? What do they find they use their prediction skills for mostly? Congratulate them on being Super Inference Detectives and Literal Patrollers!

**Extension: Activity 4 (Optional) – Draw a book cover**
- They choose one of the book titles you have written on the flipchart (unfamiliar titles).
- They circle the key words in the title to find information for drawing the cover details.

OR

- They write or draw what they think the book is about and discuss with a partner how the 'who, what, where' information and clues in the title helped them to create their book cover.

# Unit 4 (Part 1): Summarising and retelling – sequencing – overview of Sessions 30 and 31

**Lesson objectives – to be able to:**

- gather literal key words to ask and answer 'who', 'what', 'where' questions to retell stories,
- retell a story in sequence and in their own words using Three-Finger or Five-Finger prompts.

**What you need (see resources p. 219–253)**

**Items:** Flipchart; teacher – copy of graphic organisers, pens, paper, blue tack; class – red, blue, green pens, retelling word labels ('First, 'Then', 'Last'), Activity 4 envelopes
**Puppets:** Literal Patroller, Detective
**Posters:** Literal Patroller, Detective, Five-Finger Retelling Map, Using Our Senses
**Graphic organisers (pages 235–241):** Three-Finger Retelling Map, Five-Finger Retelling Map, WWW Key Word Organiser
**Pictures:** Photocopiable picture booklet *The Book Day Parade*, 'Show and Tell', p. 1, 'In the Park', p. 2, 'The Photo', p. 3, 'Sitting on the Wall', p. 4, 'The Fall', p. 5, 'The Rescue', p. 6, 'Celebrations', p. 7
**Multisensory aids:** Picture Viewer, hand signs, Riskometer, discussion cue cards, 'Brilliant Book Talk' chart

**Summary of Sessions 30–31** (teacher/class, groups, and pairs):

**Session 30** – Introducing Three-Finger Sequencing prompts ('First, Then, Last') – class discussion
**Session 31A** – Retelling a story in your own words – in the correct order
**Session 31B** – Introducing Five-Finger Sequencing – 'First, Then, Next, After that, Last'

**Consolidation/extension** – Listening to an audio version of a familiar fairy tale or short story and using the Three- or Five-Finger graphic organiser to draw or write the order of events in the boxes, then retelling the story from the information gathered

**Further extension** – Practising writing their own 'who, what, where' literal questions and answers about these stories to support self-assessment (see guidance and activities p…)

# Teacher notes

(These teaching sequences can be divided into smaller sessions as required)

### 'Read, tell, share – Who? What? Where?'

Retelling and summarising are complex skills that are a useful first indicator of a child's real engagement and basic understanding of the author's meaning. These skills help readers to 1) select the most important points from the text and pictures, and 2) to retell the key information in their own words in logical order, and with clarity, e.g., problem, events, and resolution within the story.

Unit 4 (Parts 1 and 2) demonstrates how young children can begin the process of summarising and retelling the main points of a story by first drawing on their literal enquiry skills to set the scene (e.g., 'Who is in the story?' 'What are they doing?' 'Where are they?' 'Where is the action taking place?'). Once this early retelling stage is established, the children can then include the main character's problem in their summary and 'what happens in the end'.

### Recap: Being a Detective – making predictions

(Detective puppet could ask the questions and Riskometer could be used to encourage participation)

- Super readers make predictions before, during, and after they read. Why do they do this? (*To check they understand what is happening in the story.*)
- How do you make predictions as you read? *1) We use what we know, 2) We use 'who, what, where' information, 3) We use clues on the page to work out what might happen next.*
- How do your own experiences in life help you to make predictions about what might happen to characters in stories? Give an example. (*By learning that things you do have consequences – 'cause and affect'. For example: if you go out in rain without a coat you will get wet*). Ask them to think of another situation in life.
- What word do you use to explain the reason why something happened (the cause of something happening), e.g., *I am wet 'because' I went out in the rain without my raincoat.*)
- Can they explain the purpose of the title and picture on a cover? (*To offer clues about the book's contents.*)

Explain to the class that in the next sessions they will learn how to:

- Summarise *(select the main ideas about a story or information).*
- Retell a story in your own words and in the order events happen.
- Discuss how sharing a favourite story is fun and helps you to check/show you understand what is happening and why.

## Session 30: Activity 1 – 'Little Red Riding Hood': Three-finger sequencing ('first, then, last')

**Learning objectives** – to be able to:
a. identify key information about a simple story, e.g., nursery rhyme (who the story is about, what they do in the story and what happens in the end),
b. identify the beginning, middle, and end of a simple story,
c. retell events in the correct order using sequencing words.

Begin by asking the children if they enjoy retelling stories to their friends. Do they find it easy or difficult? Why? (*Perhaps the Detective puppet could volunteer to retell a familiar fairy story in his own words, e.g., 'Little Red Riding Hood' – and muddle the order up.*)

For example:

*One day Little Red Riding Hood went to see her Granny with a basket of food.*
*A woodcutter was cutting down trees. He heard a loud scream and ran to the cottage.*
*Her Granny lived in a small cottage deep in the woods.*
*On her way she met a wolf and told him where she was going.*
*When Little Red Riding Hood walked into Granny's room,*
*The wolf ran to Granny's house and shut Granny in a cupboard.*
*She said, 'Granny, what big eyes you have!'*
*'All the better to hear you with!' said the wolf.*
*'Granny, what big ears you have!'*
*'All the better to see you with!' said the wolf.*
*'Granny, what a big nose you have!'*
*'All the better to eat you with!' said the wolf.*
*'Granny, what big teeth you have!'*
*'All the better to smell you with!' yelled the wolf.*
*He saw the wolf chasing Red Riding Hood and knocked him to the ground. He heard a rumpus from the cupboard. He opened the cupboard door, and Granny leapt out.*
*Then he ran out and was never seen again.*

- Ask them if they found this retelling of the Little Red Riding Hood story difficult to listen to. Why? (*The events in the story were retold in the wrong order.*)
- Agree that when you retell a story, first you need to summarise. Explain that summarising involves selecting the main information about the story (e.g., *who it is about, what the characters do in the story and what happens in the end*).
- Once you have gathered this key information, you can retell the beginning, middle, and end of the story in the order the events happened.
- Point to the labels on the flipchart which contain the following starter words: First (*who the story is about*), Then (*what the characters are doing in the story*, Last (*how the story ends*). Explain that by retelling it in order, the listener will have a clear understanding of the beginning, middle, and end of the story.
- Now model how to summarise and retell the Red Riding Hood story in the correct order using the starter words 'first, then, last', and finger actions 1, 2, 3 to emphasise the

beginning, middle, and end of the story. As you say 'first, then, last' – refer to each finger in turn. For example, point to:

a. the thumb on your left hand and say: *'**First**, Red Riding Hood meets a wolf on the way to her Granny's house.*

b. the next finger and say: *'**Then**, the wolf gets to Granny's house before Red Riding Hood and shuts Granny in a cupboard. When Red Riding Hood arrives, the wolf pretends to be granny and chases her round the house.*

c. the following finger, and say: *'**Last**, Red Riding Hood and Granny are rescued by a woodcutter and the wolf runs away and is never seen again'.*

- Explain that to retell a longer version of the story you might include more sequencing words, e.g., 'first, then, next, after that, last', using all five fingers to indicate the order of events from beginning to end. Tell them that they will have an opportunity to do this in the next session. First, you want them to practise using three fingers to retell simple nursery rhymes.

- Model how to retell three lines of the simple nursery rhyme (e.g., 'Hickory Dickory Dock') in the correct order using Three-Finger actions and the words 'first, then, last' to emphasise the beginning, middle, and end of the story. For example, point to the thumb on your left hand and say:

*'**First**, the mouse ran up the clock.*
(the next finger and say...)
*'**Then**, the clock struck one'.*
(the following finger, and say...)
*'**Last**, the mouse ran down.*

- Ask the children to join in with you as you repeat these words and actions.
- Then ask them to practise retelling other short nursery rhymes in their pairs using Three-Finger actions to help them identify the beginning, middle, and end of events (e.g., 'Jack and Jill', 'Little Bo Peep', and so on). For example:

(Beginning) *'**First**, Jack and Jill went up the hill to fetch a pail of water'.*
(Middle) *'**Then**, Jack fell down and broke his crown'.*
(End) *'**Last**, Jill came tumbling after'.*

**Session 31A: Activity 2 – Retelling key information ('first, then, last')**

(Activity A for less confident readers – for more able readers see Activity B)

**Learning objectives** – to be able to:

a. summarise and record key information about the characters in a story (what they are doing, where they are and what happens to them in the end),

b. retell events in a story accurately in the order they happen using their own words and sequencing word stems to guide this.

**Activity: 'Humpty Dumpty' Retelling in order in my own words using picture narrative**

*(It might be necessary to seat the children at tables for this drawing activity)*

Hand out pencils and the Three-Finger Retelling graphic organiser (see p. 237).

- Explain that the next activity will help them to practise retelling the Humpty Dumpty story in the correct order and in their own words, using 'First, Then, Last' to guide them.
- Hold up a copy of the sequencing graphic organiser. Draw their attention to the three empty boxes on the page. Explain that they will be asked to draw a picture in each box that tells the story of Humpty Dumpty at each stage of the rhyme. Show them the headings Beginning, Middle, and End at the top of each box. Tell them that these words refer to a part of the story. Then point to the words 'First', 'Then', 'Last' at the bottom of the boxes. Remind them (using the Three-Finger actions) that these word prompts will help them to retell the story in their own words in the correct order.
- Ask them to look at the copy of the graphic organiser on the flipchart. Point to your drawing of Humpty Dumpty sitting on a wall in Box 1. What is Humpty doing in this picture?
- Then invite them to recite the first line from the Humpy Dumpty rhyme out loud with you: 'Humpty Dumpty sat on a wall'. Repeat it. Then ask the children to quickly draw an image of this in Box 1 of their own graphic organisers (allow five minutes).
- Then point to your drawing in Box 2 on the flipchart and ask: 'Then what happened to Humpty Dumpty?' Recite the next line of the rhyme together (*'Humpty Dumpty had a great fall'*). Tell them to draw this in Box 2 of their organiser.
- Next ask them to look at the drawing in Box 3, 'What was the last thing that happened? Ask them to recite the end of the rhyme (*'All the king's horses and all the king's* men *couldn't put Humpty together again'*). Tell them to draw a picture of this in the last box on their graphic organiser.
- Discuss how easy or difficult they found this activity. Did they repeat the line of the rhyme in their heads to help them draw the scene? Or did they ask themselves questions to help them draw the characters and their actions? For example, 'Who is this rhyme about?' 'What do the characters look like?' 'What are they doing?' 'Where are they in each scene', and 'What happened to them after that?'
- Next ask the children if they remember the three words used with finger actions to retell a story in order. Invite them to show you. Then ask them to help you place the 'First, Then, Last' labels under the correct drawings on the flipchart.
- Finally demonstrate how to retell the story *in your own words* from beginning to end using the 'First, Then, Last' Three-Finger word prompts:

*'First… Humpty sat on a wall'.*
*'Then… Humpty fell off the wall and hurt himself'.*
*'Last… all the King's men couldn't save Humpty'.*

- Draw their attention to the words 'First, Then, Last' listed in order on their graphic organisers under their drawings. Ask pairs to take it in turns to retell the Humpty Dumpty story in their own words (in the order they have drawn their pictures), using 'First, Then,

Last' and finger actions to guide them. Emphasise 'their own words', so they don't just say the rhyme.

- Invite volunteers to hold up their pictures and retell their versions of the story to the class.
- Discuss how easy or difficult they found this activity. Did the words in the boxes, finger actions, and information in their drawings help them to retell the Humpty story accurately in their own words? If it was difficult, explain that they will be able to practise these skills further over the next sessions.

**Session 31B: Activity 3 – Introducing five-finger sequencing ('first, then, next, after that, last')**

**Learning objectives** – to be able to:
a. summarise and record key information about the characters in a story (what they are doing, where they are, what the problem is, how the characters try to resolve the problem and what happens in the end),
b. draw on knowledge of vocabulary and story structure to retell events accurately in the order they happen using their own words and sequencing word stems to guide this.

For those children who want a greater challenge than Three-Finger retelling activities, encourage them to use the retelling prompts and actions shown in the Five-Finger graphic organiser (p. 238).

These extended word prompts and actions will help them to retell a range of longer nursery rhymes and familiar short stories in the correct order. This might involve a group using finger activity to retell the story as narrators while others in the group re-enact it using play dough or story-bag figures. For example, they might like to revisit the Little Red Riding Hood story and retell the story using Five-Finger actions and sequencing words, 'First, Then, Next, After that, Last'.

*The graphic organiser has boxes for the children to draw each stage of the story in order.*
- It reminds them that you need to say *who* it is about, *what* they are doing, and *where* they are.
- Finger prompts can be added as the stories increase in length – till all five fingers are in use to retell the story in order (as a group retelling or taking turns to retell each stage), e.g., 'First, Then, Next, After that, Last'.
- As the stories increase in length, the children are then encouraged to use the sentence stem: 'In the beginning...' (rather than 'First').
- They are also prompted to identify the problem. Then how it is solved in the end, using: 'In the end...' (instead of 'Last').

For example (using Little Red Riding Hood):
   **First (In the beginning)** *a girl called Little Red Riding Hood meets a wolf on her way to her Granny's cottage in the woods.*
   **Then**, *Little Red Riding Hood tells the wolf where she is going with her basket of food and the wolf runs to Granny's cottage and shuts Granny in a cupboard.*

**Next,** *the wolf puts Granny's clothes on and waits for Little Red Riding Hood to come to the house.*

**After that,** *Little Red Riding Hood walks into Granny's room and the wolf jumps out of bed and tries to eat her.*

**Last (In the end)** *A woodcutter is chopping trees nearby when he hears a loud scream and runs to the cottage. He knocks the wolf to the ground, opens the cupboard door and Granny leaps out. The wolf runs out of the house and Red Riding Hood and Granny never see him again.*

- Tell them that they will find out how to retell the main points of a less familiar story in the correct order and in their own words in the next session.

**Consolidation/extension:** Listen to an audio version of a familiar fairy tale or short story using the Three- or Five-Finger graphic organiser to draw or write the order of events in the boxes. (It might be helpful to pause the tape to give them time to write or draw.) Then retelling the story from the information they have gathered.

**Further extension:** Practising writing their own 'who, what, where' literal questions and answers about these stories to support self-assessment. (Please see guidance and photocopiable activities on p....)

# Unit 4 (Part 2): Summarising and retelling – overview of Sessions 32–36

**Lesson objectives** – to be able to:

- identify the theme (central, recurring idea) in a familiar text,
- ask and answer literal 'who, what, where' questions to identify the main ideas in a story,
- draw on knowledge of 'cause and effect' to identify the characters' problems, and solutions to these,
- summarise the main ideas of a picture narrative in their own words,
- retelling a story in sequence using finger prompts ('In the beginning, Then, Next, After that, In the end').

**What you need (see resources, p. 219–253)**

**Items:** Flipchart, red, blue, green felt tip pens/crayons
**Graphic organisers:** large copies of 'Character's Feelings, Problem, and Solution', 'Five-Finger Retelling Sequencing Map'
**Pictures:** Photocopiable picture booklet (*The Book Day Parade*)
**Posters:** Author, Literal Patroller, Detective, Using Our Senses
**Multisensory aids:** Picture Viewer, literal questions hand signs, Riskometer, 'Brilliant Book Talk' chart

**Summary of Sessions 32–36** (teacher/class, groups, and pairs):

**Session 32** – Being a detective: Identifying the theme of a story
**Session 33** – Being a detective: Identifying characters' feelings

**Session 34** – *The Book Day Parade*: Feelings and problems at the beginning of the story

**Session 35** – *The Book Day Parade*: Recording characters' problems and solutions

**Session 36** – Retelling: Beginning, Problem, and Solution – *The Book Day Parade*

**Consolidation/Extension** – Role-play and retelling of the beginning, middle, and end of familiar tales to consolidate skills. Teacher hot-seating to encourage children's questions about stories (to support their understanding). Practising writing own 'who, what, where' literal questions and answers about stories to support self-assessment. (Guidance and photocopiable activities.)

# Teacher notes

(4 x 30-minute teaching sequences which can be divided into smaller sessions as required)

### Retelling – Beginning, Problem, and Solution

When children are taught to summarise and they are given the opportunity to listen regularly to others using this skill, their reading comprehension improves significantly. Summarising and retelling guidance helps young children to build an overall understanding of picture narrative, text information, story structure, and chronological reporting. It also provides them with a basic and familiar writing-frame guide.

Part 2 of Unit 4 focuses on consolidating children's summarising and retelling skills by modelling how to 1) identify the theme of a story, 2) select the main ideas of the narrative, 3) identify the problems and solutions for the characters, and 4) retell what happens in the story from the beginning to the end in the correct order. In addition, these sessions help young readers to understand the theme of a story by helping them to identify how the characters' emotions, behaviour, and motives link to the problems and solutions in a story.

### Recap retelling

*(Detective puppet could ask the questions and Riskometer could be used to encourage participation.)*

- What does the word summarise mean? (*Selecting the main ideas about story information*).
- How does asking literal questions help you to retell a story? (*Asking literal questions helps you to gather and retell the who, what, where information about the characters, what they are doing and where they are in a story*).
- What method helps you to retell the main points of a story in the order the events happen? (*Using each finger in turn helps you to remember the words and order for each stage of a story*).
- Why does being able to retell a story in your own words mean you understand the author's meaning? (*Using words that have a similar meaning when you retell a story shows you have understood the author's message because you have a matching picture in your head of their ideas*).
- How does a Literal Patroller retell a picture story? (*Literal Patrollers gather literal 'who', 'what', and 'where' facts about the characters and objects, their actions, and places, they then retell the story in the order the events happen from the beginning to the end of the story*).

## Session 32: Activity 1 – Being a detective: Identifying the theme of a story

**Learning objectives** – to be able to:
a. identify the theme in a familiar text,
b. make inferences drawing on knowledge of 'cause and effect' to identify the characters' problems, and solutions,
c. make inferences drawing on knowledge of other stories to identify the characters' problems, and solutions,

Explain that to retell a story you need to be both a Literal Patroller and an Inference Detective. You need to summarise the information (select the main ideas) identify the problems, and retell what happens to the characters from the beginning to the end in the correct order, for example:

a. the theme of the story (*the topic – what it is about, the moral of the story/author's message, e.g., how consequences have actions*),
b. the key 'who', 'what', and 'where' facts about the characters and objects, their actions, and places where events are happening (e.g., *gathering Literal Patroller information*),
c. the characters' problems (*why they are unhappy*) and how the problems are solved in the end (*gathering Detective clues*).

Explain that storytellers use a variety of ways to help them begin retelling fairy tales and other types of stories. First, they introduce the theme of the story to the reader (the topic, or author's message – the recurring idea in the story). For example, story themes sometimes warn the listener or reader 'not to speak to strangers', or they compare good with evil... 'even if you are small, you can still challenge a giant and win'. Ask the class if this reminds them of a story they have read or heard, (e.g., 'Red Riding Hood', 'Jack and the Beanstalk').

- Themes often ask the reader to pay attention to something that will be help them and others in life. For example, the theme in the story of Goldilocks shows how personal actions can affect others.
- Give the children a quick summary of the Goldilocks story. (*You could use picture cards here to support this*).
- Then ask them if they can explain how Goldilocks upset the Three Bears in the story and why her actions were thoughtless and unkind. They might say something like:

*Goldilocks didn't know the Bears – but she went into their house, sat at their table, ate baby bear's food, and then slept in his bed.*
*She was being selfish and only thinking of herself.*
*She gave the Bears a fright when they found her in their house. In the end she ran away and did not say sorry.*

- Remind the children of 'cause and effect' (see Prediction Sessions 25 and 26) – how thoughtless actions can cause problems, e.g., Baby Bear was hungry and upset because Goldilocks ate all his porridge.
- Ask them to think how she might have solved the problem or made things better in the end? (e.g., *Goldilocks could have said sorry and invited them to her house for tea*).

- Then discuss the theme of Goldilocks and Three Bears. What message might the author have for the reader? (e.g., *think about your actions - they can hurt others*).

## Session 33: Activity 2 - Being a detective: Identifying characters' feelings

**Learning objectives** - to be able to:

a. draw on their knowledge of other texts to identify problems and solutions for characters,

b. draw on their own experience to identify character's emotions from clues in pictures and text.

- Remind the children that in the last session they discussed the theme of 'Goldilocks and the Three Bears' (e.g., *think about your actions - they can hurt others*), and how the theme suggests the type of problem in the story before retelling the order of the events.
- Explain that not all stories have a happy ending where the characters solve their problems (e.g., *in the original Humpty Dumpty rhyme no-one could put him together again*). But if you are a Detective, you might predict how the problems could be solved if the story were told differently...
- Discuss the role of a story Detective. What is the difference between a Literal Patroller and an Inference Detective? What can a Detective do that a Patroller cannot do? (*Literal Patrollers can only see what is right there on the page. Inference Detectives can find clues and link this information with the facts about the characters and their feelings to help them identify problems and work out solutions*).
- Explain that today the children will use their Detectives skills to think more about the characters' feelings to understand how emotions are linked to problems and solutions.
- Clarify the children's understanding of the words 'problem' (*a situation that causes difficulty for the character/s*) and 'solution' (*a way to deal with the difficulty successfully*).
- Ask them to come up with five problems. Then write them down on the board and invite pairs to think of a solution for each.
- Check they can identify 'problems and solutions' in a variety of stories that are familiar to them. For example, revisit 'Goldilocks and the Three Bears' and discuss Baby Bear's problem at breakfast time. Why was he upset? (e.g., **The problem** is that Baby Bear is upset **because** Goldilocks has eaten all his porridge and he is hungry).

What could Baby Bear do to solve the problem? (e.g., *Baby Bear might ask Daddy and Mummy Bear to share their porridge with him.*)

- Ask them to describe how they think Baby Bear might feel about his problem (*sad, angry, fed up, anxious*).
- Then ask how he might feel if there is a solution? (*Relieved, happy, pleased etc.*)
- Discuss further what it feels like to have a problem. Do problems make them feel worried, for example, or fed up? Can they think of other emotions they feel when things are difficult? (*Sad, angry, bothered etc.*)
- Invite them to give examples of times when they have felt these emotions.
- Draw the children's attention to a selection of emojis on the flipchart or your own drawings of facial expressions. Discuss each expression and the feelings associated with it.

- Give them an example of body language and a facial expression that suggests you are 'happy'.
- Ask them what your expression suggests you are feeling. Then point to the 'happy' emoji on the flipchart. Talk about the situations that make you happy. Next ask them to give you some examples of times they feel happy.
- Invite them now to use facial expressions and body language to act out 'angry, sad, confused, happy' feelings, as you call each word out.
- Discuss when they have felt any one of these emotions and what happened to change these feelings.
- Explain that Detectives look for clues in pictures and text that suggest how the characters might be feeling. They link this information (e.g., *expressions on the characters' faces and their actions*) with their own experiences of emotions to help them work out what the problem and solution might be for the character.
- Show pictures from a familiar story and talk about the actions and the expressions on the characters' faces.
- Discuss how the characters' actions and facial expressions suggest they have a problem (e.g., *The characters might appear confused or unhappy when they have a problem*). In what way might their facial expressions suggest they have solved the problem? (e.g., *The characters might appear smiley at the end because their problems have been solved*).
- Tell them that in the next sessions they will be using their skills as Detectives to search for clues that suggest how the characters are feeling and what their problems and solutions might be in *The Book Day Parade* story.

## Session 34: Activity 3 - *The Book Day Parade* - feelings and problems at the beginning

**Learning objectives** - to be able to:
a. draw on knowledge of other texts to identify characters' problems and solutions,
b. draw on own experience to identify character's emotions from clues in pictures,
c. make inferences and draw on knowledge of 'cause and effect' to identify the characters' problems, and solutions to these,
   - Remind the children that in the last session they talked about character's feelings and about problems in stories and how the characters solved them.
   - Talk about the 'cause and effect' situations discussed in other sessions - that the outcome of some actions can cause problems for the characters (e.g., *Goldilocks causes a problem for Baby Bear and upsets him because she has eaten his porridge*).
   - Explain that today the children will use their Detectives skills to search for picture clues in *The Book Day Parade* story that will help them to think more about the characters' feelings, their problems, and how their problems are solved in the end.
   - Draw their attention to the *The Book Day Parade* illustrations on the flipchart. Point out that the pictures are in the order the events happen in the story.
   - Then point to the expression on the characters' faces and how they are interacting with each other. Explain that the characters' facial expressions and actions help the reader to work out how they are feeling, what their problems are, and how their problems might be solved in the end.

- Talk first about the obvious problem in the story that relates to the Humpty Dumpty rhyme and *The Book Day Parade* story (e.g., *Turtle has a problem when he falls off the wall and the Humpty Dumpty costume he is wearing is torn and he can't mend it*). Point to Pictures 5 and 6 on the flipchart and ask them to describe Turtle's expression and body language (e.g., *sad, and fed-up*).
- Then hand out Viewers to pairs and copies of *The Book Day Parade* illustrations (stapled together as a picture book).
- Invite pairs to be Detectives again and look for a character in the story who has a problem that is less obvious.
- Explain that you want them to look carefully at the first picture and examine the faces and actions of each character. Remind them to use their Viewers to help them search for clues that suggest how each is feeling and whether they have a problem in this scene. (*Remind them to place the hole of their Viewer on a character's face and body to help them focus on their expression and actions*).
- Who has the problem in the first picture? For example, who looks upset, fed up, cross, or sad? Why might they have a problem?
- Then ask the pairs to share their ideas with the class and explain why they think the character is 'unhappy' (using the word 'because').
- *It might be useful at this point to note down the children's comments on the flipchart or audio record them for reference later.*
- Explain that in the next session they will continue as Detectives to look more closely at Rabbit's problems and whether he finds a solution to them in the end.


**Session 35: Activity 4 – *The Book Day Parade* – recording characters' problems and solutions**

**Learning objectives** – to be able to:
a. draw on own experience to identify character's emotions from clues in pictures,
b. make inferences and draw on knowledge of emotions to identify the characters' problems, and solutions,
c. discuss and record character's feelings, problems, and solutions to support the retelling process later.
  - Ask the children to explain the type of clues Detectives look for in pictures that suggest how the characters might be feeling (e.g., *they examine the expressions on the characters faces and their actions*).
  - Remind them that feelings are often linked to problems and solutions for characters in stories.
  - Point to the first *The Book Day Parade* picture on the flipchart ('Show and Tell' scene). Ask the children to continue in their Detective roles from the last session and imagine they are in Rabbit's position. *'How would you feel if your friend was not listening to you?'*
  - Next ask them to check if Rabbit looks like he has a problem in the other scenes and why? Encourage the pairs to use their Viewers to examine Rabbit's expression and actions in the other pages of the story. Does he look unhappy throughout the story or does his expression change in the end?

- Then hand out the 'Character's Feelings' graphic organiser (p. 236) to pairs. Tell them that this will help them to gather information about Rabbit's problem and how he solves it in the end.
- Hold up an enlarged copy of the organiser and demonstrate how to use it.

For example:

a. Explain that in the first column ('Character's actions'), the pairs need to look carefully at the 'Book Day' pictures and take it in turns to write or draw what Rabbit is doing in each scene.

b. Then in the second column ('Character's feelings'), they need to draw the facial expression or write the word that describes how Rabbit is feeling at each stage of the story (see the 'Emotions' column).

c. Explain that the last column ('Emotions') contains examples of different expressions which offer them a guide to Rabbit's feelings. Each has a word beneath it describing the emotion it represents (e.g., *fed up, pleased, worried, cross etc.*).

- Give the pairs plenty of time to explore the pictures and note down their ideas.
- Then discuss what they have found out about Rabbit's actions and how he is feeling at the different stages of the story and record their ideas in each column on the flipchart graphic organiser.
- Ask the children why they think Rabbit is on his own in many of the pictures. Discuss how his facial expressions and actions in the columns suggest what his problem might be throughout the story (e.g., *Rabbit is still cross with the friends, he feels left out and might want to punish them – such as cycling through the puddle and splashing them.*)
- Then write down their thoughts in the 'Character's problem' box on the flipchart graphic organiser.
- Finally ask them if Rabbit's expression changes at the end. Does he find a way to solve the problem? How?
- Then, write their ideas in the 'Character's solution' box on the graphic organiser. They might say for example:

'Rabbit helps to mend Turtle's costume. This solves Turtles problem and makes them both feel much better'.
'He does not feel left out and unhappy anymore because Turtle and his friends have listened to him in the end'.
'Now they are all friends again'.

- Remind them that the problem for a character often suggests the theme of a story (e.g., the theme of 'Goldilocks and the Three Bears' could be: *think about your actions – they can hurt others*). Do they think the theme of *The Book Day Parade* might be similar and why? (e.g., *think about your actions – they can hurt or help others*).
- Explain that in the next sessions they will be using their skills as Literal Patrollers and Detectives to retell the beginning, middle, and end of a story using the clues they have found out about the characters' feelings and problems.

**Session 36: Activity 5 - Retelling - beginning, problem, and solution in *The Book Day Parade***

**Learning objectives** - to be able to:

a. ask and answer their own literal questions about the characters to identify the main ideas in a picture narrative,

b. summarise the main ideas of a picture narrative in their own words drawing on knowledge of vocabulary and information they have previously gathered,

c. retell a story in sequence using finger prompts ('In the beginning, Then, Next, After that, In the end').

- Draw the children's attention to *The Book Day Parade* pictures on the flipchart and emphasise that the illustrations are presented in the order the events happen.
- First ask the children to help you circle the 'who, what, where' information in each picture.
- Then remind them how to retell a story in the correct order using this information and the Five-Finger prompts.
- Next, invite them to retell the story with you, using the prompts ('In the beginning, Then, Next, After that, In the end').
- Model again how they need to hold their thumbs up and say *'In the beginning'* to start the Five-Finger retelling. Then point to the information in each picture on the flipchart. Remind them to look for who the story is about, what the character is doing, and where they are. For example:

  *In the beginning (who) Rabbit (what) tells his friends about sticky tape (where) in the classroom.*

  *Then, (who) Turtle and his friends (what) are wearing Book Day costumes (where) in the park.*

  *Next (who) Turtle and his friends (what) are waiting for the parade (where) in the street.*

  *After that (who) Turtle (what) tears his costume when (what) he falls off (where) the wall.*

  *In the end (who) the Queen's guards (what) cannot mend Turtle's costume (where) in the street. (Who) Rabbit (what) comes to help (where) on his bike.*

- Explain that you will now show the children how to retell the problem and solution in a story from a particular character's point of view with their help. (*The use of different animal masks and role-play might help to support retelling in the first person here.*)
- Together you will use the 'who, what, where' information and clues about feelings that the children mentioned in the last session. For example:
- (From Rabbit's point of view) Ask the children to use the Five-Finger retelling prompts with you as you point to rabbit's expressions in each picture:

  *In the beginning (the problem is that) Rabbit is upset with Turtle and his friends **because** they are not listening to him.*

  *Then Rabbit feels unhappy **because** he is not invited to join the friends in the park on their way to the Book Day Parade.*

*Next Rabbit is feeling cross with them and drives through a big puddle on his bike and splashes his friends.*

*After that Rabbit feels sad **because** Turtle and his friends have fallen off the wall and Turtle is wet and his costume is torn.*

*In the end Rabbit feels sorry that Turtle's Book Day is ruined **because** no-one can mend his costume.*

*The solution is that Rabbit helps Turtle and they are friends again **because** he mends Turtle's costume with his sticky tape.*

Or (from Turtle's point of view):

*In the beginning (the problem is) that Turtle does not listen to Rabbit **because** he wants to play.*

*Then Turtle and his friends do not ask Rabbit to play with them in the park **because** he is cross with them.*

*Next Turtle finds it difficult to see what is happening **because** his friends are crowding round him on the wall.*

*After that Turtle falls off the wall **because** he gets splashed with water and loses his balance.*

*In the end Turtle feels upset **because** his costume is torn and no-one can mend it.*

*The solution is that Rabbit mends his costume **because** he knows how to use sticky tape to put it together again – so they are all happy.*

- Then invite pairs to practise retelling the story from Turtle or Rabbit's point of view in their own words using Five-Finger prompts to help them and the information they have gathered in their graphic organisers.
- Congratulate the children on their skills as Super Literal Patrollers, Detectives, and Storytellers. They have shown they know how to share a story and check they understand the author's message. They are ready to extend their skills to include more information in the retelling process over the next sessions.

**Plenary:** Discuss how they feel now about the retelling process. What do they like or dislike about retelling? What new words or phrases do they know?

**Consolidation/extension:**
- Acting and retelling the story – Revisit the story and talk about the literal information, Detective clues, and order of events. Then invite small groups of children to dress up and re-enact *The Book Day Parade* story in the right order. Ask pairs to take it in turns to retell each stage as narrators. They will need to think who the characters are in the story, what they did, where they were, what the problem is, and how it was resolved.

For example, they may say:
**In the beginning the problem is that** *(Who) 'Rabbit (What) is telling Turtle and his friends about sticky tape (where) in the classroom, but they are not listening to him. This upsets Rabbit.*

*Then, (who)'Turtle and his friends (what) are wearing Book Day costumes (where) in the park on the way to the parade. Rabbit is upset because he feels left out.*
*Next (problem) (who)Turtle and his friends (what) are waiting for the parade (where) in the street. Rabbit is coming towards them on his bike. He splashes them all as he rides through the puddle on his bike because he is cross with them.*
*After that (who) Turtle's costume is torn because (what) he falls off (where) the wall.*
*In the end (problem): (who) the Queen's guards (what) cannot mend Turtle's costume.*
*So (solution) Rabbit comes to fix the problem with his sticky tape. Everyone is happy and they are all friends again.*

The teacher takes on a hot-seating role to encourage the children to ask them their own literal (and detective) questions about the story.

**Repeat the story retelling process** using a different fairy story or nursery rhyme (see Retelling graphic organiser for drawing or writing down events in sequence).

**Further extension:** Practising writing their own version of a different nursery rhyme using the Five-Finger Retelling organiser (see graphic organisers).

- Writing answers to 'who', 'what', and 'where' questions (see guidance and activities).
- Writing their own 'who', 'what', and 'where' questions about characters, objects, places, problems, and solutions they have identified and circled in a different picture or text (see photocopiable activities).
- Write their own version of *The Book Day Parade* with the option of changing the characters.
- **Listen to an audio version** of a familiar fairy tale or different nursery rhyme and use the Five-Finger graphic organiser to draw or write the order of events in the boxes (using who, what, where information). Then retell each stage of the story in turn in a group circle or to a partner using the finger prompts to help them.
- **Write their own** 'who', 'what', and 'where' questions and answers about the information they have in their graphic organisers (see guidance and activities). *Remind the children that written **questions** must always have a question mark at the end of the query and written **answers** must have a full stop at the end of the sentence.*

# Section 2: End-of-unit skills review plans (Units 1–4)

# Section 2: Foundation comprehension skills assessment resources

## Unit 1 (Part 1) - Book talk (listening, speaking, interacting)

The following resources provide a consistent method for reviewing pupils' listening, speaking, and communication skills over three different stages of development. For further information about assessment procedure, scoring, and analysis see Chapter 7, p. 74:

Phase 1: Baseline appraisal of listening, speaking, and interaction skills.
Phase 2: Intermediate evaluation of pupil's learning following Unit 1 'Book Talk' Sessions 1–5.
Phase 3: End of reception year assessment: Listening, speaking, and communication skills.

## Unit 1 (Part 1) – 'Book talk' review (Sessions 1–5)

Focus of this assessment:

- pupils' understanding of the importance of active listening and responding,
- pupils' understanding of the purpose of discussion and how to participate in small group and class discussion effectively.

### Sessions 1–5 objectives
To be able to:

- listen attentively and comment appropriately when being read to and during whole class discussions and small group interactions,
- make comments about what they have heard and ask questions to clarify their understanding,
- hold conversation when engaged in back-and-forth exchanges with their teacher and peers,
- participate in small group, class, and one-to-one discussions, offering their own ideas, using recently introduced vocabulary,

- express their ideas and feelings about their experiences using full sentences,
- use past, present, future tenses, and conjunctions, with modelling and support from their teacher.

## Unit 1 (Part 1) – Assessment procedure

### Reviewing listening, speaking, interaction skills – guidance for marking

Optional marking guidance is provided for Sections 1 and 2 (and space for writing responses to the questions). An example of how to award marks for each question is as follows.

If the pupil:

a. does not understand the question mark and gives no verbal response: 0 marks,
b. understands the question and gives a basic verbal response: 1 mark,
c. finds the question easy to answer and gives an articulate verbal response: 2 marks

### Section 1: Active listening (*questions/answers to support teacher–pupil conferencing process*)

Ask the following questions about the child's view and experience of listening and discussion. (You may wish to use an audio recorder to note their responses.)

Q: 1a) What are you doing when you are listening well? Can you give two or more examples of 'good listening'?

A: *'Good listening' examples: 1) I look at the person who is speaking. 2) I wait till they have finished before speaking. 3) I think about what they are saying. 4) I respond politely (respectfully). 5) If I do not understand what they are saying, I ask them to explain what they mean.*

Q: 1b) What are doing when you listen poorly? Can you give two or more examples of 'bad listening'? OR If you cannot tell the difference between 'good' listening and 'bad' listening skills, explain why.

A: *'Bad listening' examples: I don't look at the person who is speaking. I fidget or keep my hand up speak while they are talking. I interrupt them when they are speaking. I talk to someone else or change the subject in response to a question.*

Q: 1c) Can you listen carefully when you are being read to and during discussion in one or more of the following situations: one to one with an adult (*easy, OK, hard?*), with another child (*easy, OK, hard?*), in a small group (*easy, OK, hard?*), with the whole class (*easy, OK, hard?*).

**Section 1 Active listening: Total optional marks**      /6

# Section 2 (Unit 1)

Optional marking guidance is provided for Section 2 (and space for writing responses to the questions). An example of how to award marks for each question is as follows.

If the pupil:

- does not understand the question, e.g., no verbal response: 0 marks,
- understands question but needs support to answer, e.g., basic verbal response: 1 mark,
- understands and finds easy to answer, e.g., articulate verbal response: 2 marks.

**Section 2 (Unit 1) – Active discussion: Responding and engaging** (*questions/answers to support teacher–pupil conferencing process*)

Ask the following questions about the child's view and experience of listening and discussion. (You may wish to use an audio recorder to note their responses.)

Q: 2a) Can you explain how 'discussion' is different from simply 'talking'?

*A: For example: Discussion is not just about talking – it is about listening and sharing ideas with one or more people.*

Q: 2b) How does 'discussion' with others help you to learn? Can you give one or more examples?

*A: For example: Discussion helps me to:*

- *see things from a different point of view,*
- *ask questions to help me understand something better or others better,*
- *decide, plan, and solve a problem with others,*
- *think about and accept others' views,*
- *make links to other people's ideas.*


OR if you do not like taking part in discussion, please give your reason/s why.

Q: 2c) How might rules for 'good discussion' help you to talk about ideas and feelings with others?

*A: Rules for 'good discussion' examples: You think about what others are saying. You say why you agree, disagree, or want to add to what they have said. You listen and do not interrupt the person speaking. You take turns speaking. You are aware of everyone's feelings during discussion. You talk about your ideas using 'because' to explain them.*

Q: 2d) Do you ask for help when you do not understand something? Explain why you say that.

Q: 2e) Do you prefer to talk about your ideas and experiences to one person or in group discussions? Explain why you say that.

Q: 2f) Do you find it easier or more difficult to explain your feelings and ideas to adults? Explain why you say that.

**Section 2 Active discussion:   Total optional marks      /12**

**Total score for Sections 1 and 2: Listening, responding, discussion skills      /18**

Teacher comments and recommendations: _____

_____

_____

_____

**Section 2: (Unit 1, Part 1) Pupil self-assessment – Listening, speaking and interaction skills** (*aims and outcomes for pupils*)

Ask the pupil to think carefully about their listening and discussion skills. Do they find some listening and speaking activities easier or more difficult in class, paired, and group tasks? Explain that there is no 'right' or 'wrong' answer to the following questions. You are inviting them to 1) think about their learning, 2) to share how they listen to and discuss their ideas with others, and 3) to help them recognise their learning strengths and how they can improve their learning. (You may wish to use an audio recorder to note their responses.)

**1. Active listening** (with prompting and support from adults when necessary)

1a) I can tell when I am being a good listener.

Easy ☐   OK ☐   Hard ☐

1b) I can tell when I am being a poor listener.

Easy ☐   OK ☐   Hard ☐

1c) I can listen carefully when I am read to and during discussion:

| | |
|---|---|
| One to one with an adult | Easy ☐   OK ☐   Hard ☐ |
| With another child | |
| In a small group | |
| With the whole class | |

**2. Active discussion** – responding and engaging (with some prompting and support from adults)

2a) I can explain why 'discussion' is a different activity to simply 'talking'.

Easy ☐   OK ☐   Hard ☐

2b) I can explain why taking part in 'discussion' is fun and helps me learn.

Easy ☐   OK ☐   Hard ☐

2c) I can tell you some rules of 'discussion' that help me to share my ideas and feelings with others.

Easy ☐   OK ☐   Hard ☐

2d) I can argue my point of view in a discussion till it is understood…

| | |
|---|---|
| One to one with an adult | Easy ☐   OK ☐   Hard ☐ |
| With another child | |
| In a small group | |
| With the whole class | |

2e) I can comment on what I have heard in a discussion.

Easy ☐   OK ☐   Hard ☐

2f) I can ask for help if I do not understand something.

Easy ☐   OK ☐   Hard ☐

2g) I can talk clearly about my feelings, ideas, and experiences in full sentences using 'because' to explain them.

Easy ☐   OK ☐   Hard ☐

Self-assessment outcomes: Teacher's comments and recommendations:

_____

_____

_____

# Section 2: Foundation comprehension skills assessment resources

## Unit 1 (Part 2) - Reading for meaning (reviewing picture book comprehension)

This oral assessment focuses on the reader's basic concept of print, their language comprehension and unconscious use of literal, predicting, and clarifying skills over the following three different stages of development:

Phase 1: Baseline appraisal of emergent comprehension skills.

Phase 2: Intermediate – evaluation of pupil's learning after Unit 2 'Reading for Meaning' Sessions 6–8. (Note: Although the assessment primarily reviews end-of-unit (1–4) skills, it can also be helpful in assessing pre-instruction skills.)

Phase 3: End of Reception year assessment of reading comprehension skills.

Focus of this assessment:

- identifying key information about a story from the front cover of a picture book,
- understanding how picture comprehension supports the reading process,
- understanding why authors write and the purpose of reading for meaning.

**Making sense of the front cover of a picture book**

Young readers are encouraged to explore the front page of the *Little Fly and the Spider Trap* picture book with the assessor to demonstrate their ability to make meaning of unfamiliar images and print (see Teaching Unit 1 – Part 2).

FIGURE A1.1 *Little Fly and the Spider Trap*

**Illustration – setting:** An introduction to the picture book characters (see Figure A1.1).

Incy Wincy Spider is sitting on a wall with his web kit beside him. Sitting next to him is Dad Fly reading the paper, Mum Fly hovering above the wall, and Little Fly lying down on the wall in lazy pose (wearing white trainers and a baseball cap back to front). The book title and names of the author/illustrator are at the top of the page and there is a web spread across the bottom of the wall with further information about the story.

# Unit 1 (Part 2) – Reading for meaning skills (comprehending pictures and text)

### Sessions 6–8 objectives
To make sense of the front cover of a picture book by being able to:

- draw on knowledge of vocabulary to demonstrate understanding of picture narrative,
- understand that reading requires you to make meaning of both pictures and text,
- identify the key details on the front cover of a book,
- understand how pictures without words have meaning,

- identify characters, key events, and settings in picture narrative,
- identify and link information and clues in pictures and text to make meaning,
- offer explanations for why things might happen, making use of recently introduced vocabulary from stories,
- non-fiction, rhymes, and poems when appropriate.

## Assessment procedure

**Reviewing early reading for meaning skills:** Little Fly and the Spider Trap **picture book cover** (see photocopiable resource in Part 3, Section 3 p. 228)

Example of picture 'walk and talk' guidance.

*Step 1: Invite the pupil to look closely at the details on the cover of the picture book. Then follow this procedure:*

- Invite the reader to explore the cover of the 'Little Fly' picture book with you.
- Ask them if the cover is the front or back of the book. Then ask them to explain why they say that.
- Tell them to point to the title (then read it out to them – if they cannot read it themselves).
- Then ask them to locate the authors' names on the page.
- What else can they see on the cover that might give them some clues about the story inside?
- Ask them to point to the characters and describe each one in turn. Do they remind them of characters from other stories? Why do they say that? Could they belong to the same family? Why?
- Read out the title again and invite the reader to predict what they think the story might be about and why they say that.
- Do they think they might enjoy this story? Why? What do they like or dislike about the characters and why?

*Step 2: Explain that you would now like them to answer some questions about the cover of the story.*

**Assessment questions about the picture book cover** (*examples of questions/answers to support the teacher–pupil conferencing process*)

Ask the following questions about the child's view and experience of early reading. (You may wish to use an audio recorder to note their responses.)

Optional marking guidance is provided for each section.

Q: 1) Look carefully at the information on this page. Do you know if it is the front or the back of a book? Explain why you say that. *A: Example: I think it is the front of the book because it has a picture of the story, story title, and the names of the authors on it.*

*Optional mark      /1*

Q: 2) Can you tell me/point to the title and the names of the authors or illustrators? *A: The title of the book is* Little Fly and the Spider Trap. *The authors are Donna Thomson and Chrissy Morgan-Grant.*

*Optional mark      /1*

Q: 3) Can you point to 'the characters' in the picture?

A: *Example: Spider, Fly 1 lying down on the wooden fence, Fly 2 reading the paper, Fly 3 hovering above the fence.*

*Optional mark        /1*

Q: 4) Look carefully at the picture. Can you describe what each character looks like?

*Optional marks: 1 mark: accurate (simple) descriptions, 2 marks: accurate (detailed) descriptions*

Spider _____

Fly 1 _____

Fly 2 _____

Fly 3 _____

*Optional marks        /2*

Q: 5) Can you guess who the following characters are in the picture from their names? (see below) Explain why.

*1 mark for each character*

*Incy Wincy* _____

_____

*Dad Fly* _____

_____

*Mum Fly* _____

_____

*Little Fly* _____

A: *Example: I can guess who these characters are because of what they are doing and how they look.*

A: *OR I cannot guess who the characters are from their names because _____*

*Optional marks        /4*

Q: 6) Can you point to each character and tell me what they are doing?

*Optional marks: 1 mark only for incomplete answer, 2 marks for identifying what all the characters are doing.*

Incy Spider is _____

Dad Fly is _____

Mum Fly is _____

Little Fly is _____

A: *Example answer: Incy Spider is sitting, Dad Fly is reading (the paper), Mum Fly is hovering, and Little Fly is lying down.*

*Optional marks        /2*

Q: 7) Can you describe the setting of the story and where each character is in this scene (their positions).

*Optional marks: 1 mark only for incomplete answer, 2 marks for identifying the positions of all the characters.*

The setting is _____

Incy Spider is _____

Dad Fly is _____

Mum Fly is _____

Little Fly is _____

*A: Example answer: The setting is **outdoors** because the characters are **sitting on a wooden fence**. Incy Spider is **sitting next to** Little Fly **on the fence**. Little Fly is **lying down on the fence**. Dad Fly is **sitting beside** Little Fly and Mum Fly is **hovering in the air near** Dad Fly.*

*Optional mark:      /2*

Q: 8) Can you guess what the story might be about from the information on the page? Why do you say that? (Give them the title again if they cannot read it.)

*A: Example answers: The story is about Incy Wincy Spider and the Fly family because:*

- *Mum, Dad, and Little Fly are in the picture with Spider, or*
- *the title says Little Fly and the Spider Trap, or*
- *the information on the cover says the story is based on the Incy Wincy nursery rhyme.*

*Optional mark:      /2*

Q: 9) Do any of the characters remind you of another story? Why? Can you name the story or rhyme and tell me what it is about? *Optional marks: 1 mark only for incomplete answer; 2 marks for full answer.*

*Optional mark:      /2*

Q: 10) Can you tell me which character you like most and why? *Optional marks: /1*

Q: 11) Can you tell me if there is a character that you do not like? Why do you say that?

*Optional marks:      /1*

**Total Score:** Reading for meaning skills      /18

**Teacher comments and recommendations**

Teacher/pupil overview   Easy ☐   Instructional ☐   Hard ☐

Comments: _____

_____

Recommendations: _____

_____

# Unit 1 (Part 2) – Pupil self-assessment of picture comprehension (picture book cover)

### Reading for meaning – Aims and outcomes for children

Ask the pupil to think carefully about how they make sense of picture book information. What do they do when they read a picture book? Are they aware of the skills they use? Explain that there is no 'right' or 'wrong' answer to the following questions. You are inviting them to think about how easy or difficult it is to approach books and to discuss how they make meaning of images and print. (You may wish to use an audio recorder to note their responses.)

**I can…** (with some prompting and help from adults)

1) I can explain which is the front and which is the back of a book.

   I find this activity…   Easy ☐   OK ☐   Hard ☐

2) I can tell you or point to the title and the names of the author and illustrator on the front cover of a book.

   Easy ☐   OK ☐   Hard ☐

3) I can show you where the characters are in the picture.

   Easy ☐   OK ☐   Hard ☐

4) I can name characters or predict who they might be from information and clues on the page.

   Easy ☐   OK ☐   Hard ☐

5) I can describe each character I see in the illustration in detail using my knowledge of vocabulary and viewing skills.

   Easy ☐   OK ☐   Hard ☐

6) I can tell you what each character is doing and where they are.

   Easy ☐   OK ☐   Hard ☐

7) I can tell you the setting of the story and the position of each character in the scene.

   Easy ☐   OK ☐   Hard ☐

8) I can predict what the story might be about from the details on the cover of a book and explain how and why things might happen.

   Easy ☐   OK ☐   Hard ☐

9) I can explain why things might happen in a story using vocabulary and ideas from other stories, non-fiction, rhymes, and poems (when appropriate).

   Easy ☐   OK ☐   Hard ☐

10) I can tell you which character I like most and why.

   Easy ☐   OK ☐   Hard ☐

11) I can tell you if there is a character that I do not like and explain why I say that.

   Easy ☐   OK ☐   Hard ☐

**Teacher comments and recommendations – aims and outcomes for children**

Pupil's ability to comprehend details on a picture book cover:

Easy ☐    OK/Instructional ☐    Hard ☐

Comments: _____

_____

Recommendations: _____

## Assessment scoring – evaluating comprehension ability following each unit

For further information about scoring and analysis see Chapter 7, p. 74

- Easy – 70–100% (13–18 marks): Found the assessment easy overall and would benefit from a more challenging text to assess their comprehension strengths and weaknesses moving forward.
- Instructional – 40–65% (7–12 marks): Requires more explicit reading comprehension instruction at this level of text.
- Hard – 0–35% (0–6 marks): Needs to be given a less challenging text and explicit instruction that shows them how to use comprehension skills in smaller steps to support their understanding.

# Overall score for Unit 1 (Parts 1 and 2) – book talk and reading for meaning assessments

Part 1: Book talk – Listening, responding and engaging – Sessions 1–5:    Total score    /18

Easy ☐    Instructional ☐    Hard ☐    _____ %

Part 2: 'Picture Comprehension' – Sessions 6–8:    Total score    /18

Easy ☐    Instructional ☐    Hard ☐    _____ %

Book talk and reading for meaning:    Total score    /18

Easy ☐    Instructional ☐    Hard ☐    _____ %

# Section 2: Intermediate foundation assessments (Unit 2)

## Unit 2 (Parts 1-4) - Literal skills review: 'Who, what, where'

The aim of the post-instruction Unit 2 assessment ('Literacy Enquiry', Sessions 9–20), is to provide a guide for evaluating children's understanding of explicit meaning and literal self-questioning skills. This informal appraisal includes checking whether readers can 1) locate and retrieve information they see in pictures and text, and 2) gather, organise, and classify this information to respond to and generate simple literal questions following Unit 2 comprehension skills instruction. For further guidance on assessment procedure, scoring, and analysis see Chapter 7 p. 74 and go to Part 3, Section 3 of the book for photocopiable resources.

## Oral assessment of literal skills

### Unit 2 (Parts 1–4) – 'who, what, where' questioning (Sessions 9–23)

The teacher–pupil conferencing and self-assessment resources help to support the following evaluation of pupil's learning following the completion of:

Part 1 'Literal 'who' enquiry Sessions 9–12
Part 2 'Literal 'what' enquiry Sessions 13–16
Part 3 'Literal 'where' enquiry Sessions 17–20

### Focus of Unit 2 (Parts 1–4) – literal enquiry assessment

Evaluating whether the reader can…

- identify the characters in stories and gather literal information about what they are doing and where they are in each scene,

- ask and answer their own 'who, what, where' questions from the literal information gathered,
- clarify meaning of explicit information on the page using knowledge of vocabulary, other stories, and subject knowledge.

# Assessment procedure

## Using picture narrative to review literal skills

In this literal skills review, the front cover (Figure A2.1) and page 1 of the picture booklet *Little Fly and the Spider Trap* (Figure A2.2), provide reading material for reviewing pupil's literal understanding and 'who, what, where' self-questioning skills. The aim of this first part of the process is to explore some unfamiliar picture narrative with the reader to encourage them to share their spontaneous observations about the information on the pages before they answer a set of literal questions about the story. To support analysis later, it is helpful to use an audio recorder to capture the children's initial responses to the story, their retelling of the narrative and their answers to questions about the story.

FIGURE A2.1 *Little Fly and the Spider Trap*

FIGURE A2.2 **In the garden**

## Unit 2 – Picture walk and talk process for literal skills assessment

Refer to the front page and page 1 of *Little Fly and the Spider Trap* picture book (see photocopiable resources in Part 3, Section 3).

*Step 1: Revisit the* Little Fly and the Spider Trap *picture book cover and invite the pupil to look closely at the details in the picture. Then follow this procedure:*

● Discuss the character's names, what they look like, what they are doing, and where they are in the picture.
● Then ask the reader what the title says (give them the title if they cannot remember or read it).
● Next ask them to explore the illustration on page 1 of the picture book with you.
● Explain that you want them to begin by looking carefully at the picture (offer them the Picture Viewer to look through). Remind them how to use the Viewer to frame the actions and locations of the characters on the page.
● Then ask them to tell you what they can see 'right there' on the page (invite them to be Literal Patrollers). Ask them to tell you about the characters. Can they name them? What are they doing and where are they?
● Ask them to read the line of text with you, 'Incy wincy spider climbed up the waterspout', and the word in the speech bubble, 'Yum!' (without saying anything further about this).

*Step 2: Explain that you would now like them to retell what they can remember about the front cover and page 1 of the story. (See guidance on how to use the retelling graphic organiser on p. 172 to support analysis of retelling skills, Chapter 7, p. 76)*

## Unit 2, Part 4 – Consolidation: 'Who, what, where' enquiry skills

*Step 3: Explain that you would now like them to answer some literal questions about the characters in the illustration. You will then give them an opportunity to ask and answer their own literal questions if they can. (You may wish to use an audio recorder to note the child's responses). Space for noting down responses alongside marking guidance is provided. Paper and pencils are also required for pupils written responses where appropriate.*

The purpose of this part of the assessment is to establish whether pupils can:

- gather literal information about the characters, what they are doing and where they are in relation to other characters in a scene,
- answer 'who, what, where' questions about the characters (in a full sentence) and ask and answer their own literal questions using this information,
- clarify their understanding of the information they see on the page using their knowledge of the world, vocabulary, and characters' activities in other stories/rhymes.

## Examples of questions and answers to support teacher–pupil conferencing process

Optional marking guidance for each question is included.

### 1. Verbal answers to literal 'who, what, where' questions

Answer the following literal questions in full sentences (1 mark each). Indicate whether the question was easy, OK or hard for the reader to respond to in the box provided (optional).

Q: 1a) Who is in the garden? Name all the characters.

*A. Incy Wincy Spider, Bee, Caterpillar, Dad Fly, Mum Fly, Little Fly are in the garden.*

Easy ☐   OK/Instructional ☐   Hard ☐

Q: 1b) What is Dad Fly doing?

*A. Dad Fly is standing on a sandwich.*

Easy ☐   OK/Instructional ☐   Hard ☐

Q: 1c) Where is Little Fly?

*A. Little Fly is in a web inside the waterspout.*

Easy ☐   OK/Instructional ☐   Hard ☐

*Verbal answers to literal 'who, what, where' questions 1a–1c: Total marks      /3*

### 2. Written answers to literal 'who, what, where' questions

Can you write down the correct answers to these literal questions in full sentences? Indicate whether the question was easy, OK, or hard for the reader to answer in the box provided (optional).

*Optional marking for written answers – 2 marks for each answer:*

Q: 2a) Who is hovering over a sandwich in the grass?

A. *Mum Fly is hovering over a sandwich in the grass.*

Written answer: _____

Easy ☐  Instructional ☐  Hard ☐

Q: 2b) What is Little Fly doing?

A. *Little Fly is stuck/lying in Incy Spider's web.*

Written answer: _____

Easy ☐  Instructional ☐  Hard ☐

Q: 2c) Where is Incy Spider's web?

A. *Incy Spider's web is inside the drainpipe (spout).*

Written answer: _____

Easy ☐  Instructional ☐  Hard ☐

*Written answers to literal 'who, what, where' questions 2a–2c: Total marks     /6*

### 3. Own literal 'who, what, where' written questions and verbal answers

Q: 3a) Can you write down your own literal 'who' question about one of the characters in the story and give a verbal answer to your question in a full sentence? Indicate whether the question was easy, OK, or hard for the reader to answer in the box provided (optional).

(For example: *Q. Who is buzzing over a flower? A. The bee is buzzing over a flower.*)

*Optional marking: written/ verbal responses 2 marks question, 1 mark answer*

Own written 'who' question: _____

Verbal answer:_____

Easy ☐  Instructional ☐  Hard ☐

Q: 3b) Can you write down your own literal 'what' question about one of the characters in the story and give a verbal answer to your question in a full sentence? (For example: *Q. What is the caterpillar doing? A. The caterpillar is eating a leaf.*)

*Optional marking: written/verbal responses 2 marks question, 1 mark answer*

Own written 'who' question: _____

Verbal answer:_____

Easy ☐  Instructional ☐  Hard ☐

Q: 3c) Finally, can you write down your own literal 'where' question about one of the characters in the story and give a verbal answer to your question in a full sentence? (For example: *Q. Where is Incy Wincy Spider? A. Incy Wincy Spider is in the garden.*)

*Optional marking: written/ verbal responses 2 marks question, 1 mark answer*

Own written 'where' question: _____

Verbal answer: _____

Easy ☐   Instructional ☐   Hard ☐

*Own literal 'who, what, where' questions and answers 3a–3c: Total mark    /18*

## Parts 1–4 assessment – literal 'who, what, where' – literal questioning skills

**Analysing pupil responses to literal questions:**

- Does the pupil's answer relate to the explicit information in the picture narrative? Does the pupil have problems identifying literal information?
- Is the pupil engaged in the picture content? Has the pupil looked closely enough at the picture detail?
- Is prior knowledge being used in addition to the direct information in the picture narrative?
- Does the pupil understand the phrasing of the question/meaning of the vocabulary used in the story title, text, and in the questions?
- Does the pupil have problems expressing themselves?
- Does the pupil have problems with answering or asking literal questions?
- Does the pupil have problems writing down answers to explicit questions or writing their own literal questions?

### Teacher comments and recommendations

Teacher/pupil – literal skills overview Easy ☐   Instructional ☐   Hard ☐

Comments: _____

_____

_____

_____

Recommendations: _____

_____

## Assessment scoring
(See Chapter 7, p. 74–83 for further information)

**Evaluating comprehension ability following each unit**

- Easy – 70–100% (13–18 marks): Found the assessment easy overall and would benefit from a more challenging text to assess their comprehension strengths and weaknesses moving forward.
- Instructional – 40–65% (7–12 marks): Requires more explicit reading comprehension instruction at this level of text.
- Hard – 0–35% (0–6 marks): Needs to be given a less challenging text and explicit instruction that shows them how to use comprehension skills in smaller steps to support their understanding.

## Overall score for literal enquiry – Unit 2 (Parts 1–4)

*Identifying the extent the reader can locate and retrieve explicit who, what, where information from pictures and text to ask and answer questions.*

Part 1 Sessions 9–12 – 'Who' enquiry:            Total score      /8

Easy ☐    Instructional ☐    Hard ☐               _____

Part 2 Sessions 13–16 – 'What' enquiry:         Total score      /6

Easy ☐    Instructional ☐    Hard ☐               _____

Part 3 Sessions 17–20 – 'Where' enquiry:       Total score      /4

Easy ☐    Instructional ☐    Hard ☐               _____

Part 4 Sessions 21–23 – 'Who, what, where' enquiry review:   Total score      /18

Overall: Easy ☐    Instructional ☐    Hard ☐             _____

---

## Unit 2 (Parts 1–4) – Self-assessment of 'who, what, where' questioning skills

### Aims and outcomes for children – consolidating skills

Ask the pupil to think carefully about how they gather picture book information. Are they aware of the different skills they use to do this? Explain that there is no 'right' or 'wrong' answer to the following questions. You are inviting them to think and talk about how easy or difficult they feel it is to identify who, what, where information and generate and answer literal questions about information they see in a story. (You may wish to use an audio recorder to note their responses.)

Indicate whether the reader agreed that the task in the statement was easy, OK, or hard (optional).

**I can...** (with some prompting and help from adults)

1) I can identify 'who, what, where' information about the characters, actions, and places on the page to help me answer literal questions about the story.

    Easy ☐    OK ☐    Hard ☐

2) I can write correct answers to 'who, what, where' literal questions about the story in full sentences.

    Easy ☐    OK ☐    Hard ☐

3) I can identify 'who' information and write my own question about a character in the story.

    Easy ☐    OK ☐    Hard ☐

4) I can write down my own 'who, what, or where' questions about the characters in the story. I can demonstrate my literal understanding of the story by giving a correct verbal answer to my question in a full sentence.

    Easy ☐    OK ☐    Hard ☐

5) I know how to skim and scan for literal information using a Picture Viewer to help me ask and answer my own questions about characters, what they are doing, and where they are on the page.

Easy ☐  OK ☐  Hard ☐

**Teacher comments and recommendations** – Aims and outcomes for children: Literal skills

Easy ☐   OK/Instructional ☐   Hard ☐

Comments:

_____

_____

Recommendations:

_____

_____

# Section 2: Intermediate foundation assessments (Unit 3)

## Unit 3 (Parts 1-3) - Inference enquiry review

The aim of this informal appraisal is to assess whether young readers can apply the literal self-questioning and predicting skills they have learned to help them to consciously identify facts and clues, make links, and clarify meanings to support their understanding of pictures and text.

In addition, the review provides a teaching focus and a guide for assessing children's depth of understanding using picture narrative first, to support the development of text comprehension skills later. For further information about assessment procedure, scoring, and analysis see Chapter 7 p. 74 and Part 3, Section 3 of the book for guidance and resources.

The metacognitive process involved in all the inference teaching sequences helps to develop a conscious understanding of how to:

- gather literal information and clues to make inferences from the text,
- link details in titles, pictures, text clues, and their own experience to make predictions,
- predict what might happen based on what has been read so far (linked to their own knowledge and experience – cause and effect),
- draw on evidence in pictures and text to justify their answers to inference questions about the characters, actions, and places in a story,
- clarify the words, images, concepts which present the main points in a scene (who, what, where – right there!),
- draw on knowledge of vocabulary to understand texts.
- explain the writer's use of language and explain the overall effect of the text on the reader,

- ask themselves literal/inference questions, such as: What might happen next? Who? What? Where? Why?
- think about their responses, such as: 'How I know that…', 'Why I think that…'.

# Oral assessment of inference skills

### Unit 3 (Parts 1–3) – Making predictions and clarifying meanings (Sessions 21–29)

The teacher–pupil conferencing and self-assessment resources help to support the evaluation of pupil's learning after the following sessions are completed:

Part 1 Inference enquiry: Making predictions and clarifying meanings – Sessions 21–24,
Part 2 Inference enquiry: Understanding cause and effect – Sessions 25–26,
Part 3 Inference enquiry: Predictions and deductions – Sessions – 27–29.

It is advisable to audio record the readers' responses for accuracy. However, space is also provided for making notes alongside marking guidance. Paper and pencils are also required for pupils' written responses where appropriate.

# Unit 3 (Part 1) – Assessing inference skills: Predicting and clarifying (Sessions 21-24)

The front cover and pages 1–4 of *Little Fly and the Spider Trap* picture booklet illustrated by Chrissy Morgan-Grant provide the reading material for assessing pupils' inference skills (Unit 3 Parts 1–3) and their understanding of literal and inference questions ('who, what, where, why, how do you know that?') following explicit instruction.

**Focus of this assessment** includes:

- drawing on knowledge of who, what, where literal skills to begin deeper enquiry,
- identifying clues and making accurate predictions from literal information gathered,
- clarifying meanings of words, images, concepts using knowledge of vocabulary, other stories/ rhymes, and personal experiences of the world.

FIGURE A3.1 **In the garden**

## Inference skills review – picture 'walking and talking' comprehension procedure

*Step 1: Revisit the* Little Fly and the Spider Trap *picture book cover and page 1 of the book (Figure A3.1). Then follow this procedure to search for clues:*

- First ask them to read out the title on the picture book cover (give them the title if they are unsure).
- Then invite them to be Literal Patrollers. 'Who are the characters on the front cover?' 'What are they doing?' 'Where are they?'
- Next ask them to be Detectives: 'Do you think this story might be different to the nursery rhyme?' 'Why do you think that?'
- Turn to page 1 and invite them to be Literal Patrollers again. 'What can you see in the picture?' 'What is happening right there?'
- Then ask them to read the line of text with you, 'Incy Wincy Spider climbed up the waterspout.' Can they point to the 'waterspout' in the picture and explain what it is?
- Encourage them to be Detectives again. Do these nursery rhyme words link to clues in the picture that suggest there may be a problem for one of the characters? (Offer them the Picture Viewer to help them focus on the actions and locations of the characters.)
- Discuss any differences they may have noticed between the 'Incy Wincy' nursery rhyme and the unfolding story. Ask them to predict what might happen next to the characters and why they think that.

*Step 2: Ask them to retell the main points they can remember about the story so far. (They can refer to the cover and page 1 if necessary.)*

## Examples of questions/answers to support teacher–pupil conferencing process

*Step 3: Ask the following questions about the characters on page 1 (Figure A3.1) of the* Little Fly and the Spider Trap *picture book (note answers may vary and must relate to the pictures and text).*

Optional marking guidance is provided with each question. Indicate whether the question was easy, OK, or hard for the reader to respond to in the box provided (optional).

Q: 1) Look carefully at the title and the information in the picture and text. Select the key words and pictures that explain who the characters are and what is happening in the story.

*A: Example,* **Text/pictures***: 1 'Incy Wincy Spider' 2 'climbed up' / 'waterspout', 3 'Little Fly/web';* **Pictures only***: 4 Mum and Dad Fly / sandwich, 5 Bee/flower, 6 Caterpillar/leaf. (1 mark each for related key words)*

Easy ☐   Instructional ☐   Hard ☐

Total marks      /5

Q: 2) On page 1 the words say: 'Incy Wincy Spider climbed up the waterspout'. Look carefully at the picture. Can you think of another word for 'waterspout'? (2 marks)

*A: Example: 'drainpipe'*

Easy ☐   Instructional ☐   Hard ☐

Total marks      /2

Q: 3) Look closely at the characters in the garden and what they are doing. Do you think Mum and Dad Fly know where Little Fly is? Explain why you think that. (3 marks)

*A: For example: No, I do not think Mum and Dad Fly have noticed where Little Fly is. OR No, I do not think Mum and Dad Fly have noticed that Little Fly is stuck in Incy Wincy's web… because they are more interested in the sandwich.*

Easy ☐   Instructional ☐   Hard ☐

Total marks      /3

Q: 4) Look for clues on the page that suggest what Little Fly's problem might be. Then predict what you think might happen next and why.

(2 marks for clues, 6 marks for prediction)

*A: Little Fly is caught in a web, Spider is approaching and might harm him, Little Fly's parents cannot see he is in danger.*

Easy ☐   Instructional ☐   Hard ☐

Total marks      /8

**Total score 'inference' questioning skills (Sessions 21–24)      /18**

# Unit 3 (Part 2) – Assessing inference skills: 'Cause and effect' (Sessions 25 and 26)

**Focus of this assessment** – whether the reader can...

- draw on their literal skills to help them gather the facts,
- understand the meaning of 'cause and effect' in relation to predicting story outcomes,
- draw on prior experience and text clues to identify problems and explain what might happen next,
- clarify their understanding of words, images, and concepts through knowledge of vocabulary, other stories and understanding of the world around them,
- justify their predictions using 'because' to explain their ideas.

FIGURE A3.2 **On the roof**

## Inference skills – picture walk procedure

The first part of the review involves revisiting the front cover and page 1 of the picture booklet (Figure A3.1 'In the garden'). The reader is then introduced to page 2 of the picture narrative (see Figure A3.2 On the roof).

- Discuss the title on the cover and other text that refers to the 'Incy Wincy' nursery rhyme. Then ask who the characters are on the front cover. What are they doing? Where are they?
- Next introduce them to the next page. What can they see in the picture? What is happening 'right there'?
- Ask them to read the line of text with you, 'Incy Wincy spider climbed up the waterspout'. Can they point to the 'waterspout' in the picture and explain what it is?
- Discuss any differences they may have noticed between the 'Incy Wincy' nursery rhyme and the story.
- Can they predict what might happen next to the characters in this story and why they think that?
- Turn to page 2 and invite them to be Literal Patrollers once more. (Offer them the Viewer to help them patrol the two scenes in the picture for 'who, what, where' information). What can they see 'right there' on the page? Who is in the top scene? What are they doing?
- Then ask them to read out what Dad Fly is saying in the speech bubble ('Oh No!').
- What does the image in the thought bubble suggest Mum Fly might be thinking? Discuss the expressions on their faces and what this may mean.
- Then ask them to read the text in the main picture with you, 'Down came the rain…' What do they predict might happen next? Why do they say that? For example, *What might happen when the rain comes down? Will Little Fly escape the web? If so – how?*
- Next ask them to retell the points about the story they can recall so far.
- Finally explain that you will ask them a range of detective questions about the characters and what is happening in the story. Then you will give them an opportunity to ask and answer their own literal and detective questions about the characters and events if they can.

## Examples of questions/answers to support the teacher–pupil conferencing process

*Ask the following questions about the characters on pages 1 (A3.1) and 2 (A3.2) of the* Little Fly and the Spider Trap *picture book (note answers may vary and must relate to the pictures and text).*

Optional marking guidance is provided with each question. Indicate whether the question was easy, OK, or hard for the reader to respond to in the box provided (optional).

Q: 1) Why do you think Dad and Mum Fly are looking down the waterspout? (2 marks)

*A: Example: I think Dad and Mum Fly are looking down the waterspout because they are looking for Little Fly.*

Easy ☐   Instructional ☐   Hard ☐

Total marks      /2

Q: 2) Do you think Mum and Dad Fly can see Little Fly is in danger? Explain why you say that. (2 marks)

A: Example: Yes, I think they can see Little Fly is stuck in a web and in danger because Dad is saying 'Oh No!' and Mum Fly is imagining him lying on a plate ready to be eaten.

Easy ☐   Instructional ☐   Hard ☐

Total marks      /2

Q: 3) What do you predict might happen if they cannot solve Little Fly's problem? Explain why you say that. (2 marks prediction and 2 marks for justified answer)

A: Example: I think Incy Wincy Spider will climb up the spout and eat Little Fly if Mum and Dad Fly cannot solve the problem because Little Fly is stuck in the web and cannot get out without help.

Easy Instructional Hard

Total marks      /4

Q: 4) Dad Fly is pushing a leaf down the waterspout as the rainwater pours in. How do you think he plans to rescue Little Fly? (3 marks for prediction)

A: Example: I think Dad Fly plans to push a leaf down the waterspout so Little Fly can float out on it and escape the web.

Easy ☐   Instructional ☐   Hard ☐

Total marks      /3

Q: 5) What do you predict might happen next to Incy Wincy Spider in this story? Explain why you say that. (1 mark prediction for reference to nursery rhyme and 3 marks for own justified prediction)

A: Example: I predict that Incy Wincy Spider will escape down the waterspout because the nursery rhyme says he was 'washed out'. I predict that Incy Wincy Spider might run out of the waterspout if he sees the water rushing towards him. I say that because spiders do not like water and there is a lot of rainwater going down the waterspout.

Easy ☐   Instructional ☐   Hard ☐

Total marks      /3

Q: 6) Give two reasons why we make predictions about stories. (2 marks for each logical reason given)

A: Example: 1. Predicting helps me to think ahead and ask questions. I am more interested in a story when I am thinking about what might happen next. 2. Predicting helps me to understand the story better and to make connections with my own experiences.

Easy ☐   Instructional ☐   Hard ☐

Total marks      /4

**Total score 'inference' questioning skills (Sessions 25 and 26)      /18**

# Unit 3 (Part 3) - Assessing inference skills: Deducing and predicting (Sessions 27-29)

**The focus of this assessment** – whether the reader can:

- identify solutions and make accurate predictions about outcomes using their knowledge of emotions to understand the characters' motives,
- search for evidence by linking images and word clues to make logical deductions about the characters' motives,
- ask and answer in-depth questions to check their understanding of the text and author's intention,
- clarify their understanding of words, images, and concepts using the context to support this.

## The picture 'walking and talking' procedure

FIGURE A3.3 **Down the drain**

FIGURE A3.4 **Out came the sunshine**

The first part of the 'picture walk' involves revisiting the front cover, pages 1 (Figure A3.1) and 2 (Figure A3.2) and introducing pages 3 (Figure A3.3) and 4 (Figure A3.4) of *Little Fly and the Spider Trap* picture narrative to the reader as follows:

- Ask them to look at the picture book cover. Discuss the title and other text on the cover.
- Talk about the characters, what they are doing, and where they are in the story.
- What do they think will happen after this scene from the information they have gathered?
- Does it remind them of another story? Ask them to explain why they say that.
- Invite them to scan over the next two pages. What can they see in the pictures? What is happening 'right there'?
- Next ask them to read the line of text on page 1 'Incy Wincy Spider climbed up the waterspout'. Then on the following page, 'Down came the rain'. Can they point to the waterspout in the pictures and explain what it is and what they think its purpose might be?
- What is happening in the story on page 2? What are Mum and Dad Fly doing? Can they predict what might happen next to Little Fly and Incy Wincy Spider and give their reasons?
- Turn to page 3 and offer them the Picture Viewer to help them patrol the scene for 'who, what, where' information.
- Then ask them to read the line of text with you, '… and washed the spider out'.

- Invite them to discuss the details they can see on the page. What is happening? What are the characters doing? Was their prediction about Little Fly correct? Do they think this will create a problem for Incy Wincy Spider? Why do they think that?
- Finally ask them to turn to page 4 and look carefully for details in the pictures using the Viewer to help them. What can they see 'right there'? Who is in the scene? What are they doing and where are they in relation to each other?
- Then tell them to read the lines of text with you, 'Out came the sunshine… and dried up all the rain. And Incy Wincy Spider climbed up the spout again'.
- Ask them if they can find clues that suggest what is happening. Why do they think Incy Wincy Spider is climbing up the spout again? What do they predict might happen after this scene?
- Next invite them to retell the main points of the story.

Finally explain that you will ask them a range of detective questions about the characters and what is happening in the story. Then you will give them an opportunity to ask and answer their own literal and detective questions about the characters and events if they can.

## Examples of questions/answers to support teacher–pupil conferencing process

*Ask the following questions about the characters on pages 3 (Figure A3.3) and 4 (Figure A3.4) of the* Little Fly and the Spider Trap *picture book (note answers may vary and must relate to the pictures and text).*

Optional marking guidance is provided with each question. Indicate whether the question was easy, OK, or hard for the reader to respond to in the box provided (optional).

Q: 1) 'Incy Wincy Spider was 'washed out' of the waterspout?' Explain in your own words what happened to Spider in the waterspout. (1 mark: basic answer, 2 marks: articulate answer)

*A: Example: 'The words 'washed out' mean… 'poured out', 'flushed out', 'pushed out'. The water was flowing so fast it flushed Incy Wincy out of the waterspout.*

Easy ☐   Instructional ☐   Hard ☐

Total marks      /2

Q: 2) Little Fly and Incy Wincy Spider were 'washed out of the spout' together. Who do you think enjoyed it most? Why do you say that? (1 mark answer, 2 marks for a justified answer)

*A: Example: I think Little Fly enjoyed going out of the waterspout most because he had escaped from the web/because he looks like he is having fun floating out on the leaf.*

Easy ☐   Instructional ☐   Hard ☐

Total marks      /2

Q: 3) How do you think Incy Wincy Spider was feeling when she came out of the spout? Why do you say that? (1 mark answer, 2 marks for a justified answer)

*A: Example: I think Incy Wincy Spider was shocked when she came out of the spout in all the water because she looks upset and surprised / I think Incy Wincy was feeling fed up when she came out of the spout because Little Fly had escaped from her web.*

Easy ☐   Instructional ☐   Hard ☐

Total marks        /2

Q: 4) Was it still raining when Incy Spider went back up the spout? How do you know? (1 mark answer, 2 marks for a justified answer)

A: Example: No, it was not still raining when Incy Spider went back up the spout because it says 'Out came the sun and dried up all the rain. So Incy Wincy Spider climbed up the spout again'.

Easy ☐   Instructional ☐   Hard ☐

Total marks        /2

Q: 5) If Dad Fly could ask Little Fly a 'why?' question in the story, what question do you think he would ask him? What answer do you think Little Fly might give him? (2 marks for their own question, 2 marks their justified prediction)

A: Example: Q: 'Why did you go into the waterspout Little Fly?' A: 'I went into the waterspout because I wanted to see what was up there Dad'.

Easy ☐   Instructional ☐   Hard ☐

Total marks        /4

Q: 6) Look at the clues in the picture. Why do you think Incy Wincy climbed up the spout again? Give your reason. (2 marks for answer and 2 marks logical reason given)

A: Example: I think Incy Wincy climbed up the spout again to mend her web because she wanted to catch another fly for tea. I say that because the bag on her back says 'web kit' and the picture shows she is thinking about fixing the web.

Easy ☐   Instructional ☐   Hard ☐

Total marks        /4

Q: 7) Can you think of another way the author could have said 'climbed up the spout'? (2 marks for clarification)

A: Example: Another way the author could say 'climbed up the spout' is 'crawled up the spout'.

Easy ☐   Instructional ☐   Hard ☐

Total marks        /2

**Total inference score (Sessions 27–29):        /18**

## Assessment scoring and analysis

For further information about assessment scoring and analysis see Chapter 6 p…

Evaluating comprehension ability following each unit:

- Easy – 70–100% (13–18 marks): Found the assessment easy overall and would benefit from a more challenging text to assess their comprehension strengths and weaknesses moving forward.
- Instructional – 40–65% (7–12 marks): Requires more explicit reading comprehension instruction at this level of text.

- Hard – 0–35% (0–6 marks): Needs to be given a less challenging text and explicit instruction that shows them how to use comprehension skills in smaller steps to support their understanding.

# Unit 3 overall assessment scoring – inference skills

Part 1 Sessions 21–24 – 'Predicting' enquiry:       Total score       /18
Easy ☐     Instructional ☐     Hard ☐             _____

Part 2 Sessions 25 and 26 – 'Cause and effect' enquiry:   Total score       /18
Easy ☐     Instructional ☐     Hard ☐             _____

Part 3 Sessions 27–29 – 'Deductions and predictions':   Total score       /18
Easy ☐     Instructional ☐     Hard ☐             _____

## Parts 1–3 assessment analysis – deduction and prediction skills

- Does the pupil's answer relate to the information in the picture narrative?
- Are they simply guessing or referring to personal experience only to give an answer?
- Has the pupil looked closely enough at the picture detail?
- Is prior knowledge being used in addition to the information in the picture narrative?
- Does the pupil have problems with making links?
- Does the pupil understand the meaning of the vocabulary used in the story title and in the questions?
- Does the pupil have problems with story structure or sequencing?
- Does the pupil have problems expressing themselves?
- Is the pupil engaged in the picture content?

### Teacher comments and recommendations

Teacher/pupil – skills overview   Easy ☐   Instructional ☐   Hard ☐
Comments: _____
Recommendations: _____

## Unit 3 (Parts 1–3) – Pupil self-assessment of inference skills

### Making predictions – Aims and outcomes for children

**I can...** (with some prompting and help from adults)

1) I can link key words in the title with information in the pictures and text to explain what is happening in the story and why.

   Easy ☐   OK ☐   Hard ☐

2) I can explain what the difference is between literal 'who, what, where' information and detective clues on the page.

   Easy ☐   OK ☐   Hard ☐

3) I can make sense of unfamiliar words and ideas by using my background knowledge, clues in the picture and text, and my knowledge of vocabulary.

Easy ☐  OK ☐  Hard ☐

4) I can find clues that suggest what the characters might be thinking and feeling.

Easy ☐  OK ☐  Hard ☐

5) I can link the clues and literal information on the page to explain characters' motives and what is happening in the story.

Easy ☐  OK ☐  Hard ☐

6) I can ask and answer my own 'who, what, where, and why' questions and use my background knowledge to help me spot the problem in a story. I can then make an accurate prediction about what might happen next using this information.

Easy ☐  OK ☐  Hard ☐

7) I can ask and answer my own simple 'who, what, where, and why' detective questions about pictures and text using 'because' to explain 'how I know' or 'why I say that'.

Easy ☐  OK ☐  Hard ☐

8) I can ask and answer my own simple detective questions about picture narrative and text using my knowledge of similar and opposite meanings in the story.

Easy ☐  OK ☐  Hard ☐

---

**Teacher comments and recommendations – Aims and outcomes for children (inference skills)**

Easy ☐   OK/Instructional ☐   Hard ☐

Comments: _____

_____

Recommendations: _____

_____

# Section 2: Intermediate and end-of-foundation-year comprehension skills assessment

## On completion of Unit 4 (Parts 1 and 2) - summarising and retelling skills review

The aim of Unit 4's Summarising and Retelling Skills Assessment (Sessions 30 –36) is to establish whether young readers can 1) combine their knowledge of literal and detective skills, vocabulary, story structure and self-questioning to identify the main points of a story, and 2) retell the narrative in sequence, with accuracy and coherence.

The systematic process involved in evaluating these skills provides teachers and practitioners with an effective tool for assessing children's overall comprehension ability and conscious understanding.

## Oral assessment of summarising and retelling skills

### Unit 4 (Parts 1–2) – Summarising and retelling (Sessions 30–36)

This post-instructional Unit 4 review marks the end of the assessments for Teaching Units 1–4 and provides a useful end-of-year comprehension assessment. The review includes teacher–pupil conferencing and self-assessment resources for summarising and retelling the following sessions:

Part 1 Summarising and retelling: Sequencing skills – Sessions 30–31A/B
Part 2 Summarising and retelling: Beginning, problem, solution – Sessions 32–36

## Focus of Unit 4 (Parts 1–2) – Assessing summarising and retelling enquiry skills

Evaluating whether the reader can:

- select key information about a simple story to support retelling of the main events, e.g., nursery rhyme (who the story is about, what they do in the story and what happens in the end),
- identify the beginning, middle and end of a simple narrative,
- use Five-Finger prompts to retell events in the correct order using sequencing words ('In the beginning, Then, Next, After that, In the end').
- identify the theme (central, recurring idea) in a familiar text,
- ask and answer literal questions about the characters (and objects), actions, and setting to help identify the main ideas in a story,
- draw on knowledge of inference ('cause and effect') to identify the characters' problems, and solutions,
- summarise the main ideas of a picture narrative in their own words drawing on knowledge of vocabulary and information they have gathered,
- draw on their knowledge of vocabulary and other texts to retell coherently,
- clarify their understanding or words, images, concepts using contextual clues and knowledge of vocabulary.

# Assessment procedure

## Picture 'walking and talking' comprehension procedure

*Step 1: Revisit the* Little Fly and the Spider Trap *picture book cover and pages 1–4 of the book using the following procedure:*

- First, ask the reader to look through the *Little Fly and the Spider Trap* picture book pages to discuss the contents of each page with you.
- Ask them to tell you what they can see (allowing for only occasional prompts such as: Who are the characters? What are they doing? Where are they? What is happening? How do you think they feel? Why do you say that?).
- Then ask them to retell the story in their own words using the Five-Finger Retelling Map (Figure A4.1) to support this.
- Finally ask them to answer a range of questions about the characters and what is happening in the illustrations using the Retelling Map of the story to help them.
- Then invite them to ask and answer their own literal and detective questions about the narrative.

## Summarising and retelling process

**Step 2:** *Show the pupil a copy of the picture summary of the* Little Fly and the Spider Trap *narrative (Figure A4.1 see completed Five-Finger graphic organiser in Part 3, Section 3 of the Learning Support Resources) and explain that they can refer to this to help them retell the main points of the whole story.*

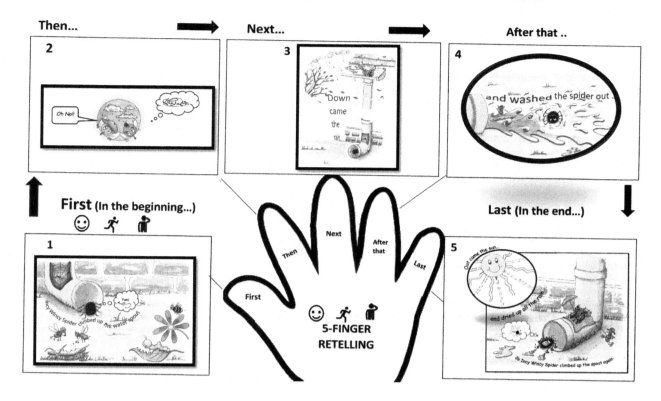

FIGURE A4.1 **Completed Five-Finger Retelling Map (images from *Little Fly and the Spider Trap* by Donna Thomson and Chrissy Morgan-Grant)**

As before, you may find it helpful to use an audio or video recorder to keep a record of the reader's responses to the 'picture walk' and retelling of the story for analysis. A 'Pupil's reading behaviour can then be recorded and assessed using the table in Figure A4.3. Following this, a transcript of their retelling can then be entered into Figure A4.2 to assess their retelling skills.' The table lists the key elements of retelling to provide a useful guide for identifying 1) pupils' knowledge of story structure and language, and 2) their ability to summarise and retell the main points of a story clearly and in sequence. In addition, the optional marking system offers a method for highlighting pupils' summarising and retelling strengths and weaknesses. For further information about assessment scoring and analysis see Chapter 7 p. 74

## Examples of questions/answers to support teacher–pupil conferencing process

*Step 3: Finally explain that you will ask them a range of literal and detective questions about the story. Then you will give them an opportunity to ask and answer their own literal and detective questions about the characters and events if they can.*

Space is provided for noting down responses to the questions and there is marking guidance with each question with boxes to indicate if the reader found the question easy, OK, hard to respond to. However, if you wish pupils to give written responses where appropriate, paper and pencils will be required.

**Retelling Analysis Record**

*See Figure 7.3 for example of retelling analysis (Adaptation of Parkin, Parkin, and Poole's 1999 PROBE -Taxonomy of Question Types, Reading Assessment New Zealand': Triune Initiatives)*

**Name:**

**Book Title:**

**Date:**

**Transcript of reader's retelling:**

| Elements of retelling skills<br>Total score poss: 18 points | None<br>0 points | Poor<br>1 point | Average<br>2 points | Good<br>3 points |
|---|---|---|---|---|
| Main ideas – characters, actions, *setting, problem, resolution* | | | | |
| Coherence – logical | | | | |
| Sequencing of events/plot | | | | |
| Use of descriptive vocab. | | | | |
| Direct reference to title and pictures | | | | |
| Connections with own experience | | | | |
| Total Score: /18 | | | | |

**Observations:**

**Recommendations:**

FIGURE A4.2  Analysing retelling skills

| Reading Behaviour Assessment | |
|---|---|
| **Reading Behaviour Assessment**<br><br>Assessing the different aspects of reading behaviour<br>*Tick the following for 'yes' or cross for 'no' in the boxes on the right* | ✓ or X |

| What Reader Says | |
|---|---|
| <u>What Reader Says</u> *(their narration skills and knowledge of story structure)*<br>For example, | a) |
| a) Did they need to be frequently prompted for responses? | b) |
| b) Could they identify who the characters are, their actions, locations, emotions, problems and how difficulties are resolved? | c) |
| | d) |
| c) Was their narration of the story logical? | e) |
| d) Could they make predictions? | f) |
| e) Could they retell the events in order in their own words? | g) |
| f) Could they use descriptive vocabulary? | h) |
| g) Could they repeat vocabulary used in story? | Total |
| h) Did they refer to their own experiences in relation to the story events? | /8 |
| Comments _____<br>_____ | |

| What Reader Does | |
|---|---|
| <u>What Reader Does</u> *(gesture, gaze, inflection, pausing)*<br>For example, did they, | ✓ or X |
| a) scan the pictures for information? | a) |
| b) pause for reassurance (to check whether responses are right or wrong)? | b) |
| c) point to details in pictures? | c) |
| d) shrug in response to your question prompts…? | d) |
| e) use other physical responses…..? | e) |
| Comments: _____ | Total<br>/5 |

| How the reader makes meaning | |
|---|---|
| <u>How the reader makes meaning</u> *(searching, cross-checking, rereading, self- correcting).*<br>For example, could they, | ✓ or X |
| a) identify explicit information, | |
| b) identify clues, | a) |
| c) make links using prior knowledge and experience, | b) |
| d) check if their ideas make sense, | c) |
| e) correct themselves if they do not make sense. | d) |
| | e) |
| Comments _____ | Total |
| Recommendations _____ | /5 |

FIGURE A4.3

Ask the following questions about the characters on pages 1–5 of the *Little Fly and the Spider Trap* picture book. (Note answers may vary and must relate to the pictures and text.)

Q: 1) Look closely at the information in the title and each picture. What is the theme of the story? (2 marks)

A: *Possible answers: The theme of the story is about luck. What is good luck for some is bad luck for others. Or the theme of the story is about family. Families look after each other.*

Easy ☐   Instructional ☐   Hard ☐

Total marks      /2

Q: 2) The title says, *Little Fly and the Spider Trap*. What do you think the author means by 'Spider Trap'? Explain why you say that? (2 marks for clarification)

A: *Possible answer I think the 'Spider Trap' is a spider's web. I say that because webs are sticky and they catch insects in them like a trap.*

Easy ☐   Instructional ☐   Hard ☐

Total marks    /2

Q: 3) Look closely at the main characters in the first scene at the beginning of the story. What are they doing? Where are they? (1 mark for literal information)

A: *Example: At the beginning of the story Incy Wincy Spider is in the garden and climbing up the waterspout. Little Fly is stuck in Incy Spider's web in the waterspout.*

Easy ☐   Instructional ☐   Hard ☐

Total marks      /1

Q: 4) Point to clues in the pictures that suggest Little Fly has a problem and give your reasons why. (2 marks for inference – clues)

A: *Possible answer: The clues that suggest Little Fly has a problem are 1. Mum and Dad Fly think Little Fly is in danger of being eaten because he is stuck in a spider's web. 2. Incy Wincy Spider is thinking 'Yum' because he is hungry and hoping to find a fly in his waterspout web.*

Easy ☐   Instructional ☐   Hard ☐

Total marks      /2

Q: 5) What do Dad and Mum Fly do to solve the problem? How do you know that? (2 marks for inference – making links)

A: *Possible answer: Dad and Mum Fly help to rescue Little Fly. I know that because as the rain pours down the waterspout, they push a leaf down the waterspout to free him from the web and help him float out of the drain.*

Easy ☐   Instructional ☐   Hard ☐

Total marks      /2

Q: 6) What happens to the main characters in the middle of the story? (1 mark for a literal answer)

A: *Example: Little Fly and Incy Wincy Spider are washed out of the waterspout by the rainwater / Incy Wincy Spider tumbles out of the spout in the rainwater and Little Fly surfs out on a wave behind him and escapes.*

Easy ☐   Instructional ☐   Hard ☐

Total marks      /1

Q: 7) Is it a happy ending for all the characters? Why do you say that? (2 marks for inference/ evaluative response)

A: *Possible answer: No, it is not a happy ending for all the characters because Incy Wincy has to go back up the spout to mend his web while Little Fly and his Mum and Dad are enjoying the sunshine.*

Easy ☐   Instructional ☐   Hard ☐

Total marks      /2

8) Own literal question and answer – Literal Q: 1 mark and A: 1 mark

Q: *Example: What did Incy Wincy do when the sun came out?*

Easy ☐   Instructional ☐   Hard ☐

A: *Example: Incy Wincy climbed back up the spout when the rain came out.*

Easy ☐   Instructional ☐   Hard ☐

Total marks      /2

9) Own detective question and answer – Inference Q: 2 marks and A: 2 marks

Q: *Example: Why do you think Incy Wincy climbed up the waterspout at the beginning of the story?*

Easy ☐   Instructional ☐   Hard ☐

A: *Example: I think Incy Wincy climbed up the waterspout at the beginning to see if he had caught a fly for dinner. I say that because the word 'Yum' and the picture of a fly in the thought bubble suggested he was thinking this.*

Easy ☐   Instructional ☐   Hard ☐
Total marks      /4

**Total score: Literal and inference summarising skills      /18**


# Assessment scoring and analysis

(See Chapter 7, pages 74–83 for further information)
Evaluating comprehension ability following each unit.

- Easy – 70–100% (13–18 marks): Found the assessment easy overall and would benefit from a more challenging text to assess their comprehension strengths and weaknesses moving forward.
- Instructional – 40–65% (7–12 marks): Requires more explicit reading comprehension instruction at this level of text.
- Hard – 0–35% (0–6 marks): Needs to be given a less challenging text and explicit instruction that shows them how to use comprehension skills in smaller steps to support their understanding.

# Overall score for summarising, retelling skills - Unit 4

Retelling – 'Picture walking and talking':    Total score /18 (Reading Behaviour Analysis)
Easy ☐    Instructional ☐    Hard ☐         _____

Summarising and retelling skills             Total score /18 (Retelling Analysis)
Easy ☐    Instructional ☐    Hard ☐         _____

Summarising and retelling enquiry            Total score /18 (Literal and Inference summarising skills)
Easy ☐    Instructional ☐    Hard ☐         _____

# Assessment analysis

**Analysing pupil responses to comprehension questions:**

- Does the pupil's answer relate to the information in the picture narrative?
- Is the pupil engaged in the picture content?
- Has the pupil looked closely enough at the picture detail?
- Is prior knowledge being used in addition to the information in the picture narrative?
- Does the pupil have problems with making links?
- Does the pupil understand the phrasing of the question/meaning of the vocabulary used in the story title and in the questions?
- Does the pupil have problems with story structure/sequencing? Does the pupil have problems expressing themselves?

**Teacher comments and recommendations**

Teacher/pupil – skills overview    Easy ☐    Instructional ☐    Hard ☐

Comments: _____

_____

Recommendations: _____

_____

## Pupil self-assessment early comprehension skills: Units 1–4

Ask the pupil to think carefully about how they gather picture book information and clues. Are they aware of the different skills they use to do this? Explain that there is no 'right' or 'wrong' answer to the following questions. You are inviting them to discuss how easy or difficult it is for them to identify specific information, make predictions, retell stories, and generate and answer literal and inference questions about the characters and events to support their learning. (You may wish to use an audio recorder to note their responses.)

## Summarising and retelling – aims and outcomes for children

**I can...** (with some prompting and help from adults)

1) I can find key information about who the story is about, what they are doing, and where they are in a scene and identify the theme of a story.

Easy ☐   OK ☐   Hard ☐

2) I can check my understanding of words, images, and ideas using my knowledge of vocabulary and clues in the story.

Easy ☐   OK ☐   Hard ☐

3) I can use my understanding of 'cause and effect' to identify characters' problems, and solutions.

Easy ☐   OK ☐   Hard ☐

4) I can make deductions and predictions about a story using my prior knowledge and by linking clues on the page.

Easy ☐   OK ☐   Hard ☐

5) I can sum up the main points of the beginning, middle, and end of a simple story.

Easy ☐   OK ☐   Hard ☐

6) I can ask and answer questions about characters, their actions, places, problems, and solutions to help me retell and check my understanding of a story.

Easy ☐   OK ☐   Hard ☐

7) I can use Five-Finger prompts to retell the beginning, middle, and end of stories in the correct order using sequencing words.

Easy ☐   OK ☐   Hard ☐

8) I can use my knowledge of vocabulary and other texts to retell with clarity.

Easy ☐   OK ☐   Hard ☐

**Teacher comments and recommendations – Aims and outcomes for children**

(Summarising and retelling skills)

Easy ☐   OK/Instructional ☐   Hard ☐

Comments: _____

Recommendations:

_____

# Section 3: Learning support resources

## Picture books

# The Book Day Parade

by Donna Thomson
Illustrated by Jake Biggin

An adaptation of the Humpty Dumpty Nursery rhyme

Humpty Dumpty sat on a wall

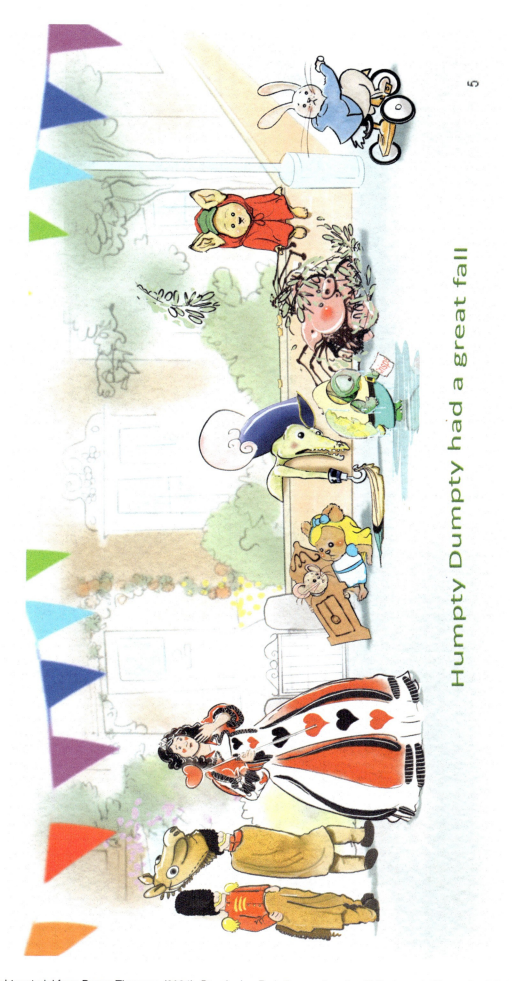

Humpty Dumpty had a great fall

All the king's horses

and all the king's men

couldn't put Humpty together again

# Little Fly and the Spider Trap

*Donna Thomson * Chrissy Morgan-Grant*

The Incy Wincy nursery rhyme retold in pictures

and washed the spider out ....

3

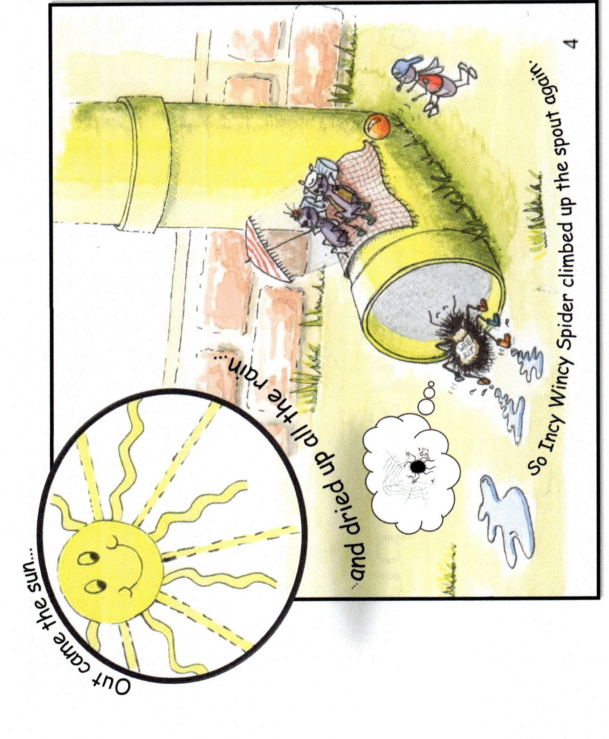

So Incy Wincy Spider climbed up the spout again...

...and dried up all the rain...

Out came the sun...

4

# Part 3: Learning support resources

## Graphic organisers

# Brilliant Book Talk smiley chart

1. Write your child's name in the first column of boxes.
2. Award them with smiley points for using any of the following SPEC skills before, during, and after reading:

- 😊 Summarising (retelling)
- 😊 Predicting,
- 😊 Questions/answers, or
- 😊 Clarifying (making sense)

| Name/s | Summarising Retelling. 😊 | Predicting What might happen next? 😊 | Enquiry Questions and answers.' 😊 | Clarifying Making sense of images, words and ideas. 😊 | Date........ Spectacular Score One point for each ........ 😊😊😊😊 Total points........ This week    Score so far |
|---|---|---|---|---|---|
| ⭐ | | | | | |
| | | | | | |
| | | | | | |
| | | | | | |
| | | | | | |
| | | | | | |
| | | | | | |

# 'Characters' feelings in the story

| Character's actions | Character's feelings… | Emotions |
|---|---|---|
| 1 In the beginning | | 🙂 fed up |
| 2 Then | | 😊 pleased |
| 3 Next | | 😟 worried |
| 4 After that | | 😠 cross |
| 5 In the end | | 😄 happy |
| | | 😢 upset |
| | | 😮 shocked |
| | | 😆 excited |
| | | 😢 sad |

| Character's problem… | Character's solution… |
|---|---|
| | |

Name: _____

**Retelling in order**   Story: _____

| Beginning | Middle | End |
|---|---|---|
| First... | Then.... | Last ....... |
| 1 | 2 | 3 |

# Retelling events in order: Who, What, Where? Problem and Solution

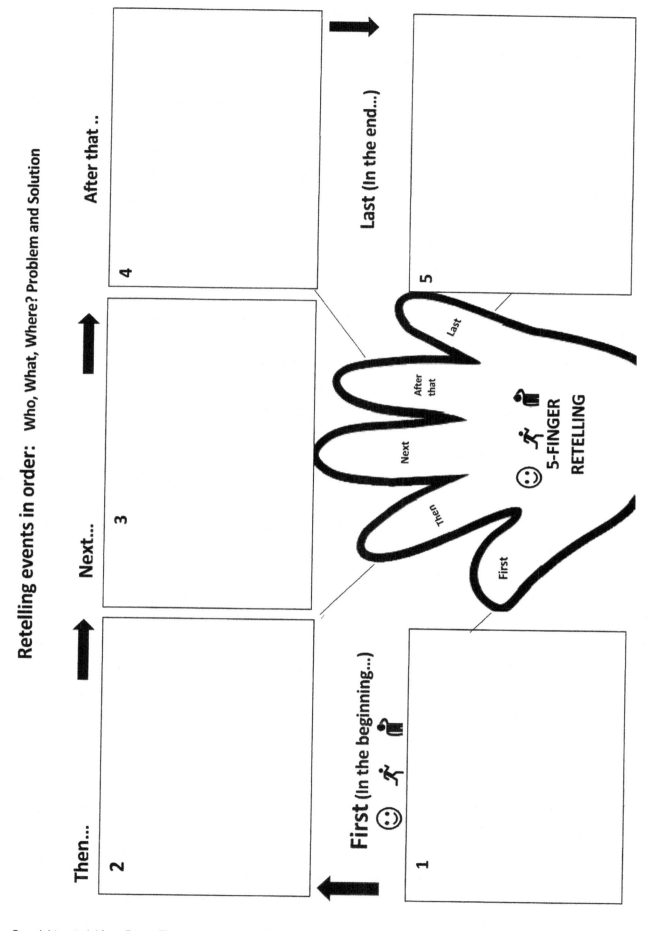

**Then...**

2

**Next...**

3

**After that ..**

4

**Last (In the end...)**

5

**First (In the beginning...)**

1

5-FINGER RETELLING

First

Then

Next

After that

Last

# Retelling events in order: Who, What, Where? Problem and Solution

# WWW Literal Keyword Organiser

■ Look for Who, What, Where key words in the pictures and text

# Key word information box

Draw or write this key information in the boxes below…

| **Who** is involved? 😊 | **What** are they doing? | **Where** are they? |
|---|---|---|
| Example: Goldilocks | is eating porridge | in the kitchen |
| | | |

Ask and answer your literal questions using this key information:

Who _____

Your answer: _____

What _____

Your answer _____

Where _____

Your answer _____

# WWW Literal Keyword Organiser

■ Look for Who, What, Where key words in the pictures and text

# Key word information box

■ Draw or write this key information in the boxes below…

| Who is involved? | What are they doing? | Where are they? |
|---|---|---|
|  |  |  |
|  |  |  |
|  |  |  |

Ask and answer your literal questions using this key information:

Who _____

Your answer: _____

What _____

Your answer _____

Where _____

Your answer _____

# Section 3: Learning support resources

## Graphic templates

1. Cut out arrow.
2. Fix arrow to riskmometer using a paper clasp to make it moveable.
3. Move arrow up a level to indicate good debate (and risk-taking from reluctant speakers during the discussion).

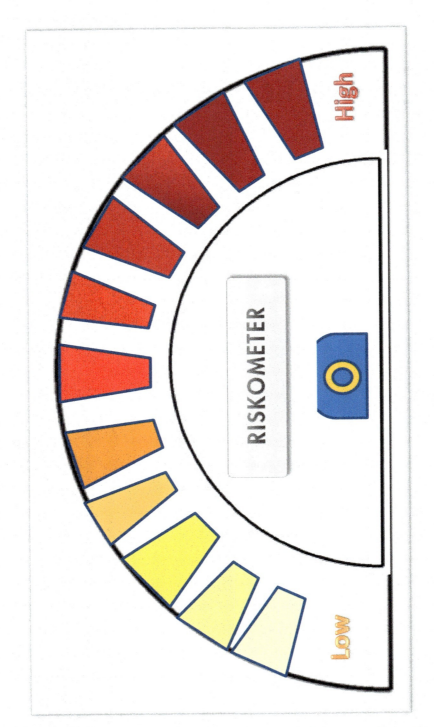

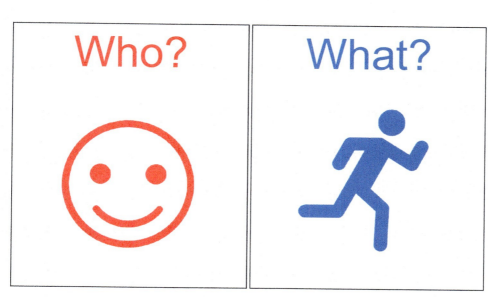

# Section 3: Learning support resources

## Posters

illustrated by Jake Biggin

# Language of discussion poster and cue cards

I agree
with you
because…,

I disagree
with you
because…,

I would like to link to
your idea …

I think…
because…,

I would like to add
to your point
and say……

# The Author Poster

Authors write to entertain you - to share ideas, feelings, and information with you.

We have a picture in our heads as we write.

We choose words carefully to paint the picture for you.

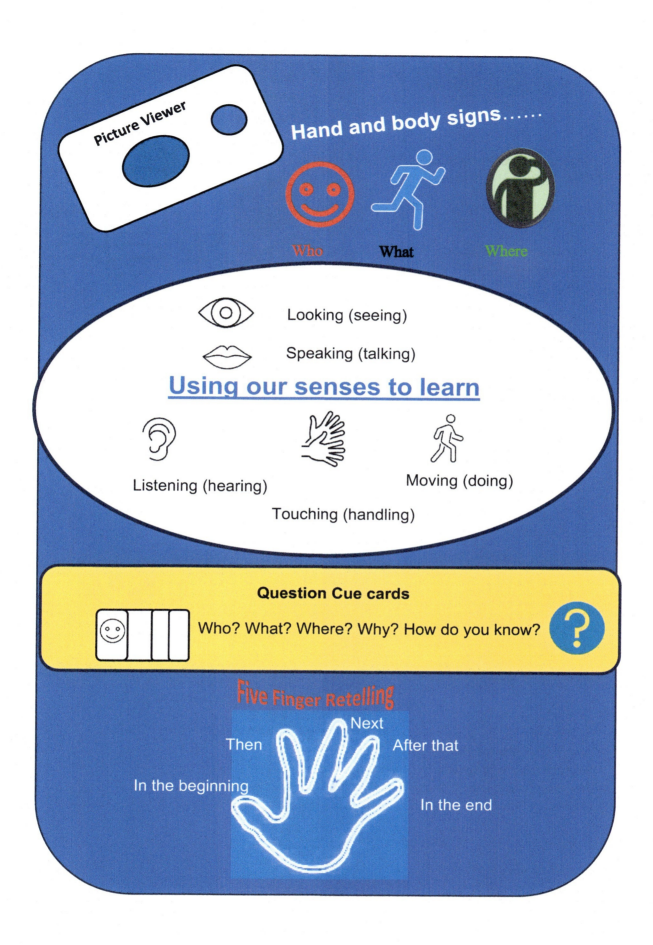

Picture Viewer

Hand and body signs......

Who   What   Where

Looking (seeing)

Speaking (talking)

**Using our senses to learn**

Listening (hearing)

Moving (doing)

Touching (handling)

**Question Cue cards**

Who? What? Where? Why? How do you know?

Five Finger Retelling

Next

Then   After that

In the beginning

In the end

# The Literal Patroller

The Literal Patroller knows where to look for literal key words in a book.

He knows that literal who, what, where is on the page – yes, right there!

He is always on the case - noting the characters, action, and place.

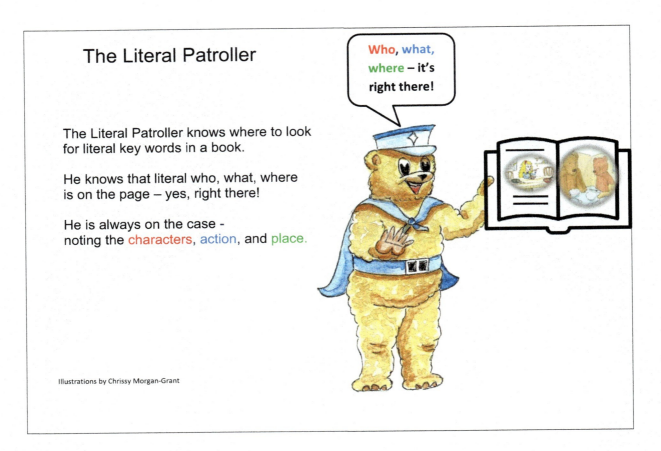

Illustrations by Chrissy Morgan-Grant

## Prediction Poster – The Inference Detective Clooze

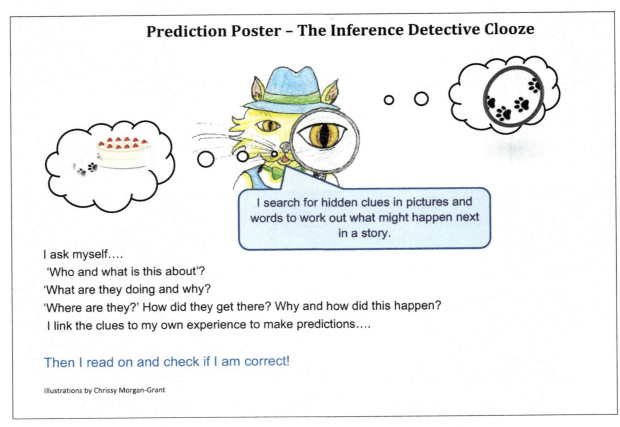

I ask myself….
'Who and what is this about'?
'What are they doing and why?
'Where are they?' How did they get there? Why and how did this happen?
I link the clues to my own experience to make predictions….

Then I read on and check if I am correct!

Illustrations by Chrissy Morgan-Grant

# Section 3: Learning Support Resources

## Assessment frameworks

# Reading Behaviour Assessment

*See Figure 7.5 p. 82 for example of 'picture walk' analysis: Reading Behaviour and Reading Comprehension Skills Revision of assessment method based on Lysaker and Hopper (2015) adaptation of Clay 2005 Early Print Strategies running record design.*

| Assessing the different aspects of reading behaviour<br>Tick the following for 'yes' or cross for 'no' in the boxes on the right | ✓ or X |
|---|---|
| **What reader says** (their narration skills and knowledge of story structure)<br>For example: | |
| a) Did they need to be frequently prompted for responses?<br>b) Could they identify who the characters are, their actions, locations, emotions, problems and how difficulties are resolved?<br>c) Was their narration of the story logical?<br>d) Could they make predictions?<br>e) Could they retell the events in order in their own words?<br>f) Could they use descriptive vocabulary?<br>g) Could they repeat vocabulary used in the story?<br>h) Did they refer to their own experiences in relation to the story events?<br><br>Comments: _____ | a)<br>b)<br>c)<br>d)<br>e)<br>f)<br>g)<br>h) |
| **What reader does** (gesture, gaze, inflection, pausing)<br>For example, did they:<br>a) scan the pictures for information?<br>b) pause for reassurance (to check whether responses are right or wrong)?<br>c) point to details in pictures?<br>d) shrug in response to your question prompts…?<br>e) use other physical responses…?<br><br>Comments: _____ | ✓ or X<br>a)<br>b)<br>c)<br>d)<br>e) |
| **How the reader makes meaning** (searching, cross-checking, rereading, self-correcting)<br>For example, could they:<br>a) identify explicit information?<br>b) identify clues?<br>c) make links using prior knowledge and experience?<br>d) check if their ideas make sense?<br>e) correct themselves if they do not make sense?<br><br>Comments: _____<br><br>Recommendation:_____ | ✓ or X<br>a)<br>b)<br>c)<br>d)<br>e) |

## Retelling analysis record

*See Figure 7.3 p. 76 for example of retelling analysis... (Adaptation of Parkin, Parkin, and Poole's 1999 PROBE -Taxonomy of Question Types, Reading Assessment New Zealand': Triune Initiatives)*

**Name:**

**Title of Book:**

**Date:**

**Transcript of reader's retelling:**

| Elements of retelling skills<br>Total score poss: 18 points | None<br>0 | Poor<br>1 | Average<br>2 points | Good<br>3 points |
|---|---|---|---|---|
| Main ideas – *characters, actions, setting, problem, resolution* | | | | |
| Coherence – logical | | | | |
| Sequencing of events/plot | | | | |
| Use of descriptive vocab. | | | | |
| Direct reference to title and pictures | | | | |
| Connections with own experience | | | | |
| Total score: /18 | | | | |

Observations:

Recommendations:

# Glossary

**Reading comprehension** – reading for meaning involves a range of tasks to support understanding before, during and after reading. These activities include extracting themes, recalling and re-organising information from pictures and text, engaging in higher order thinking skills, constructing a mental picture of text, and understanding story structure.

**Emergent comprehension** – pre-school stage of early meaning-making through picture reading activities which extends to later comprehension of text.

**Language comprehension (listening comprehension)** – a precursor to reading comprehension, language comprehension focuses on 1) being able to make sense of the different elements of spoken language, such as the meaning of words, how words are put together to form sentences, and 2) being able to make connections between new information and one's own knowledge to support understanding.

**Reading comprehension strategies** – deliberate use of cognitive tactics which help readers to reason strategically when they encounter difficulties with comprehension as they read.

**Reciprocal reading framework** – (based on Palincsar and Brown's 1984 model) provides an interactive and strategic method for constructing meaning. Young readers learn how to use predicting, clarifying, questioning, and summarising strategies both independently and collaboratively to support their understanding of text.

**Explicit instruction and modelling skills** – direct and structured teaching methods that provide step-by-step explanations about what to do and how to do a task. This involves detailed demonstration of skills, plenty of practice and teacher–pupil feedback.

**Self-questioning skills** – asking yourself a range of questions to check your understanding as you read. For example: literal (Who, what, where?) questions, inference (Why? How do I know that?) questions, and evaluation (Why are the characters thinking and feeling that way? Why do I think that?) questions.

**Metacognition, self-regulation and self-monitoring** (learning awareness) – involves conscious thinking about how you learn, developing strategic control of your own learning and checking understanding during the learning process.

**Scaffolding and gradual release of responsibility** – instructional methods teachers use to 1) demonstrate how to successfully use a strategy or memorising technique to support a task, then 2) gradually transferring the responsibility of a task from themselves to the student.

**Literal, inference, and evaluative questioning** – different levels of questioning and response.

- Literal enquiry: Identifying and retrieving explicit information; responding to and generating direct 'who, what, where?' questions about pictures and text.
- Inferential enquiry: Identifying clues and implied meaning. Asking 'why?' and 'how do you know that?' questions about pictures and text and responding with evidence from the text using 'because' to explain how you know.
- Evaluative enquiry: Making links to personal experience to explain events or characters' actions, feelings, and behaviour in a story. Asking 'why?' questions about pictures and text and responding with evidence from the text using 'because' to justify the answer.

**Multisensory learning** – learning through a combination of sensory activities, such as visual and auditory (observing, listening, and speaking) and kinaesthetic and tactile ('doing', moving, and touching). For example:

- Visual learning: Using the sense of sight to understand information and concepts when they are presented in visual form, e.g., diagrams, concept maps, illustrations, symbols.
- Auditory learning: Using sense of hearing to understand new ideas. This happens when the information is explained out loud, either by the child doing the speaking, or by others doing the talking.
- Tactile learning: Using the sense of touch to make meaning of ideas by moving things around and by manipulating objects that represent the concepts they are learning.
- Kinaesthetic learning: Using body movement to keep focused. Movement is also used to support understanding and interpretation of ideas in a variety of ways (e.g., role-play, dance) or to mimic a concept they are learning (e.g., hand and body gestures).

# Index

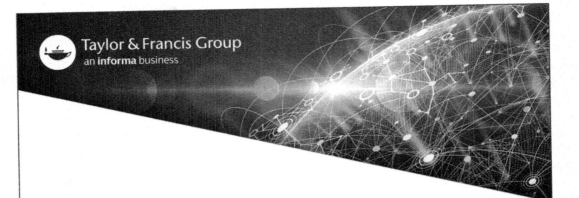